the art
of risk

the art
of risk

the art of risk

Richard Harris

SCRIBNER

London · New York · Sydney · Toronto · New Delhi

SCRIBNER

THE ART OF RISK
First published in Australia in 2023 by
Simon & Schuster (Australia) Pty Limited
Suite 19A, Level 1, Building C, 450 Miller Street, Cammeray, NSW 2062

10 9 8 7 6 5 4 3 2 1

Sydney New York London Toronto New Delhi
Visit our website at www.simonandschuster.com.au

 A catalogue record for this
book is available from the
National Library of Australia

ISBN: 9781761424052

Cover design: Bradley Graham
Cover illustration: Afry Harfy / Shutterstock
Typeset by Midland Typesetters, Australia
Printed and bound by CPI Group (UK) Ltd, Croydon, CR0 4YY

MIX
Paper | Supporting
responsible forestry
FSC® C171272

This book is dedicated to all the risk 'managers' who were generous in sharing their stories, and to the passionate group of cave explorers whom I am proud to call my friends. And of course, to Fiona – it is far easier to be the one at risk than to stay behind and worry about the risk-taker.

CONTENTS

INTRODUCTION

'H' AS IN HARRY

My name is Dr Richard Harris – or just 'Harry' to my mates. If you meet me at a party, that's what I'll be introduced as.

'This is Harry,' the host will probably say. And then, more likely than not – 'you know, the doctor from the Thai cave rescue'.

In June 2018, with the eyes of the world watching, I dived into a remote cave in northern Thailand, in an attempt to rescue a Thai youth soccer team who had become trapped by flash flooding.

I was part of a global rescue effort that involved thousands of people. Amongst them were civilian volunteers, fearless soldiers, brilliant engineers and one opinionated billionaire. And by several weird twists of fate, a bunch of middle-aged cave-diving enthusiasts. They were proponents of an obscure hobby that most of the world had never heard of, whose specific set of skills and highly specialised equipment proved key to the rescue.

Long story short, I used my experience as a recreational cave diver to traverse kilometres of the subterranean Tham Luang Nang Non cave system, and my professional knowledge as an anaesthetist to sedate the stranded boys so they could be dived and carried to safety.

The story of how the Wild Boars soccer team and their coach were rescued in the most improbable circumstances is an inspiring one. For the weeks the boys were trapped underground, the best of human nature was on show as people from disparate nations and walks of life worked together to find a way to bring them out. Around the globe, millions of people were united with concern for the kids and celebrated as one when they were rescued. It was an improbably happy ending to an extraordinary adventure, for which I managed to score front-row seats. Even if I hadn't been involved, I think it would still make a cracking good yarn. Of course, I was involved – which is why, for better or worse, I will be best known as the cave-diving anaesthetist who went to help rescue the kids.

It was a privilege to be involved, but it came with an uncomfortable amount of attention. In the greater scheme of things, my dive buddy Craig Challen (now the world's best-known cave-diving veterinarian) and I played only a small part in an extraordinary show of global solidarity to rescue the boys. We were two blokes in the right place at the right time who then found themselves in the limelight.

Craig and I had barely got our wetsuits off before people started pinning medals on us. Amongst them was the Star of Courage, a bravery decoration honouring 'acts of conspicuous courage in circumstances of great peril'. That made me a little uneasy. I don't consider what I did particularly courageous. Conspicuous, sure – when I popped up from the cave there were television cameras as far as the eye could see – but courageous? Not so sure.

To my mind, courage means doing something that frightens you. Observers of the rescue story often assume that I'm brave. They saw me and the other divers put on our scuba tanks and disappear underground to rescue those boys and think it must have taken courage. The idea of being underground, underwater, unable to see and with a finite air supply is something most people have a healthy, primeval fear of. The thing is, I quite enjoy it.

2

Because I am comfortable cave diving, I didn't feel like I was in any great physical danger, hence I didn't need to be courageous. I certainly don't think of myself as a particularly brave man. If anything, I'm rather sensible – I just happen to have an unusual set of skills.

I was able to succeed in the Thai cave because of decades of experience, comprising thousands of hours of careful planning, risk assessment and management. You won't catch me doing something dangerous unless I've thought long and hard about every possible way it might play out – I love to dive, but not in the deep end. At least, not without ascertaining what might be under the surface! I don't crave adrenaline. Nor do I give in to flights of fancy or irrational fear . . . unless there's a spider involved. Then all bets are off.

So, when people start throwing around the 'H' word, it makes me uncomfortable. Firefighters, ambos, volunteers – those are the people I'm happy to pin the 'hero' word on.

At best, I would describe myself as an enthusiastic adventurer. I like to explore, to live life to its fullest, to take chances – once I've done everything to make sure the chances favour me coming back alive.

I believe that a life without adventure and risk is a waste. I suppose you could call me an advocate for *sensible* risk-taking, as I believe the greatest risk most people will ever face is letting their lives pass them by.

*

Six months after the rescue, when Craig and I were named joint Australian of the Year (a whole other story), I found myself suddenly called upon to advocate for something I truly believed in.

'I am proud to call myself an explorer,' I said in my acceptance speech, 'but I do fear for kids today who, living in a risk-averse society, will not learn to challenge themselves and to earn the grazed knees and stubbed toes that really are necessary to build resilience and confidence.'

'I think a need for adventure resides in all of us. The answer for some is found in reading books, and for others by watching the screen . . . for me, or for us, it is about caves.'

As joint Australian of the Year, I'd been gifted a shiny new soapbox and I was going to use it for something I'd long been concerned about. Cave diving has given me a depth of contentment and joy that I now can't imagine my life without.

I'm an adventurer today largely because I was raised by parents who inducted me into a life where a few cuts and bruises weren't something to be avoided. It breaks my heart a little when I see a generation who might miss out on the immense privilege of spending time in the ocean or in the bush as kids. I used my time in the spotlight to advocate for more youth to follow Craig's and my example.

I got some laughs from the crowd for suggesting that kids might like exploring caves, not long after having rescued some kids from underground. But I stand by my message. Cave diving just 'clicked' with me. I can't say why, or how, and I know it's not for everyone. But I truly believe that everyone has something similar, waiting for them to tap into the potential to be found there.

Kids do need to be kids. They need to be allowed to find their own boundaries and test their own limits – to unlock their capacity for exploration. Craig and I spent our tenure as joint Australian of the Year by encouraging kids and their parents to do just that – for kids to find their inner Hubert Wilkins or Amelia Earhart, and for parents to relax a little and let them have the freedom to undertake that discovery.

As Craig said in his acceptance speech, 'There is a temptation to take the easy road, to think that life would be better if we mould it to be as comfortable as possible. But there is a real and serious risk in doing this – the risk that we miss the opportunities that present them-selves. Missing a chance to lend a hand and help others. A risk of never knowing our own strength and what we are capable of.'

Our thesis was that a life without risk was a life half lived. We hit the road to spread the message as best we could. Hopefully, we inspired a few people to go out and try new things, to explore new parts of the world and facets of themselves. To be part of a bigger, better life.

Then, of course, the COVID-19 pandemic took hold of the planet and life as we knew it ended. Where I live, in Adelaide, we were mercifully isolated from the worst of it and my family rode out the first waves of the pandemic in relative safety. It was an immensely privileged position to be in and I was grateful that we were safe.

But having said that, it was a little boring. I went from spending my weekends zooming around the countryside with my mates going on one adventure or another, plus those few months of unexpected limelight, to spending a great deal of time at home. I found myself getting restless. As time wore on, I started thinking about something a comedic video meme had warned me about just after the beginning of the pandemic. 'Everybody's doing it,' it said, 'but no matter what you do, no matter how strong the temptation, please don't start a podcast.'

*

My podcast, *Real Risk*, went live in May 2020. It was more frightening to me than jumping into a cave. I was aware it was a presumptuous and self-indulgent thing to do – no excuses there, but at least it would keep me close to home. Part of me was worried I'd be making another piece of digital trash to be ignored, dismissed and forgotten. Part of me was more hopeful.

Here's a great piece of advice an author once gave me: write the book you want to read. I figured that advice was easily transferred to the format of a podcast. I wanted to make something that people like me would enjoy.

When I look over at my bookshelves there's a theme. There's *Touching the Void* and *Lost in the Himalayas*, stories of incredible feats of survival in the frozen wilderness. Next to them, a chronicle of some jokers attempting to row tiny boats across vast oceans and one about a gruelling journey by bike across the Sahara. How did a middle-aged Aussie doctor get obsessed with all these rather painful and dangerous pursuits? They are the bookshelves of someone who seems to have a bit of a ghoulish interest in other people's suffering, which perhaps, is not what people want from their doctors. At least part of my fascination for the titles was always the thought – would I have it in me to do *that*? And what makes these people different?

I figured there were other people out there with bookshelves like mine, who read these stories not for the grisly details, but for the inherent truth in them. Each of the stories of adventure contains some element of questing, of personal catharsis, of spiritual betterment. Every adventurer seemed to be learning something about themselves as they pushed the boundaries of what they could do – of what all humans can do. I wanted to pursue that feeling, having experienced some facet of this myself.

In over twenty years of technical diving, with a particular focus on deep-cave exploration, I've gotten pretty used to people telling me I must have a death wish. It's hard to explain that the opposite is true – I love life and cave diving is the part of my life that reminds me of that the most. The sport is a way to recharge and to grow as a person. In the middle of a successful cave dive, while death is possible, I am living my life to the fullest and the sensation I feel is one of calm. I imagine it must be similar to the feeling some people experience during meditation.

But I understand why people think I'm out of my mind. Hey, I feel the same way about the people who BASE jump, or who climb sheer rock walls without a rope. I doubt they woke up one day and said, 'Today I'm going to do something so outrageously difficult that I will surely die doing it.' I reckon they would find what they did perfectly logical and sensible – even if to me, they seemed batshit crazy.

I wondered if other risk-takers – the ones I considered crazy – have the same approach as me to risk. The people who jump off cliff tops wearing flight suits, or ride motorbikes at bone-shattering speed around blind corners, or fly combat jets – do they get the same pleasure as I do from consciously ticking off a safety checklist? Surely not.

So, I started the podcast to satisfy a curiosity and to find like-minded people. I had questions I wanted answers to. I wanted to ask these risk-takers: why do you do what you do? Why do you climb mountains, sail through storms, go to war, dive the deepest oceans? What fundamental part of our biology and psychology makes us want to go faster, and harder, and experience the soaring highs of risk-taking? What is it about cheating death that makes us feel so alive?

The more answers I got to those questions, the more I learned about why we take risks, the more I began to believe that my hunch was right – that risk is an important part of what makes us human. The more I understood how risk is essential to our wellbeing, the happier I was that I'd set out on the journey. Starting a podcast scared the hell out of me, but like every time I've gone out of my comfort zone, I discovered something new about myself. There was more to the story than the audio format allowed. It turned out, in making my podcast, I was actually starting a book. The book you're holding now. Thanks for taking a risk on it. Let's dive in.

PART ONE

METAL

When I set out to explore risk – different facets of it, various ways that individuals experience, adjust to and live with risk – I had an idea that I wanted to start with the elements. To be specific, those people who test themselves against the elements.

Once upon a time people thought the world was made up of four elements: earth, water, air and fire. They thought everything that existed in the world was composed of different combinations of these elements.

In what became China, they believed wood and not air was an element. They also believed in a fifth element that was essential to the makeup of everything on Earth – metal.

Metal is the element that represents rigidity, but also flexibility, as it may undergo metamorphosis. In ancient engineering, the raw ore taken from the Earth was forged with fire, water and air to become whatever alloy humanity needed it to be – from brutal iron to beautiful gold. As a symbol, metal represents both mastery of the elements and of our own desire to improve upon the world with technology. It represents our better nature.

Personally, there are aspects of this philosophy that appeal to me. As a bit of a gadget man, I have a strong appreciation for gizmos, inventions and technology – those metal creations that have helped humanity strive to go further, faster and higher than we ever thought possible.

It's a practical sort of admiration, but I find an undeniable kind of poetry to a perfectly tuned straight-six engine in a beautiful classic car. It's testament to many, many hours of soulful mechanical design and human ingenuity.

I'm hardly the first to talk about the link between human mastery of metal and the individual. The English phrase, 'to test your mettle', to test your own strength and resilience, goes back to the 13th century, when the words 'metal' and 'mettle' were used interchangeably.

It's an apt metaphor to explain how some extraordinary individuals, by taking on risk, find themselves similarly changed. Just like forged metal, they are harder, stronger, more resilient. And more malleable when that is what life requires.

I wanted to meet those people, to talk to them about how they test their own mettle, what they learned and what they could teach me. But I suppose it's only fair that I start by discussing my own mettle-testing adventure, where I strapped on my dive gear to be part of something much bigger than myself.

CHAPTER ONE

HEAVY METTLE

To be perfectly frank, I didn't think much of our chances. From the moment the idea was first put to me, until pretty much the moment the final boy was rescued from the Thai cave, I did not expect any of the children to survive. When I weighed the risks, tried to envision everything that could go wrong, I thought the chances of successfully sedating the boys and diving them out were vanishingly small. But to be fair, the fact I was in Thailand in the first place was a million to one.

*

The first I heard of the Wild Boars soccer team and their coach being trapped in the cave by rising floodwaters was a tiny news article I read in an Adelaide paper. Just a few lines mentioning that a team was lost in a remote cave in northern Thailand. Naturally enough, that piqued my interest. Because of my love of cave diving and my interest in cave rescue, any article involving a flooded cave was relevant to me. As it happened, I had some contacts in the cave-diving community in Thailand.

Just a year earlier, Craig and I had been on an expedition with a guy called Ben Reymenants, a Belgian expat who runs a diving business in

Thailand. I messaged Ben asking him if he knew what was going on, if he was involved and if there was anything us Aussies could do to help.

We weren't the only ones to do so. The cave-diving community is a pretty small pool of people – particularly in the circle of cave explorers. Text messages pinged around the world as the situation became clearer – and each revelation made it increasingly clear that the boys were in terrible danger. Assuming they were even still alive and hadn't drowned in the initial flood event.

*

To reach the chamber where the boys were eventually discovered meant painstakingly navigating through nearly two and a half kilometres of narrow passages, flooded with an underground river that appeared with the early and unseasonal start of the monsoon season. Hardened Thai Navy SEALs, along with expert US military divers, were unable to make headway.

Early on, Vern Unsworth – a British caver based in Chiang Rai and part of the international community of recreational explorers – entered Tham Luang to make an assessment. The rapidly rising floodwaters he witnessed generated the callout for the UK's finest cave divers. The community rallied and those who were similarly qualified to safely plumb the cave began to mobilise to head to Thailand. Imagine the dismay of the Thai authorities when these scruffy middle-aged men from the UK and elsewhere started showing up with their home-made diving gear and unsolicited advice.

On 2 July, the British diving duo of Richard 'Rick' Stanton and John Volanthen located the boys alive and well on an elevated offshoot in the cave. The next day, seven Thai Navy divers, including Doctor Pak Loharnshoon, dived in with medicine and other supplies. Four of them, including Doctor Pak, would stay with the boys and ultimately be the last to exit the cave.

The sense of euphoria that came with discovering the team was short-lived, as it became clear there was no safe way to extract the boys. Without specialist cave-diving experience, even some of the toughest, most focused divers on the planet were unable to ford the length of the cave. A child, with no experience of scuba diving, would almost certainly panic, start to thrash and most probably drown themselves – along with any rescuers attempting to guide them out.

Faced with this extraordinary challenge and with time running out, our team of cave divers floated a proposal which was unorthodox, to put it mildly. On 5 July, I was exchanging messages with Rick, who wanted to know if it would be possible to sedate someone and dive their comatose body through a cave. My immediate response was that it was not. 'Sedation is not an option,' I wrote back.

*

I could think of a dozen ways a child could die in those circumstances. Barring equipment failure, such as a hose coming loose or a mask leaking, there were countless anaesthetic dangers: the child's chin would need to be kept up to keep the airway clear as the slightest nudge could obstruct it and lead to suffocation, the sinuses could fill up with blood, they could choke on their own saliva. I asked my wife Fiona, also a medical doctor, if she thought it was possible. She responded with an incredulous laugh – she said the idea sounded ludicrous.

Later that day, I had a proper conversation with Rick, and he convinced me to give it some thought. I said I'd come to Thailand to help the children, but not to sedate them. I figured I could pitch in with my diving and medical expertise, or volunteer some of our cave rescue gear acquired or designed over the years.

In all honesty, part of me was excited at the possibility. Frankly, I saw the trip as an adventure as well as a humanitarian act – and I didn't want to miss out. Craig and I were both as keen as mustard and champing at the bit to put our training into use. We'd been preparing for a situation along these lines for a long time.

*

It's actually more common than you'd think for people to become trapped in caves by sudden flooding. Since the rise in recreational caving seen in the past fifty years or so, it's been known to happen. So, the Thai cave incident was not an isolated event. It was, however, uniquely problematic.

The usual strategy is to wait for the water to recede, or if it looks like further flooding is likely, you send in a diver with equipment and an extraction plan. Craig and I had procedures in place for such cave rescues and had run extensive practice drills to help prepare for the day we might have to help extract a friend or caving colleague who found themselves stuck by subterranean flooding.

None of that was much help now. Our contingency plans were always based on the assumption that we would be rescuing an experienced caver. Here, we were looking at thirteen kids trapped two and a half kilometres underground, who were not expert cavers and in fact had no diving experience whatsoever. Oh, and we didn't speak their language.

*

I was willing to do what I could, but Rick was adamant that the only way I was going to be able to help these boys was through his plan to sedate them.

Down the phoneline, from the rescue site in Thailand to the operating theatre in Adelaide, Rick levelled with me. 'I can hear you're a little bit excited about coming over, but I just want to give you a word of caution. You're going to swim to the end of the cave, you'll meet the boys, and they'll seem quite healthy at the moment, quite smiley and happy,' he said. 'And then you're going to turn around and leave and there's almost certainly no way we're going to get them out of that cave. If you're not prepared to sedate them, they're almost certainly going to die. So, think about that before you rush in.'

I doubt I've ever had a more sobering conversation. With Rick's warning ringing in my ears, my dive buddy Craig Challen and I soon received a call from the Australian Government. Within hours we were on a plane to Thailand.

*

Before I left Adelaide, I'd been to visit my dad at the nursing home where he'd recently taken up residence. He'd only been in care for a couple of weeks, a decision we'd arrived at reluctantly. He and I were very close and for my whole life he'd been very much a hero to me. He was a great dad and a respected surgeon in his day. He was a gentle man, a vascular surgeon who loved a smoke and a drink, a bloke with a big belly and a bigger laugh, with a genuine love of life and the people around him. He had friends from all walks of life and respected everybody on their own terms. Everyone has a story, he taught me, and you should be open to all of them.

For my whole life he had been a great supporter of mine, even if he didn't exactly love my hobby. He never understood the appeal of cave diving and wasn't too thrilled about the dangers it involved. Over the years, his wariness about my sport had evolved into a running joke between us.

Every time I told him I was off on an expedition he'd look concerned, and I'd tell him not to worry because after this dive I was going to hang up my fins and retire. He'd look relieved and then a smile would slowly cross his face as he realised I was pulling his leg. This time was no different, and he laughed and wished me luck on the trip to Thailand, which by now was all over the news, blaring on the TV in the nursing home.

*

By the time Craig and I arrived at the cave, the kids had already been trapped for fourteen days. My mind was still not made up on whether anaesthesia was viable. I wanted to see the situation for myself before I decided, and as I inched down the cave following the guide rope laid by the British divers, I tried not to think how terrifying it all must be for the children. From the time they'd first become trapped to when they had been located, ten days had passed. That's ten days without any food at all. Ten days drinking cave water. Ten days of near-total darkness, broken only by the occasional dim beam of torchlight as they rationed their batteries.

When I surfaced, the filth floating in the water alerted me to the fact I was in the right chamber. The smell of that many males trapped in an airtight cave for two weeks is not something I will forget in a hurry. When I first saw the kids, I was struck by how painfully thin they were. I could hear a moist cough from a couple of them, and there were some minor abrasions which, while not serious yet, could turn nasty in an environment which grew less sanitary by the hour. They looked weak to me, but incredibly brave and in good morale. Just like Rick had promised, they looked happy and wore huge smiles in the darkness. And sure enough, I had to decide if I could live with what was asked of me.

*

Oxygen levels in the cave were already dropping. The kids didn't have enough food and they were cold. Above ground, the monsoon rains were about to recommence in earnest. According to the meteorologists, we had just a few days. The window for a rescue was almost closed.

The only viable alternative was to leave the boys in the cave through the rainy season until the floodwaters receded and they could walk out. That would mean having to dive in more than 2000 meals and once the rain started again, divers would not be able to reach the boys to resupply.

From a medical point of view that would have been a nightmare. Even if adequate air and food could be brought to them, illness would start to spread before long. What would happen when they started to succumb, one by one? What would the children do with the bodies of their dead friends? It was unthinkable. It was clear they needed to get out of there quickly. I realised I had to get on board with the plan to sedate the children and carry them out.

*

Personally, I didn't think I was at any individual physical risk. We wouldn't normally dive in a cave that was actively flooding, so our senses were on high alert, but I never felt I was in serious danger or putting my own life at risk to save others. What I was doing was in many ways much worse – I was putting the boys' lives at risk on the off chance I could save some of them.

Their survival was far from guaranteed. I was almost certain not all of them would make it out alive. To be honest, I thought they would all die under the effects of my anaesthetic. Which would mean their deaths would be on my conscience for the rest of my life. The proposal was akin to euthanasia.

Then there was the small matter of getting the Thai authorities to give us the go ahead, which would require its own epic struggle.

To convince them, I came up with a very simple combination of drugs which we could use to dose the children – Xanax to help their anxiety while we got them suited up, atropine injected in one leg to stop their salivation so they didn't drown in their saliva in the full-face mask and ketamine in the other leg to put them to sleep.

The Thai authorities asked me lots of questions – about the drugs, the doses, the risks. I had to keep emphasising to them that nobody had ever done this before. I felt like a used car salesman trying to sell an old bomb to an unsuspecting customer.

The only real guarantee our guys could give the Thai minister in charge was that if we didn't dive, the entire soccer team was sure to perish. As one of the US Pararescue team told them, 'We don't envy you sir. Both choices are terrible, but one is worse than the other.'

*

The night before the first rescue day (which incidentally was my 28th wedding anniversary), I called Fiona and talked her through the plan. 'I don't think it's going to work,' I confessed. 'I think they're going to drown under anaesthetic.'

I slept very badly that night. I couldn't stop thinking, 'Who am I to take this risk?' But the alternative was to let those children perish slowly in the dark and I had a moral obligation to try.

When faced with a dilemma like that, I would try and consider what my dad would do. The thing I got from my father more than anyone else was how to treat people – he was a very generous man. It was a great lesson in how to navigate through life. Doctors take a vow: 'First, do no harm.' Some take it more seriously than others, admittedly. Nobody took it more seriously than Dad. And during that long night in Thailand, I kept coming back to the truth of the matter. To put the kids under and dive them out presented a terrible risk of harming them, but not to do so would be a certain death sentence.

The one thing I am proud of myself for is finding the courage to make that decision to proceed with our objectively flawed plan. It came down to a very binary decision. Either I took the risk with the dive, or walked away and left those kids to die a dreadful death in the darkness. To my mind, that would have been much worse. I knew I wouldn't be able to live with myself if I did that. Ultimately, there was only one choice to make.

*

In the morning we put on our gear and with the eyes of the world on us went into the cave to get the boys – a motley team of thirteen volunteer cave divers, including the British contingent, the local expats, Craig and myself. The plan was to kit the boys up in wetsuits, harnesses and full-face masks. A cylinder of oxygen would be clipped to their front, which would serve as a keel to keep their faces down and hopefully their airways clear.

If everything went to plan, the boys would remember nothing. From their point of view, they would take a Xanax pill administered by Doctor Pak, I'd give them a bit of a sting in the leg with a needle, and they'd wake up topside. Doctor Pak explained this to them in Thai – that they would be given medicine which would make them sleep so they could be carried through the cave. They would go to sleep and wake up with their families.

I'd decided to bring the largest, fittest boys out first, as they stood the most chance of surviving the journey and of recovering if something went wrong on the first run. For the sake of our own morale, to prove our improbable plan might work, we had asked for the biggest, healthiest boy to volunteer.

Unbeknownst to us, that message had been ignored. The boys had chosen amongst themselves on the basis of who lived furthest from the cave, and it was agreed they should go first. They assumed that when they got out, they would have to ride their bikes home! They didn't have any clue about the thousands of people up above, the ambulances, helicopters and military units all waiting for them to emerge.

I helped the first boy onto my knee and gave him the injections. His eyes slowly closed and he went limp. Once he was unconscious, fitting a dive mask on him was like dressing a rag doll. Then, the first test. To say it felt very wrong, pushing an unconscious child underwater and then tying his hands behind his back, would be an understatement. An action that goes against all human and nurturing instincts; it certainly felt like euthanasia to me.

Once the children were on their way, there was nothing I could do. It was a one-way trip. If the guys carrying the children ended up taking a body out of the cave, that's what they would have to do.

Like ants underground, our team of divers worked to bring the boys out, diving them through water and hauling them through dry sections of the cave, chamber after chamber. When necessary, they changed over their air cylinders. Once or twice, they had to get them breathing again when it seemed they had stopped.

*

The dose of ketamine I'd administered would last 30–45 minutes, however the journey through the cave would take around three hours. When the boys started to show signs of wakefulness, the guys would have to inject another dose of ketamine. Every so often as the divers floated the unconscious children through the tunnels and hauled them through the dry chambers where gravity would kick in and slow their progress, they would have to stop and readminister the ketamine to the boys.

We'd prepared pre-filled syringes with ketamine, and I gave the other divers a crash course in how to administer the drug with an injection to the outer thigh. They practised on plastic bottles so they could get the feel of punching through the wetsuit and skin.

'Straight through the wetsuit, into the muscle,' I said, cheerfully. 'Doesn't matter if you hit the bone, just go for it. You can't go wrong.' I was lying through my teeth. Anything could have gone wrong, but it was to give them the courage to actually do it. I was asking them to do something nobody had attempted in history as far as I knew. 'As long as you inject the boy and not just the wetsuit, it will work.'

On the first day, we sent out four boys in total. Working in the foul-smelling chamber, I helped them kit up, put them to sleep and sent them on their way with one of the four English rescuer divers. Then, there was nothing I could do but wait and try not to dwell on the enormous risk we were taking with the lives of these boys. You can't imagine how relieved I was when Rick surfaced in the chamber and swam over to me with the news: 'It's all good, Harry. The first two kids have come through their initial dive. So far so good.'

Two hundred people then helped haul the boys out once they reached chamber three, which signalled the diving sections were complete. Applause greeted the unconscious boys as they were carried to the exit by army medics and then into waiting ambulances.

It was unbelievable. Although I'd pretty much kept it to myself, I'd thought there was little to no chance of the boys surviving. The first four had made it. The next day, four more. And on the final day, the last four boys and their coach made it safe and sound.

When I dived out myself for the final time, I had no idea of the rollercoaster waiting for me on the surface. Wild applause, a bottle of whisky passed around (and gratefully accepted), and a bunch of slightly sheepish looking blokes from around the world grinning stupidly at each other, unable to comprehend what had just been achieved.

After four days spending twelve hours at a stretch underground, followed by late night meetings with the Thai government and only then snatching a few hours of sleep, my exhaustion was overwhelming. At that point, I was running on pure adrenaline.

When I finally got back to the hotel and had a chance to call Fiona, I was just babbling, completely pumped full of endorphins. I must have gone on for at least ten minutes before I finally drew breath. That's when she burst into tears. She told me my dad had just died a couple of hours before, right about the time we were carrying the final boy from the cave.

I didn't know what to feel. It was a massive emotional swing from euphoria to disbelief. I'd just seen Dad a few days earlier and made him smile with the joking promise that this time, after a quick rescue effort in Thailand, I was done with diving. Now I'd never hear him laugh again.

I sat on the edge of the bed, with poor Fiona listening to me sob down the phone from across the world. Often, when I've been on a particularly emotional dive such as a recovery operation, I've managed to hold all the emotions at bay until I'm back on dry land. Then it all comes out in this big outpouring.

Of course, though, never to this scale – to go from what might have been the happiest day of my life, to this crushing news. It was a tough blow. But, as I sat with it, I started to feel better. I realised that for the chance to see him one more time and say goodbye, I would have done almost anything. But I would have still gone to Thailand, still gone down the cave, because I knew that this job had my name all over it. And it was the right thing to do, and Dad would have approved.

I quickly came to see his death as a good thing. Not that he had died, but the *way* he had died. With his cancer diagnosis the end might have been pretty grim, so to suddenly keel over without warning was a blessing. He and I agreed strongly on the concept that quality, not quantity of life, is most important. Who said, 'It's better to burn out, than fade away'? Every one of us is going to die, so a good death should be celebrated as much as a good life. Hence, I decided to stay in Thailand and celebrate – both for the boys who had lived and for Dad who had reached the end of his life.

He'd died peacefully, the way he wanted to. He believed in living life and would have known what we did was worth the risk. And he certainly would have wanted me to stay on in Thailand and celebrate. So that's what I did. And boy, did we party!

*

The hangover in the morning was pretty ordinary, but it faded and in time I've been able to look back at the whole adventure with some perspective. I'm not religious and I don't tend to use the word 'miracle', even though that's how a lot of people describe what happened in those two weeks. I prefer the term 'exceptional'.

It was a triumph of hard-working enthusiasts, passionate about their craft, who rolled their sleeves up, made some tough choices then got on with it. An example of superb teamwork across multiple disciplines, cultures and nationalities. I'm not just talking about the divers, but the thousands of people around the site on the mountain and in offices around the world supporting the complex logistics of this enormous undertaking.

In retrospect, I can look at the entirety of the rescue and see how and why it worked, even though everything I knew about anaesthesia and cave diving told me there were so many reasons it should fail. But we succeeded, which I put down to a bunch of very courageous, very practical people, giving it a crack.

The rescue effort involved upwards of 10,000 people. These included more than 100 military, commercial and recreational divers, representatives from about 100 government agencies, 900 police officers and 2000 soldiers.

We, the cave divers, were the most visible element in the story, true. We played our part and all held a great pride in what we did. We helped to save thirteen lives, and, on a more selfish level, we enjoyed the validation it gave for our dedication to a minority sport that nobody ever took seriously before.

We were the tip of the spear, if you like, but we weren't heroes. We were just moving parts in an extraordinary machine that took on mammoth odds and found a way to manage the risks. Nothing any of us did – or could have done – was half as impressive as the bravery and strength the boys in the cave showed the world. They were the heroes – a group of kids who survived the indescribable and who did it with smiles on their faces.

I can't imagine how I would have coped if I'd been faced with such a challenge at that age. Probably not as admirably. It's safe to say the cave rescue was a transformative experience for them – I know it was for me. A good old-fashioned test of mettle for us divers – but something else entirely for the boys. The hardship and risk tested us. But the fact is we'd had our whole lives to prepare for it. The Wild Boars were thrown in the deep end without warning and their attitude to the hardship only deepens my respect for their strength of character. You don't really know what you're made out of – what alchemical reaction the worst day of your life will bring out in you – until it happens. But I know, from long experience of dragging my own rusted-on mettle around the world, that you can take steps to be ready. And you can have fun doing it.

CHAPTER TWO

SHED GUYS

You may have heard the famous story about George Mallory, who, when asked by the *New York Times* in 1923 why he wanted to climb Mount Everest, replied, 'Because it's there.'

It's gone down in history as one of the great one-line quips, but, like most pithy quotations, it's been a little shaved down over time. Mallory went on to explain, 'The answer is an instinctive part, I suppose, of man's desire to conquer the universe.'

For me, that quote defines the visceral need to explore. It explains my need to pursue the sport of cave diving. When asked the same question about why we do what we do, my friend Craig Challen likes to say, 'If you have to ask the question, you wouldn't understand the answer.'

In this, as in many aspects of cave diving, I defer to Craig's wisdom. He's right – you either get it or you don't.

I first 'got it' back in the year 2000, when I was working at the diving and hyperbaric unit of the Royal Adelaide Hospital. My daughter Millie had just been born and things were fairly hectic in the Harris household. On the occasions I got a chance to sneak away for some R&R, I would head down to the south-east to do a bit of tuna fishing.

One of my friends and colleagues, a former police diver named Ron Jeffery, suggested that if I was out that way, I should pop over to a privately-owned sinkhole simply known as 'Kilsby's'. It was where the police divers did their training and was one of his favourite spots for diving.

Honestly, I hadn't given much thought to cave diving over the preceding years. My first experience with it had been back in 1986, when, as an enthusiastic member (and president) of my university dive club, I decided along with a few others that we were bored swimming around the same old wrecks and signed up for a cave-diving course.

Together, we went down to Mount Gambier for what turned out to be a very robust and arduous training course, with an emphasis on safety over fun.

It was winter; rainy and cold above and fifteen degrees in the water. My wetsuit was old and not up to the task, and the caves themselves were grimy holes full of silt and weeds. Half the time we were blindfolded. Often, through the endless lost-line drills where we scrabbled in the mud for a thin piece of nylon cord, I found myself wondering why anybody would voluntarily spend their time this way. I enjoyed the training, but where was the reward?

This unpleasant, introductory training was supposed to culminate with a dive in a famous coastal spring called Piccaninnie Ponds – first named in a less progressive time and now affectionately called 'Pics'. 'Pics' is known for its crystal-clear water, striking green algae and blinding-white walls. A chasm runs to over 100 metres far below, in which the azure shade of the water deepens as one descends.

It was supposed to be a glorious sight to behold, but we never got to see it. Unfortunately, the authorities closed the cave just before we could visit, due to concerns about the impact of divers on the aquatic plants. So, my first experience was underwhelming. I joined the Cave Divers Association of Australia but, after a few years, I let my membership lapse.

That was that I thought to myself. The whole experience was pretty ordinary. A few years later in 1990, my girlfriend Fiona and I married, and she was not unhappy to hear that I had given away this aspect of the scuba diving that was perceived by so many people to be highly dangerous. I didn't give it much more thought.

That all changed in the year 2000. Ron's suggestion to visit Kilsby's sinkhole would be a game changer for me. He had set things up with Ross Kilsby, the owner of the property boasting the sinkhole. At the end of the successful fishing trip, I dragged my old mate Sam Hall over to the farm for a quick dive.

For a life-changing adventure it was remarkably brief. We plunged through an unassuming pond in the ground into an astonishing submarine world. Astonishing and frigid, around sixteen degrees, and I only had a wetsuit and a single scuba tank. I went for a shallow, quick dive and that was all it took. I was hooked.

The water was the colour of an expensive bottle of gin – crystal clear with a touch of blue. The sun shone down in shimmering bliss from the mouth of the cave. I dropped only twenty metres and marvelled at the depths that fell away below me. The moment I climbed from that sparkling water, I turned to Sam and said, 'Oh my God, what have I been missing?'

At the next opportunity I rejoined the Cave Divers Association and repeated my basic training. Once I'd managed to convince Fiona that I wasn't going to drown myself and leave her a widow with three young children, I started going cave diving at every opportunity. I took every advanced course I could find – rebreathers, mixed gas, more cave courses – and soon made friends with vastly experienced divers and cavers who were pioneers in the field. I suddenly felt like I had found my tribe.

I think in those early days there were three people in particular who took me under their collective wing. I'd like to say it was because they felt I showed some potential for the sport but, to be honest, I think it was more about enthusiasm and an insatiable thirst for knowledge and new experiences. The first was Peter 'Puddles' Horne. His nickname was given to him because he would literally dive into anything more than puddle-sized in case it led into an underground labyrinth. Peter filled books with his maps and scientific observations based on many years of early diving in the Mount Gambier region of South Australia. Peter generously taught me the basics of mapping caves and taught me that a cave had not truly been explored until it had been *mapped* and explored.

The second person was John Dalla-Zuanna ('JDZ'), a senior cave-diving instructor who showed me all the different configurations that cave divers use, including 'side-mount' diving where tanks are mounted on either side of the diver, rather than on their backs. It allows for penetration of tight sections of cave, and would quickly become my preferred way of diving.

JDZ was also an early adopter of closed-circuit rebreathers (CCRs), a more complex device compared to standard scuba, which recycles the breathing gases, scrubbing out the diver's exhaled CO_2 and replenishing the oxygen metabolised by the diver. The result is a very efficient system which massively extends the range and depth for cave exploration. A CCR is in many ways very similar to an anaesthetic machine in the way it provides a fresh flow of life-preserving gas. As an anaesthetist, it seemed to me an immediately intuitive and logical way to dive.

Finally, my dear friend Ken Smith, one of the most experienced cave divers I know. Ken is akin to James Bond's 'Q'. He has a planet-sized brain and is constantly inventing or developing gadgets and gizmos to further our exploration projects. But it is Ken's side-splitting humour that makes him an essential part of any expedition!

Shed guys

With such extraordinary mentors, I began to develop my passion for diving in caves. Under the supervision of these very experienced friends, I was quickly tutored from raw beginner to an apprentice explorer.

*

In 2004, Fiona, three young children and I left Australia to spend two years living and working in Vanuatu. Fiona threw herself into the school community and fundraising initiatives. Meanwhile, I was officially employed as a doctor working with AusAid at the Vila Central Hospital, but I was also drawn by rumours of amazing caving and cave diving.

The island republic had only been independent for twenty-four years and many of the eighty-three islands remained undeveloped and out of reach of tourists and travellers. That included what turned out to be an abundance of unexplored caves nestled amongst the archipelago.

On arrival, it became clear from discussion with Ni-Vanuatu people that caves abounded on most of the islands. A simple drive down the eastern half of Espiritu Santo island revealed numerous crystal-clear streams and tell-tale blue water holes by the roadside.

On some islands you could hardly throw a stone without it dropping into some beautiful, fascinating, water-filled cave. As far as I could tell, no human being had ever penetrated more than a few metres into many of them and it seemed like I was just about the only person in the whole country who had any interest in diving them.

Best of all, the constrictive web of permissions required to access a cave had not yet descended on Vanuatu. Usually, all it took was asking the permission of the local chief to access their land.

I couldn't believe my luck – my own set of virgin caves. I would be the first person ever to dive many of them. That was the second bite of the bug. That was it for me. Obsession took over. I found genuine exploration to be completely addictive.

31

I loved every minute of it. The slow decent from sunshine into darkness. Squeezing through narrow passages and endless limestone mazes, only to emerge into still, open pools and amazing geological formations. I explored tunnels which bloomed into vast chambers closer to a cathedral than that dank cave I first dived – almost like artworks sculpted by flowing water from raw limestone over eons. Caves no other human being had ever laid eyes on. Caves I could lay the first ever guide-line into.

*

In the sport of cave diving, your life is always on the line – quite literally. Whenever you advance into a cave, you follow a guideline which also represents an essential, physical path back to the safety of the entrance.

The guideline, or line, is a thin, durable cord, usually made of nylon and white or brightly coloured – although colour is irrelevant when a silt-out or light failure takes away all visibility. On those occasions, your life depends on your ability to stay calm, locate the guideline with your hand and follow it back to safety.

As you might surmise, this only applies to caves that have been explored by divers on a previous occasion, who have laid down the line to find their own way out and left it in place for the benefit of future divers.

The funny thing is, there are few things in the world as comforting to me as the sight of an old length of line. No matter how gnarly, cold and difficult a cave appears to be, the psychological boost of knowing that someone else has been there before means that it must be diveable. It makes it feel 'safe'. But that all changes when you reach the end of the line.

When I'm exploring a cave and I get to the end of the line, it means I've reached the limit of previous exploration. The stretch of cave in front of me might look identical to that behind me, but psychologically, it's a whole new world. A world that no human being has ever seen or touched before.

At that point, I always feel a significant elevation in awareness and vigilance – a state of elevated arousal. Whatever hazards lie ahead, they are unknown. And I will be the first to ever navigate them. Anything could be waiting ahead – jagged or unstable rock, deep silt that, once disturbed, will obscure my vision, or a cavity too small to turn around in to safely escape.

Most likely it will be more cave, much like that already swum through, but that doesn't stop the spike of excitement you feel when you start rolling your line off the reel. From then on, that cave is yours – and every human being who will ever go down that passage will follow in your footsteps.

It's difficult to describe the sensation – the sheer overwhelming excitement of that moment. In some ways, that's the most dangerous part of the sport, because it takes a great deal of self-control to turn back at that moment.

At times, I've reached that point where exploration starts and realised I've reached a pre-determined limit – my air reserves are getting low, or my friends back at base camp are expecting me back. It takes a lot of self-control to do the sensible thing and turn for home. It can be enormously frustrating. The temptation to continue – to venture just a minute or two deeper, to see what's around the next stretch of rock and water – can be overwhelming.

The feeling is something that's always been part of me. As a kid, I was blessed with a classic Aussie happy childhood, dotted with beach holidays where we would go snorkelling and fishing. That's where my love of the ocean started – as well as my desire to test the boundaries.

I remember being out on a boat, fishing with Dad and lobbying him to motor further out. He was perfectly happy to stick close to the shore and catch a few whiting for dinner. But I was not. All day I'd kept pitching the idea of going out to deeper water or to the distant islands where the fish might be bigger. Who knows, we might even catch a shark!

So, that restless ambition has always been there, as has the love of all things underwater. I still get the same buzz every single time I put the regulator in my mouth, stick my head in the water and find I can breathe and move around. It's just such a cool thing to be able to do.

*

Cave diving is a selective pursuit. It takes a certain type of person to be drawn to the sport and those who are dedicated explorers are even rarer. Cave divers are often independent and individualistic people – methodical, analytical folk who not only tolerate but enjoy physical risk and discomfort. I've met few individuals in my lifetime that fit that description better than my friend and long-time dive buddy Craig Challen.

We first dived together in 2006, on a six-man dive into Kija Blue, a massive deep-blue sinkhole in the remote Kimberley region of Western Australia. The dive got tighter and siltier as we went deeper and deeper. I turned back at 111 metres where it seemed to choke out at a boulder pile, one that might have killed me, had things gone the other way.

As I squeezed down the cave, a large rock that I must have dislodged fell behind me. It broke the all-important guideline and obscured my vision in a massive cloud of red Kimberley silt.

My training kicked in and in the blanket of darkness, I took out my small safety reel – carried for emergencies like this – tied it to a rock projection and searched the area, eventually locating the broken end of the guideline which led me out to safety.

It was a bit of an incident, but well worth it . . . It was on this trip that Craig and I identified a common interest in exploring deep underwater caves and that became the basis of numerous future trips.

The other site that cemented our friendship was the exploration of Cocklebiddy Cave beneath the Nullarbor Plain of Western Australia. The Nullarbor is a remote and featureless desert, but hauntingly beautiful. A vast aquifer lies ninety metres below the surface and sporadically, large voids in the limestone have opened forming windows into it. The most famous of these is Cocklebiddy Cave, which for many years attracted explorers from Australia and overseas – a cave divers' paradise in that there was always something new to find as the tunnels grew longer and longer with every foray.

Finally, in 1995, South Australian veteran Chris Brown made a modest extension to the most distant tunnel – ending in what seemed to be a passage too tight to navigate. Brown declared the cave finished at the restriction, just over six kilometres from the entrance and so closed the final page on an historic chapter of Australian cave exploration.

However, Craig and his buddy Karl Hall weren't ready to accept that reality until they had a look for themselves. In 2003, using the new closed circuit rebreather technology, they dived to another restriction near the end of the cave where Craig waited for Karl. Karl removed his cumbersome back-mounted rebreather and forged ahead using a more traditional side-mounted scuba set. Craig waited fifty-two minutes for Karl, babysitting his rebreather.

Karl reached the end of Chris Brown's line and looked at the very uninviting hole before him. With his streamlined kit he managed to push through and noted the cave widening and continuing ahead. It was still game on at Cocklebiddy! However, equipment issues for both Karl and Craig would result in that dive being aborted and no exploration being claimed beyond Chris Brown's exploration point.

That was the state of Cocklebiddy's exploration history when, over a bottle of red wine in an Adelaide pub, I foolishly offered to support Craig's return to Cocklebiddy to finish the job. In 2008, Craig and I made a nineteen-hour return push to the end of the cave, eleven of them in the water. Craig forged ahead at the underwater restriction that had stopped Chris Brown, while I waited underwater in the pitch-dark nursing Craig's rebreather. Seventy-five very long minutes passed (fifteen minutes overdue in fact), before Craig reappeared, having laid another 120 metres of line into unexplored tunnel – a satisfying result and a 'bonding experience' to say the least for Craig and myself.

Even then, it was clear we made a great team. Cave diving, despite its emphasis on individual responsibility, is still very much a team sport. Perhaps the ultimate team sport for someone like me, whose general lack of coordination did not make me a sought-after asset on the footy field, despite my enthusiasm.

The teams are small, but vital. The bonds between divers are forged in the dark and the cold, where split-second decisions might mean life or death.

When you are hundreds of metres underground in a fast-moving current, with zero visibility and your rebreather has just conked out, you really need to be able to trust who you're diving with. For such outings, you tend to be pretty fussy who you dive with. And for even more critical risky ones, you may even be safer alone.

When I first got the call about going into the Thai cave as part of the rescue effort, I refused to even entertain the idea unless Craig was with me.

Our relationship is really more than an adventuring partnership, closer than friends. It's fraternal in a way – he's like a brother to me, right down to the fact that half the time we irritate the hell out of each other. Like any important relationship, there are pebbles in the road.

We manage to find ways to insult and annoy each other whenever we don't have a regulator in our mouths. We've been known to exchange some heated or hurtful words. Having said that, you'd have to work pretty hard to hurt Craig's feelings.

In many ways we have very different personalities. I try to be jocular, maybe play the fool and bring morale up whenever I can on an expedition. Craig is more intense, I would say. He's highly intelligent and doesn't suffer fools. He is almost immune to extremes of emotions – not to say we don't share plenty of laughs.

I think our personalities and skillsets complement each other. Together we've embarked on some very, very deep dives. You know going in that if anything goes wrong, rescue may not be on the cards. In the event of an emergency, we have discussed the possibility that it may be too dangerous to assist the stricken diver. As part of our partnership, we have discussed what would happen in a situation where one of us had to be abandoned in order to get the other safely to the surface.

That's a tough, but necessary, conversation to have with your dive buddy. To openly discuss the possibility that an attempt to assist or rescue your mate could well turn a fatality into a double fatality. But high-altitude climbers have known this for decades. Rescuing a partner in the 'death zone' above 8000 metres may be nigh on impossible. Far better to have considered the possibility *before* an event occurs, because rational thought and clear decision-making will be elusive when panic is inevitably drawing in.

*

Our deepest bond – in both the figurative and literal sense – involves the Pearse Resurgence. A resurgence is essentially the mouth of a river – the place where water reaches the surface after emerging from an underwater aquifer. Imagine a river as a gushing fountain – a resurgence dive would be a little like swimming down the pipes feeding that fountain to find the source of the water – in this case, the Pearse River in New Zealand's Kahurangi National Park. The Pearse River is a brisk, refreshingly cold thread of water spanning some of the most beautiful country on Earth. The cave it emerges from is one of the deepest, coldest and most dangerous in the world. At six degrees, the water is formidable, and I believe there is no other site dived at these depths at these kinds of temperatures. It's a place Craig and I have returned to again and again.

I first dived the site in 2007 with Dave Apperley, Craig Howell and Rick Stanton. On that trip the cave was extended from 125 metres to 177 metres in depth by Dave and Rick, who took my breath away with their seemingly casual dives into the underground river.

That trip had a profound effect on me. It opened my eyes and shattered my whole perspective on what was possible in cave diving. On a technical level it was mind-blowing – but as a feat of skill and courage, it was beyond my comprehension. I went away for a little soul-searching: 'Okay, well, is that something I could ever do?'

I went back the next year with a couple of mates. Our initial intention was for me to go just a bit further past my previous dive to 137 metres in the cave. I wanted to test my mettle, to find out something about myself. To prove to myself that I was capable of those sorts of depths in this very intimidating site.

I dived past the previous record of 177 metres down to a new level at 182 metres. I was pretty happy with that. But I knew someone who would be even happier to go even deeper.

'I think you need to come to New Zealand,' I said to Craig, next time we spoke. 'It's got massive potential to be one of the great exploration sites on Earth.'

Naturally, Craig then went in for a bite at the apple and broke my record by 12 metres, reaching 194 metres in a nine-hour dive. And naturally, I felt I had to reclaim my record.

As a community, we go out of our way to actively manage the healthy urge to compete before it becomes dangerous. Competitive cave diving is not smart. Especially for tight teams like Craig and myself, it's an extremely dangerous motivation to push into a cave just to try to beat someone else. It can be the fastest way to a lonely death. In an environment where a dropped reel of guideline or an overenthusiastic fin kick can lead to a fatal silt-out, racing down into the unknown is really not a logical way to go about it. It's not good for friendship, and it's got a good chance of killing you.

So, we split the difference. If we're diving together, someone will be in front, someone behind, but we'll dive as a team. If Craig and I lay another ten metres of line into an untouched cave, then we'll log it as us both reaching the depth or distance simultaneously. That way, neither of us is tempted to sneak past the other for another little bit of glory. I believe it is okay to push yourself to achieve your goals, but not to push another person in a dangerous environment.

Reaching those sorts of depths is a deeply analytical pursuit. There's some physical discomfort, sure, but the real challenge is overcoming the obstacles that arise as you progress further into a cave. And the biggest obstacle is often psychological. The problem with going where no one has gone before is that there's no instruction manual on how to get there – or how to safely return to the surface.

Deep-cave underwater exploration is a constant battle to minimise dozens of persistent and often competing risks. There are obvious issues – managing cold, fatigue and breathable gas – as well as less obvious, but vital issues. How will we maintain nutrition and hydration when we are underwater for many hours at a time? If we don't see sunshine for days, how do we manage sleep hygiene in the permanent darkness? What happens when nature calls? What about mental health? The acute psychological stress – of being so far underground, cold and wet and effectively blind – can wear down even the most resilient minds. If you lose your ability to stay calm, concentrate and think through problems as they arise, then the level of danger skyrockets. In cave diving, panic is death. It is the greatest killer of any factor by far.

Over the years, hundreds of technically skilled and experienced divers have died because they succumbed to panic.

Next to panic, the ever-present danger is decompression sickness. The science around this is fascinating, as is the physiology of breathing super-dense exotic gas mixtures under such pressures. Each of the gases used (oxygen, helium and nitrogen) has its own benefits and drawbacks – it is a very delicate balance. The deeper we go, the more narcotic and dense nitrogen becomes. At a certain point, we substitute helium for the nitrogen as helium is easier to breath at depth and is far less narcotic. Helium allows divers to safely explore to ever greater depths, but it comes with its own drawbacks. Firstly, it robs you of body heat much faster than nitrogen. Secondly, it gives you a squeaky voice. There is something grimly comical in dealing with an emergency situation when you sound like a chipmunk.

Algorithms used to calculate decompression are untested at these depths except in saturation diving, so deep explorers like us have become our own 'guinea pigs', cautiously evaluating how we feel as we gradually increase the depth of our dives and adjust safety margins. And the community of divers around the world with whom to compare notes is alarmingly small.

That sort of self-experimentation is not for everyone, but it is fascinating. Craig and I both have a shared interest in the physics and physiology of the dives. Between our medical and technical educations, we spend many hours trying to thrash out all the issues we might encounter and how to overcome them before we jump in the water.

The exploration dives usually occur at the end of the trip, once the cave has been 'set up' with all the life-support systems necessary to allow the push divers to spend upwards of sixteen hours decompressing on their ascent from the depths.

On any deep dive, it takes a lot longer to come up than to descend. A waypoint that takes thirty-five minutes to descend to might take fifteen and a half hours to safely return from. The deeper you go, the longer it takes to decompress, especially as you get closer to the surface. It follows a logarithmic curve and gets slower right up to those last few metres before the surface.

Our last dive in the Pearse to 245 metres meant it would take far longer to decompress than is practical to stay in the cold water. With a water temperature of only six degrees, it is not actually possible to stay fully submerged for up to sixteen hours at a stretch.

So small decompression 'habitats' are positioned at four different depths in the cave. On the way back to the surface, the divers stop at each habitat where they can get the top half of their body out of the water and thus prevent excessive heat loss. Think of the habitats as upturned buckets, fixed in place at different depths and filled with air to create little underwater hotels.

They are basically refuges, these little habitats where Craig and I are able to climb in, eat, drink and rest. Their location is determined mathematically, contingent on a delicate balancing of necessities for survival – decompression, heat loss and fatigue. We'll spend ninety minutes in one, then a couple of hours in the next one, then more in the next and so on and so forth.

That means hours and hours sitting side-by-side in silence on a little perch, our legs in the water, waiting to jump back in and swim up to the next habitat. Conversation is possible; however, we need our regulators to breathe the correct gas. To be honest, I go into a bit of a trance. The dive is the job at hand, so the hours mostly pass in peaceful silence. My longest thus far is sixteen hours and eight minutes in the Pearse waters. Craig once did seventeen hours on a shallower dive.

Year after year we returned, leapfrogging each other's records: 182, 194, 207, 221 metres. At that point, we worked out we could manage the logistics of supporting two divers at once and so we resumed exploring the cave as a buddy pair. The world seemed a lot nicer down there with a friend!

At the time of writing, our record stands at 245 metres and the cave shows no sign of ending. The only thing that stopped Craig and I after 2020 was the COVID-19 pandemic which shut the world down. We plan to go back at the next opportunity. The wisdom of that plan is open for debate amongst our loved ones.

*

I began this chapter with the famous 1923 quote from Mallory about the glory of exploring the unprecedented and pushing forward the limits of human experience. It's not lost on me that the famous mountaineer died the next year, on the north face of Everest, where his body remained undiscovered for another seventy-five years. It remains unclear whether he ever reached the summit or if he died in the attempt. His legacy remains one of intrepid adventure and honour, but it comes with a tacit lesson – nothing will kill you faster than the quest for glory.

So, we take our time. We manage every conceivable risk we can imagine before we even think about strapping on our gear. The idea is to push the sport forward, to add to the shared bounty of exploration and scientific knowledge.

Most of the equipment used by the divers is heavily modified or even home-made to improve life-support systems for the depths targeted. Part of the thrill in the sport is at home in the shed – the gear we must design and create as we explore further and realise that we need more specific items to survive those temperatures or depths. Like the early cave-diving pioneers, we've had to tinker with or invent our equipment from scratch.

One of the early (and still active) legends in our sport, William 'Bill' Stone, began his cave-diving career with the goal of reaching the end of an unexplored flooded cave in Mexico. Back then, in the 70s, he strapped on a scuba tank, which was the only option available at the time. As the sport progressed, the technology advanced and Stone was often at the forefront.

In December 1987, he caused a stir in the wider diving community when he demonstrated the Cis-Lunar MK1 model rebreather – a device originally envisioned for space exploration that recycled spent air, eliminating carbon dioxide and replenishing oxygen molecules. Bill went on a rebreather dive which lasted twenty-four hours and used only half of the system's capacity. When he surfaced, the world of cave diving had changed forever.

'You know, if I could have walked into the hardware store and said, "Hey, please give me a redundant rebreather," I would have bought it,' he recalls. But in the mid-80s, when he first became interested in the technology, the closest tech available was through the navy, required military clearance and cost $50,000. 'So, I kind of went back to the drawing board. Well, okay, I guess we're going to have to start from scratch.'

Since then, Bill, who has a PhD in engineering, has participated in over forty international cave and diving expeditions and has had a storied career in developing technology for exploring both under the Earth and far above it. These days, he is President and CEO of Stone Aerospace, developing deep-sea submersible technology and other projects designed to scour Jupiter's moon Europa for signs of life. In this capacity, he works with NASA – another extraordinarily fruitful partnership, although they differ a little on their approach to risk.

He points to a similarity between cave diving and NASA's approach in space exploration – where the priority is to assure zero risk. But no matter how well prepared a team is, once you reach the furthest point of human exploration, survival ultimately rests on the individual. 'Every single person is responsible for themselves. You can't have a mission control looking over your shoulder every second.'

Bill's attitude to risk does not surprise me. He's not a cowboy – he's amongst the most methodical and well-prepared people I know. For a particularly ambitious 1994 expedition to the Huautla cave system in Oaxaca, Mexico – which took 135 days and a team of forty-four people – Bill took extraordinary precautions. His team identified a Florida cave system with a similar shape to what was expected in Mexico and spent four months living there. Day-after-day they rehearsed: dragging seventy-kilogram haul-sacks through dark caves wearing their rebreathers, putting on their gear in the dark and running drills on any problems that might arise.

He wanted his team to be ready for any eventuality and they were. Despite all efforts, he stressed that risk, in exploration, as in life, can never be zero. 'You're only given so many days here on this planet. If you're going do something, then follow through, put the effort in. Is there a risk that you know somebody is going to die? Hell yeah.'

On balance, Bill does it anyway. After decades of risking his life in the pursuit of exploration, he takes a pragmatic approach to the possibility of serious injury or death. To him, the key is a rational assessment of what is irrational fear and what is a clear and present risk. 'If you can extract the element of fear through training and rehearsal, then you are much more able to quantitatively assess the risk and say, "You know what, we can do this. *And* we're going to come back alive."'

Bill is representative of what draws me to cave diving. Rugged and individualistic, he's a team player who takes responsibility for every decision he makes. His dedication is apparent to me as we talk. It's evident in the extraordinary machinery he creates in the pursuit of exploration. He is, for lack of a better term, what our community calls a 'shed guy'.

Shed guys and girls are cut from the same cloth and are well repre-sented in caving. They show a curious mind and the desire to take things apart, see how they are built and how they might be done better.

Some of us know how to work a lathe, others are handy with a welder, others with electronics. The most important thing is to want to push the technology forward, to find solutions for previously unsolved problems.

In my own shed, there's a small arsenal of dive and caving gear: from ropes to heated dry suits, gas cylinders, dive lights, underwater scooters. Some of it is off the rack, much of it is customised – built to spec by a member of our community, mates like Ken and JDZ.

It's a healthy little collection, but it's limited by the acreage available. Craig, who lives on a large block on the outskirts of Perth, has a fine collection of sheds.

Of course, like any shed guy, I dream of what would be possible with far greater resources. As it happens, I know someone who has maybe the biggest 'shed' imaginable.

The good news story that was the Thai cave rescue was great for the sport of cave diving. And in raising the profile of the sport, it also opened some doors for me. The opportunity I have valued the most is the chance to meet some fascinating people.

Amongst them is one of the world's most enthusiastic and renowned underwater explorers, filmmaker James Cameron. I had actually already met Jim through the small world of cave diving and a mutual friend by the name of Andrew Wight. I have long admired Cameron's development and deployment of deep-sea submersible craft. In deep-sea diving communities, he is famous for sending submersibles to the alien world at the bottom of the Mariana Trench and for successfully exploring the wreck of the *Titanic*. To most of the world, he is famous for making the iconic Hollywood movie *Titanic*.

For me, I saw an opportunity to talk underwater exploration with one of the greats of the field, perhaps the most prolific and successful shed guy in the world.

CHAPTER THREE

HOMEMADE SUBMARINE

You might have heard of the filmmaker James Cameron. At the very least, you've probably seen one of his films. I've spent many weekends of my adult life literally under a rock, but I've still managed to enjoy a film or two of his over the years. *Terminator, Aliens, Avatar*, Cameron has a history of making era-defining Hollywood blockbusters. I think it's fair to say that Cameron is one of the most influential filmmakers alive today.

Like most storytellers, certain themes occur again and again in his movies: strong female protagonists, laconic tough guys (and their guns), advanced robotics and surprisingly often, the ocean.

Perhaps his best-loved film, *Titanic*, tells the story of star-crossed lovers on history's most famous doomed ocean voyage. My personal favourite is *The Abyss*, a science fiction speculation of what mysterious things might lurk in the deepest recesses of our oceans. His love of the sea and the mysteries beneath it is evident throughout his body of work. It's a fascination he and I share.

What's even more impressive to me, though fewer people know about it, is Cameron's extraordinary life as a hardcore underwater explorer.

Cameron is a skilled submersible and remote operated vehicle (ROV) pilot and has undertaken expeditions that were once the stuff of science fiction. He has visited – by ROV or in custom-built submersibles – deep wrecks such as the *Bismarck* and the *Titanic*, and explored the lightless depths of the deep hydrothermal vents, where strange life thrives in the most extreme environments.

He completed perhaps the ultimate quest: a solo dive to the Mariana Trench, the deepest place on Earth, in the *Deepsea Challenger* submersible.

For his efforts, he has been recognised by the Explorers Club of New York and in 2012, received their 'Explorer of the Year' medal. He has also been a National Geographic Explorer-in-Residence and has been awarded their highest honour, the Hubble Medal. These are honours that sit alongside his three Academy Awards for *Titanic* (which won 11 Oscars in total). Not bad for a kid from small-town Canada.

James Cameron (Jim to his mates) grew up in the mid-1960s, at a time when underwater exploration was first coming into the public consciousness in a serious way. The filmmaker and scientist Jacques Cousteau led the charge, using film to take the world on one big collective dive adventure. For Cameron, watching from his childhood home, it seemed impossibly romantic and exciting that people could swim with sharks, explore long-lost shipwrecks and spend their days discovering new species.

'He and his guys were running around in their silver wetsuits with underwater scooters and diving saucers,' recalls Cameron. 'It was like a science fiction fantasy coming true. My personal response was to pester my father until he'd let me learn how to scuba dive.'

Easier said than done. At the time, Cameron lived in Chippawa, Ontario, a small village which is now part of the City of Niagara Falls – hundreds of miles from the ocean with no scuba training available for miles in any direction. He eventually ended up getting trained and certified to dive in a YMCA swimming pool in Buffalo, New York – a fifteen-year-old high school kid taking adult night classes his dad had to drive him across the border to attend. Interestingly, that's the same age I was when I learnt to dive in urban Adelaide, with my mum driving me to attend the lessons.

He wouldn't actually dive the open ocean until he moved to California a couple of years later. 'My first open-water dive was amazing. It wasn't a training dive – just me with whatever I had learned in a pool, going into the ocean and seeing kelp for the first time. Of course, I almost died. Of course, I kept getting tangled up in the kelp, but I somehow survived all that and learned the hard way.'

Like many before him, the young man was fascinated with the world beneath the waves – or it might be more accurate to say, the world beneath that. 'Coral reefs, kelp beds, there's so much beauty, such amazing fauna. It's fascinating, it's enriching; [although] it's what hasn't yet been seen that is most interesting to me. Personally, I always want to go beyond. To see the thing that people haven't seen.'

It's safe to say that Cameron has achieved this goal. He is amongst a handful of people who have looked upon the very deepest, most alien environment on Earth, something that was impossible until he took great personal and creative risks to make it happen.

*

Since 1984's *Terminator*, when he first cast an Austrian bodybuilder as a time-travelling robotic assassin, each film Cameron has made has pushed the envelope – not just of limits of what we imagine possible, but what we can achieve with our technology. His influence in Hollywood is profound – and in diving and oceanic circles, he's just as revered.

He and I first met when I was moonlighting as a utility diver on *Sanctum*, the 2011 drama about a cave-diving disaster that Andrew

'Wighty' Wight experienced attempting a record dive in Pannikin Plains Cave on the Nullarbor Plain. Andrew was, until he sadly perished in a 2012 helicopter crash, a storied cave-diver and explorer, as well as a gifted filmmaker and frequent collaborator of Cameron's. Wight co-wrote and produced the film, which was directed by Alistair Grierson, with an Australian cast and crew – including me.

'We should note that I was only exec producer on that,' Cameron reminds me, 'I think I was the only non-Aussie in the bunch.' That said, having James Cameron executive produce your film isn't a bad thing.

Over the years, he's used his considerable resources and clout to create a suite of documentaries and features about exploration and diving, as well as funding the development and creation of some of the most advanced submersibles the world has ever seen. Even before that, long before he first set foot in a submersible, he'd already logged upwards of 3000 hours underwater at normal scuba depths. In short, he's earned his stripes in the water.

*

A few of us in the underwater exploration community have wondered out loud whether Cameron's true passion was in fact the deep-sea, and whether his multi-Oscar-winning career was a way to fund his exploration of the ocean. At the first chance I got, I asked him exactly that. 'I think there's a large element of truth to that,' Cameron says. 'I think I made *Titanic* because I wanted to go *dive Titanic.*'

Cameron, long fascinated with the mythos and tragedy of the *Titanic*, had always dreamed of seeing it with his own eyes. However, for many years, he was limited by the technology. In 1985, an expedition led by oceanic explorers Jean-Louis Michel and Robert Ballard had located the wreck, which lay on the seabed at 3700 metres – depths impossible to dive with conventional gear.

Cameron decided the problem was not insurmountable. This has been a pattern in his career. Many things are only impossible until they are not.

On three separate occasions, Cameron has set new records for directing the most expensive movie in the world, each time pushing technology and the people around him to do things that weren't considered possible.

It is rumoured that Cameron's demands of his crew are rivalled by few in Hollywood. A profile in *The New Yorker* states that when Arnold Schwarzenegger disappeared from the set of *True Lies* without permission, Cameron got within an inch of his face and shouted, 'Do you want Paul Verhoeven to finish this motherfucker?'

Cameron, when asked about this, notes it was 'more like a foot than an inch'.

*

The set of *The Abyss* is legendary in Hollywood for the technical ambition of the project. Forty per cent of principal photography took place underwater in a custom-built tank – and cast and crew shot seventy-hour weeks for six months. Just the technical training required for the actors to dive safely and successfully in hard hats took four weeks. Cameron himself logged an estimated 600 hours of dive time while filming *The Abyss*, which he directed from inside a custom-made dive helmet, modified so his voice could be transmitted to the actors underwater.

Aesthetically it was designed by Ron Cobb, a Hollywood designer with solid engineering chops, but it was built and the guts of the regulator were designed by the legendary Bob Kirby, who designed the most used 'hat' or diving helmet in the commercial diving world, the Superlight 17.

Taking an entire production underwater – with a large cast logging thousands of person-hours under the surface – had never been done. Impressively, it was executed with 100 per cent safety – which required such discipline and attention to technical precision that exaggerated myths about the production continue to circulate three decades later.

One rumour holds that a memorable scene where Ed Harris' character breathes liquid oxygenated fluorocarbon in order to dive to impossible depths – taking liquid into his lungs instead of gas – Ed really had to do it. 'I have a reputation as being rough on actors, but I didn't require Ed to actually breathe the oxygenated perfluoro-carbon,' says Cameron. 'But we did require little Beanie the rat to do it. He didn't get a vote in it.'

As a student, Cameron had attended a lecture on the potential use of perfluorocarbons as a liquid breathing medium and the idea had fascinated him. A successful American research program actually existed, funded by the USA's Office of Naval Research, with Dr Johannes Kylstra as its lead scientist. Kylstra had successfully tested the theory on rodents and dogs. The first human volunteer was commercial diver Frank Falejczyk who became the first person to breathe oxygenated liquid. Jim was so impressed by a subsequent presentation by Falejczyk, he included the concept in *The Abyss* script.

During production, he saw his chance to use the film to experiment. He tracked down Dr Kylstra at North Carolina's Duke University. This was only about fifty miles from the production, so Cameron drove over to ask how it could be done on a live subject.

Dr Kylstra gave Cameron instructions on how to submerge a rat into body-temperature super-oxygenated liquid with its feet down and head up to help it transition into fluid breathing and how to retrieve the rat by picking it up by the tail and letting the fluid drain harmlessly out so it would resume breathing normal air.

Cameron conducted the experiments on set in front of the cast and crew, for footage that makes it into the final cut of the film. 'We did it with five rats. And they were fine,' says Cameron. 'Except for rat number five.'

When Cameron pulled rat number five – 'Beanie' – from the liquid, he showed no sign of life. 'He was limp,' says Cameron. 'Just the deadest rat I ever saw in my life.'

Cameron recalls looking up from Beanie's body and seeing the entire crew staring at him. He'd broken one of the cardinal rules of filmmaking, which is that one never *ever* harms animals for a movie.

So, he did what any diver would do if one of their crew had drowned: he performed CPR. He put his hand around little Beanie's chest and started palpating his rib cage at a high rate. Suddenly, the fluid shot out of Beanie's nose, and he gasped back to life. 'He shook himself off and he was fine.'

After that, Cameron adopted Beanie as a pet for the rest of his natural life. 'He died of old age, but I'm not sure he ever forgave me.'

*

In researching and producing *The Abyss,* Cameron worked with some of the luminaries of deep-sea exploration. Around 1987, he connected with renowned oceanographer Dr Robert Ballard, who first discovered the location of the wreck of the *Titanic.* Ballard and the engineers and scientists at Woods Hole Oceanographic Institution were world leaders in the field of deep-sea exploration. That team had already built and developed *Jason Junior,* a small ROV, and were developing *Jason,* one of the first big 'work class' ROVs built for extreme depth.

As he became more involved with these oceanographic explorers, he was struck by the potential of their work and technology. 'I was a fan,' Cameron says simply. 'I got to know them and I thought, "Wow, I could do this for real, what we only showed fictionally in *The Abyss*."'

It didn't strike Cameron as more complicated than the movie productions he'd been involved in. Both fields involve high levels of engineering, integration between different tech streams, building complex systems and so on. It dawned on him that a long-held dream might be within his reach. 'For real, I could go to the *Titanic* and make a film there. How cool would that be?'

So, Cameron put a pitch together for a Hollywood studio. He wrote a *Romeo and Juliet*-style story of star-crossed lovers set on the doomed *Titanic* ('a movie the studio couldn't resist') and convinced the studio of the necessity to fund an expedition. They would charter highly capable *Mir* submersibles from the Russian Institute of Science that could reach the final resting place of the *Titanic* and film it where it lay on the seabed.

'I told them that they're either going to spend four million dollars on visual effects to recreate the shipwreck, or we could just go film it [for the same cost].'

The studio agreed to stake four million dollars on an expedition and were rewarded with the iconic shots of the *Titanic*'s hull emerging from the gloom of the deep that made it into the movie, as well as an invaluable harvest of free publicity that came with it.

'Hollywood is about, I think, inspiring the imagination. And the idea that a bunch of filmmakers would go down to the *Titanic* shipwreck and shoot it for real for a fictional film was kind of amazing. It was a good story hook,' he says. 'I think it helped us a lot in promoting the film. But I think there was a definite grain of truth to the idea that I made that movie so that I could literally dive *Titanic*.'

To film the *Titanic*, Cameron's team developed not only an ROV that could reach a depth of 12,500 feet – a functional ROV dubbed *Snoop Dogg* that features in the movie – but a way to film it. That meant developing a camera that could withstand the harsh environment and capture satisfactory footage.

The 1992 documentary *Titanica* had filmed the wreck using IMAX cameras bolted inside the viewport of two *Mir* submersibles. Cameron needed a camera outside the craft, in the water, in order to get the shots he planned.

'I wanted to pan this thing around and do cinematic shots,' says Cameron. 'Nobody had ever done stuff like that before. So, I had to put my engineering hat on and got some engineers to figure it out.'

Cameron's brother Mike (who built play-forts and homemade rockets with him as a child) happened to be a very gifted engineer. For the first expedition, he designed the housing for a movie camera with good optics that could withstand deep sea pressures.

'Mike's camera weighed about 100 pounds (45 kilograms) and was mounted on a pan-tilt system we built for the movie,' recalls Cameron. The camera was bolted onto *Mir* 1, so Cameron could operate it from within the submersible. This gave him the ability to film precise, controlled, cinematic shots of *Snoop* from where it was being piloted from inside *Mir* 2. That footage – later to become part of the legendary Oscar-winning film – was the result of twelve dives with the twin *Mirs*, with Cameron inside one of the two craft. Each dive needed intense concentration, professionalism and discipline. At the depths the wreck lay, the margin for error is negligible.

The subs would take the ROV down to depth, where they would 'park' on the wreck at 12,500 feet – usually on the roof of the officers' quarters or boat deck.

From there, they could deploy the ROV, spooling out a disposable fibre-optic tether through which the pilot would steer. The tether, about the width of dental floss, allowed the ROV to roam anywhere around the wreck – inside or out.

Cameron had made an ironclad promise that they wouldn't pilot *Snoop* inside the Titanic because of the high risk of it becoming entangled and lost. 'I promptly broke that promise,' says Cameron. 'Once we'd gotten all the footage we knew we really needed, we flew inside the ship and saw wondrous things. Things people didn't even know existed.'

Homemade submarine

I know well the pleasures of designing, prototyping and building a piece of kit in order to unlock further capacity for exploration. Any tinkerer knows the familiar sensation of taking apart a gadget and working out how to repair or upgrade it.

There's an extra level of satisfaction in deploying a breathing apparatus or life-support system that started in your home workshop and ends up accompanying you on a journey into a place human eyes have never seen. You feel a certain pride in knowing your creation is not only going to make your goals possible, but possibly those of the next generation of explorers as well.

Cameron shares the same passion, albeit on a much larger scale. 'It becomes quite addictive to discover these amazing mysteries of the deep [by] working with very talented engineers,' he says, with a careful qualifier. 'That got the wheels turning for the next expedition and then the next one after that, and so on.'

Subsequent expeditions followed, producing enthralling documentary films. The 2002 expedition to survey the wreck of the German battleship *Bismarck*, used two *Mir* submersibles to provide a detailed portrait of its dramatic wartime downfall.

Then there were four expeditions to hydrothermal vents, home to extremophiles, organisms that thrive in environments toxic to most life forms.

To put this in context: the upper layer of the ocean is called the photic zone – the depth that sunlight can penetrate. It varies depending on the murkiness of water, but can be up to 100 metres on average. At these depths, photosynthesis allows for plant life, and herbivores and carnivores, and the complex matrix of predation that sustains life. Without light, life is much harder to sustain, and so up to ninety per cent of life in the ocean is in the first layers.

Below that, where the sun cannot penetrate, things are very different. While it is too dark for humans to see, there are creatures who can perceive light at depths of up to perhaps 1000 metres, where bioluminescent creatures hunt in the darkness. The creatures down there are every bit as fascinating and frightening as anything science fiction has dreamed up. Even further below, clustered around the vents of the Earth's core, are stranger creatures still.

Conditions at the vents are thought to resemble those elsewhere in the solar system – hinting that life on other worlds waits to be found – so Cameron recruited a NASA astronaut and three researchers from NASA's Jet Propulsion Laboratory to collaborate with. One of them, Dr Kevin Hand, now runs their Europa science group. The other two provided support for a laser spectroscope experiment built for the expedition, to test 'life detection' technology in the deep ocean – in preparation for future expeditions to Europa and other icy moons. Much of the technology applicable to our deepest oceans has potential in future explorations of other planets.

'I've been fascinated by the deep ocean for a long time, really, since high school,' says Cameron. 'In my mind, there is outer space and there's oceanic inner space. And they're kind of equal.'

The major difference between the exploration of outer space and the deep ocean seemed to be money. Specifically, governments are willing to invest heavily in space exploration because the technology developed can go on to be adapted for weapons systems. That's less true in oceanography. The military application of underwater combat is so specialised that funding deep-sea biology and geology are not a priority for military-industrial development.

Given that oceanographic exploration is given short shrift by the powers that be, Cameron felt he had a responsibility to contribute to the field of science that had inspired him in the first place. He decided it would be amoral of him to spend millions of dollars going into the deep ocean to shoot films solely for his own curiosity and that of the viewer. So, he emulated his childhood hero Jacques Cousteau and brought the scientists along with him.

'Cousteau always brought scientists with him. And the condition? They had to publish,' says Cameron. 'I just made the same deal with our scientists.'

Over sixteen months, Cameron and his team made forty dives across ten locations in the Atlantic and the Pacific. One of the NASA scientists kept a sleep log and averaged three hours a night. Some of the team found themselves tired and stressed. But Cameron had the time of his life.

Then there was the 2012 *Deepsea Challenger* expedition, which saw Cameron become the first human being to travel to the bottom of the Mariana Trench since the bathyscaphe *Trieste* in 1960. The Challenger Deep in the Pacific Ocean is the very deepest part of the seabed, with a depth of 10,098 metres. In the custom-built *Deepsea Challenger* submersible – a long submarine designed to drop through the depths like 'a vertical torpedo' – Cameron was encased in a sphere just large enough to keep him alive for the journey. But whether he would survive wasn't a given.

The craft had been tested time and again, and every foreseeable variation accounted for. Earlier designs for a human-occupied vehicle had been rejected due to the risk of sympathetic implosion, where the smallest implosion, say in the tiniest of buoyancy devices, could produce a shockwave in the pressurised depths leading to a chain reaction which would crush Cameron inside his sphere. 'All it takes is one failing, and they all go like a string of fireworks. An entirely new buoyancy system was designed and built, in order to avoid that possibility.'

When Cameron finally undertook his dive, which he has described as like 'going to another planet and back in a day', he says he was fairly certain he was coming back. He had faith in the submersible, trusted his team and had gamed out every foreseeable disaster. Which, in my experience, is what separates people like Cameron – who write themselves into the history books and live to tell the story – and those who perish in the attempt. Being clear-eyed about the risks is key.

'It doesn't make you reckless, but it does put you in a certain class of people who are willing to take what most would consider to be extraordinary risks and go through extraordinary steps to mitigate them. We spent seven years designing and building that sub. And there wasn't one failure scenario that we could imagine that we didn't engineer against,' says Cameron. 'Now, there's always that X factor – the thing you didn't imagine or didn't see coming. That's true of any human endeavour. It shouldn't hold you back.'

The fact is, exploration is not easy. It's impossible to eliminate all risk, no matter how careful, or smart, or brave and resourceful and well-resourced you are. Cameron knows that. Shackleton likely did, too. I know it, all too well. With that in mind – why do I love it so? Why do I keep pushing myself – to reach ever deeper depths? What drives a person to strap on a scuba tank and dive through a wrecked ship? To design and build a vessel that can go into the extreme depths and explore environments that human beings were never meant to see?

Most explorers have their own, personal answer to this question, but few can answer it as well as Cameron. He's quite a storyteller – there's a reason he's amongst the most successful filmmakers on the planet. The passion and eloquence with which he talks about exploration captures something I've long tried to articulate – why we do what we do and take on the risks inherent with it.

You go on an expedition to bring back some knowledge to contribute to the greater trove of human experience. You also find out things about yourself as you probe those limits of human experience. We make ourselves bigger.

What Cameron has experienced has certainly changed his perspective on himself and the world. He likens flying an ROV through the rooms and corridors of the *Titanic* to an out-of-body experience, in which he can physically sense the robot's physicality as he controls it remotely. He describes a sense of synaesthesia where his senses become coupled with the craft – a state in which the limits of human experience are extended by the human framework of the robot.

'I always say that the soul of the engineer is in the machine,' he says. 'At the end of a seven-hour dive with the ROV and you're deep inside the *Titanic*, your mind *exists* in the machine.'

Cameron describes the distinct feeling of flying the little bot back up to the bigger submersible, and, through its eyes, catching sight of the lights of the *Mir* sub above, where it was parked on the deck of the wreck and thinking to himself, 'Oh, there are those guys over there in the sub', whilst being fully aware that he *was* the guy in the sub – or at least, his body was. His mind felt as though it was housed in the machine, slowly ascending towards Cameron's biological body. 'It's the strangest thing I have to say. I could totally understand how maybe in the future, if we ever do find a way to upload our consciousness into a machine, that that shit's gonna work. Let me just say, I know because I've seen a glimpse of it. You can have a machine body. It doesn't even have to be a human-shaped body.'

Which, increasingly, looks like it might be the future of exploration. Cameron has his sights on a collaboration between Bill Stone and NASA to send an autonomous remote-operated vehicle to Europa – one of Jupiter's moons. Bill is building prototype testbeds for the type of tech needed to go through the ice and explore the ocean of Europa.

There, theoretically, it would punch through the frozen ice on the planet and scour the bottom of the planetoid's moon for hydrothermal vents and the life they hope to find there. That, I have to admit, is a mission I'm unequipped for, as exciting as it would be.

'We are hoping to get his new THOR (Thermal High-voltage Ocean-penetrator Research) 'cryobot' down to Antarctica to go through a thousand feet of ice down to a lake under a glacier,' says Cameron. 'But we are years from being able to do such a thing on Europa, where the ice is ten miles thick. You need a nuclear reactor and tens of billions of dollars for that hat trick.'

Closer to home, Stone has already prototyped an underwater exploration craft that will be able to dive depths not safe or sensible for any technical diver. In a cave system that would take Craig and I countless expeditions to slowly unlock the depths of, this craft will be able to make its own decisions on navigation – to zip through the depths without worrying about decompression, or staying warm, or staying fed and hydrated.

As excited as I am about technology, I admit to mixed feelings about what it could mean for my own adventuring. Nobody wants to be put out of work by a machine.

Talking to Cameron about his adventures, I can't help but catch his contagious, unbridled excitement about the future and what barriers technology will soon be able to smash when combined with the old-fashioned human need to explore and understand the unknown.

The way Cameron tells it, some of the most moving moments of his life occurred on the bottom of the ocean. During the first dive to the *Titanic*, Cameron had been fully focused on locating the wreck and establishing the shots he needed to take home for the movie. 'I was thinking like a director, there was an intellectual barrier,' he recalls. 'I had my shot list and all my plans; I'd researched and rehearsed every shot with a model.'

It was on the second dive that Cameron, as he looked out the viewport of the *Mir* sub, realised he was sitting exactly where the five-person orchestra had played music to keep people calm as the ship sank underneath them. He carried on, completed the dive, and returned to the support vehicle overhead. It was there, in the cabin of his ship, that his composure cracked.

'I just stopped. Everything went out of my head, the mission, everything,' says Cameron. 'That's when the emotion hit me. I got back to my cabin and sat by myself and just wept. This wasn't some science project. This wasn't a space mission. This was a tragic site where people died. And if I couldn't connect to that, then I had no business making the film. From then on, I always kept that in mind when I was making the movie – that this was about people. About heartbreak, loss and separation. That's the appeal of the story, and if you can't connect to that, then you shouldn't be doing it.'

The epiphany did not come on the first dive, or the first time Cameron laid eyes on the *Titanic*. It came – as all my own big emotional moments in caves or on shipwrecks – in the quiet moments of the aftermath, when the enormity of the task seizes you.

Cameron says he's had many epiphanic moments looking at a video screen while driving a robot inside the wreck of the *Titanic,* usually a blend of awe and excitement – the thrill of seeing something no one else has ever seen. 'And I've had emotional reactions driving the bots around the *Bismarck* – a much grimmer, sadder wreck than the *Titanic* – because on the *Titanic* there are no human remains. Almost all who died on the *Titanic* floated off the ship and died of hypothermia at the surface after the ship departed for the bottom of the ocean. On the *Bismarck* you saw leather coats and boots blown apart and blasted into the jagged wreckage by exploding shells and you knew you were seeing all that was left of men, after the bones had long dissolved in the calcium-depleted deep water.

'There are times when diving a shipwreck, especially one that remains more-or-less unexplored, when one finds some little human echo – an empty boot, or a book, or a teacup resting in the silt on the bottom of a derelict cabin. For me, the appeal of swimming through

61

the wreck of a ship lies not in the twisted junk, which to be honest, represents human litter in an otherwise pristine seascape. It is the small pieces of humanity that immediately take you to the moment before the sinking and the suffering that may have followed. It is impossible not to feel a connection with the passengers or crew and wonder what emotions they felt as their vessel sank below the waves.'

As is his way, Cameron articulates that feeling much better than I can. 'I think it's the juxtaposition of being so far from human experience, in an alien world, and discovering something familiar. There's something surreal about going to the most remote place you can imagine. And what you find there is us.'

PART TWO

EARTH

There's an element of discovery to climbing a mountain. I don't mean that a mountaineer will stumble across undiscovered country – most mountains have previously been summited. I mean in the existential sense. Climbers endure exhaustion, thirst, nausea, breathlessness and bone-chilling cold in what can only be a personal quest. The need to summit must surely be more about exploring something deep within themselves.

My own experience of mountains is limited, but I've done enough to know that such a journey is a profoundly grounding experience. Perhaps it is the danger that makes us feel alive. It could be the vast perspective that climbing to the highest summits of the world provides. Although I don't like to be anywhere near the edge of a cliff without a safety harness bolting me to the Earth, I feel a certain affinity with climbers. I suspect that as they climb above the clouds, they experience a similar restorative sense of peace to that which I find in caves, when all problems dissolve and life slows down to the truly essential.

To better understand that feeling and the psychology of those who pursue it, I talked to those at the apex of climbing, to find out what grounds them so deeply to the mountains that they want to return again and again.

CHAPTER FOUR

FREE SOLO

My dive buddy Craig Challen received a technical diving award at a conference one evening. During his acceptance speech he said something that both struck a chord and inspired me. 'It's true our group has enjoyed some success in our diving, but we are definitely nothing special. Ninety-five per cent of being an explorer is just showing up. You've just got to get off your bum and do it.'

That day, in his blunt way, Craig articulated one of my core beliefs – anyone can achieve extraordinary things. You've just got to have the drive to get out there and give things a go. No one is an expert on day one.

Take American filmmaker and adventurer Jimmy Chin – somewhat of a legend in rock-climbing circles. A top climber himself, he's taken visibility of the sport to new . . . well . . . heights, with his film career. As a mountaineer, he's famous for both big-wall climbs in the USA and high-altitude climbs in the Himalayas. Plus, he's a renowned adventure photographer and cinematographer – a career that started with one tremendous photograph – one that he happened to be in the right place and the right time to snap. How? Because he had the gumption to climb a sheer rockface.

*

Jimmy is someone I admire greatly, not least because he's found a way to combine his love of adventure and professional passions into a sustainable career. He works with his wife, fellow filmmaker Elizabeth Chai Vasarhelyi. Together, they have made some truly epic productions. I met the husband-and-wife team when they interviewed me for *The Rescue*, a Netflix documentary on the Thai cave rescue which I suspect will stand the test of time as the standout film version of that story. It is testament to their talents as filmmakers that they managed to string along and crank up the narrative tension even for a viewer like me, who for obvious reasons knew how it ended. Their films tend to be startling, definitive statements on extraordinary events.

Jimmy and Chai's 2018 documentary *Free Solo*, which won both an Oscar for Best Documentary Feature and a BAFTA – is one of the scariest movies I've ever seen. *Free Solo*, which captures one of the most terrifying athletic feats a human being has ever undertaken – a free-solo climb of El Capitan, a 3000-foot (914 metre) sheer rockface – which is to say, a climb done entirely without safety harness, rope or any specialised climbing gear – attempted by Jimmy's friend and fellow climber, Alex Honnold.

Naturally enough, when the opportunity arose to turn the tables and interview Jimmy and Alex about their adventures and the world of elite rock-climbing they both inhabit and capture so majestically, I jumped at the chance.

*

Jimmy grew up in south-western Minnesota. 'About as far away from any mountains as possible. Not exactly a hotbed for high altitude, big wall climbers,' he recalls. He was a typically athletic American child and excelled at competitive swimming and martial arts, with a focus on achievement, excellence and competition. It wasn't until college that he discovered and fell in love with climbing – of being in the outdoors, pushing himself in this new and different way that turned the focus inwards. 'With climbing, it wasn't competing against other people. You were kind of competing against yourself.'

Like many young climbers, back in the days before the internet was omnipresent, he read climbing magazines and idolised the people who documented their adventures there. 'I was really inspired by the adventurers and climbers that went out to explore these really remote ranges and were doing first ascents, climbing things that no one had ever climbed before.' He recalls reading about an expedition to the Sherpa Valley in Pakistan and thinking, 'That's where it's at. If you're going to be the best in this space, that's what you do.'

Getting there would be a longer road. He learned the ropes on the stark walls of Yosemite National Park – in many ways, the centre of the rock-climbing world, and home to the iconic El Capitan, affectionately known to climbers as 'El Cap'. El Capitan is a 3000-foot granite monolith. Its sheer size and dramatic vertical face make it an iconic destination for rock climbers, who are known to spend days scaling its face, camping on ledges as they go.

It was on his second climb of El Cap – with friend and mentor Brady Robinson – that Jimmy took his first professional photo. Brady had a camera and was taking photos of the expedition, with a view to selling them afterwards. Along the way, he showed Jimmy how to use the camera and Jimmy snapped a photo of Brady in his sleeping bag, snoozing on top of El Capitan – which turned out to be the only one that sponsors wanted to buy.

I know that feeling Brady must have experienced. Once – on the trip to the Kija Blue sinkhole in Western Australia – I was diving with Craig when I passed him my underwater camera rig to take my photo. I'd set the shutter speed and f-stop, got the strobes angles right and then posed above him with the sun at my back. I could picture the image in my mind. He pressed the shutter release then passed the camera back. The image became the cover shot for the expedition article in our cave-diving quarterly. At least Jimmy got the credit for his shot. And he did manage to get paid for it.

'I made $500 selling that one photo,' he said. To Jimmy, then in his early 20s, that represented about a month's wages, so it was a lot of money for him. 'I thought "Wow, I just have to take one photo and I can keep living like this for the rest of my life,"' he says with a laugh.

This formative moment for Jimmy – the serendipity of him being in the right place at the right time to discover his phenomenal talent – is one of my favourite things about living adventurously. You never know what you will discover about yourself. It just happened that Jimmy is one of the greatest living nature photographers – but I wonder if he would have known it if he'd never taken up climbing?

Jimmy spent the money on a camera of his own and started his ascent – professionally, in the world of adventure photography, as well as literally heading up in the world – setting his sights on some of the world's most remote and forbidding climbs.

He realised that big walls in America were just stepping stones to the big league. He decided if he was going to be the best possible climber, it meant testing himself by going on an expedition. He wanted to challenge himself with alpine, high altitude, big-wall climbing in the wild peaks of the Himalayas.

For one of his first big professional assignments, he decided to follow his dream to go to Pakistan's Karakoram Range. In 1999, Jimmy organised an expedition himself and convinced a few mates to join him. They applied for grants, sold fund-raising t-shirts and somehow cobbled together enough to pull off the expedition, where he and three others made the first ascent of the 3000 foot (914 metre) alpine tower Fathi Brakk.

Jimmy's career was underway, although his parents initially did not understand the life he'd chosen. Refugees from the Chinese Communist revolution who endured terrible hardships and rebuilt their lives first in Taiwan and again in the USA, they were somewhat confronted when he told them he would spend the next few years travelling and climbing.

'Shocked is probably one way to put it ... disappointed,' says Jimmy. 'They could not relate at all to what I was doing.' He recalls them telling him there was no word in Chinese for someone who climbs mountains for a living. 'There was just no cultural tradition of climbing as a sport in Chinese culture in any way.'

What they did understand was the extraordinary risk involved. Not only was he walking away from a 'normal' life of college, work and family and all that entailed, but he stood to lose far more than just fiscal security. On that first expedition to the Karakoram Range, in a year when Pakistan went through both armed conflict with neighbouring India, a military coup d'état, and subsequent withdrawal from the Commonwealth – Jimmy didn't even have a cell phone.

'I just remember saying, "Well, don't worry, I'm going to the Karakoram, which is in northern Pakistan and I'm going high-altitude, big-wall climbing, and we're trying to climb things that have never been climbed before. And, you know, I'm leaving in June. And I'll be back, hopefully, by the beginning of September."'

*

Fast forward a few years, some of them lean, seven spent living in his car – 'I didn't even have a van. I lived in a little hatchback Subaru,' says Jimmy, now one of the world's most celebrated adventure photographers. His friends and community comprised of the most intrepid and celebrated big wall and alpine climbers in the world and Jimmy forged a name capturing their feats, as well as his own. After all, he can't shoot a mind-blowing photo of an epic climb unless he's up there hanging off the wall himself.

Photography led to film work and new opportunities beckoned. Jimmy met his wife and creative collaborator, Elizabeth Chai Vasarhelyi, in 2012 when both were working on the adventure documentary *Meru*, in which Jimmy and his fellow climbers try to conquer a 4000-foot (1220-metre) wall known as the 'Shark's Fin'.

Some reading this story might think it is in itself an unreasonable risk to start dating a colleague at the very start of what would prove to be a year-long production, but their partnership speaks for itself.

'I'm blown away by her ability to capture the hyper-specific details of the human experience and find the universal emotional resonances in it – without having to inject needless drama,' says Jimmy of his wife's work. 'I thought I knew where the bar was and the bar she set was so much higher.'

Hearing Jimmy articulate this, I was pleased to realise I was talking to someone who shares my own mistrust of hyperbole. I like to think I'm pretty thick-skinned, but there are few things that appal me more than over-dramatised depictions of cave diving.

It's rare to find depictions of cave diving in pop culture that don't depict it as a kind of waking nightmare. I've watched some very mediocre movies depicting my sport. Some of them are . . . misguided, let's say. Others are cheap, nasty and exploitative. In any case, these films don't come close to depicting the tranquillity and joy that cave diving brings me and other divers.

The reality is that cave diving, for all the apparent risks and inherent dangers, is ninety-nine per cent tranquillity and one per cent pure adrenaline. I'm not sure how you're supposed to capture that on film, but Jimmy and Elizabeth found a way when they directed the factual story of the Thai cave rescue.

I particularly enjoyed a sequence about the people who are drawn to cave diving – a humorous few minutes introducing the foibles and weird personality types the sport throws up. Despite coming from a wide variety of backgrounds and lifestyles, there are commonalities: most of us were active individuals but not great at team sports, most a bit 'different', more of loners. It resonated with me, and I think it will with a lot of outdoor adventurers and enthusiasts – that subset of people who are obsessed with a pursuit that others consider wildly dangerous, or at least extremely unpleasant. And who keep doing it despite the high risks and the occasional tragic loss of one of our own.

Now and then, when learning about my sport and what it entails, people tell me I must be crazy. It turns out there are many people – who are otherwise perfectly polite – who aren't shy of making this assessment. To the best of my knowledge, none of them were practising psychiatrists, but that doesn't stop them from editorialising about my mental health. I'm not a psychiatrist either, just a humble anaesthetist. But I don't think I'm insane. I don't think any of my friends or dive-buddies are either – I wouldn't get in the water with someone I don't have absolute confidence in.

That said, I can appreciate their perspective. Spending hours upon hours in the dark and cold, and breathing recycled air is not everyone's idea of an ideal weekend. It takes a certain temperament to be drawn to the sport in the first place, and there are similarities amongst those of us for whom it becomes an obsession. We tend to be introverted, focused, intently logical people, in my case maybe a little anxious in our day-to-day lives. I'd be the first to tell you, as would many people who cave dive, that we can be nervous before a dive. However, moments after I get in the water any anxiety melts away.

At times I've wondered if people like me are somehow neurologically 'different' to the general population – if there is something in our biology or neurochemistry that allows us to enjoy an activity that other people would run screaming from.

One of my key motivations to seek out and interview other risk-takers was to see if they, too, found a sense of peace and release through their activities. To see what made them tick. To that end, I wanted to speak specifically to people who accomplish near-impossible feats while pursuing activities that scare the living daylights out of me. People who do, and thoroughly enjoy, things that I would consider 'crazy'.

The top of that list would have to be anything involving heights. I'm not fond of public speaking either – although the events following the Thai cave rescue have allowed me to become more comfortable with that. I still don't love it, but I'm at a point in my life where I'd be happier speaking at a funeral than being in the box! Heights, though, continue to unnerve me.

Probably the most frightened I've ever been was a cliffside incident as a teenager. My friend Sam and I were spearfishing along a coastal cliff in South Australia, when the weather turned. The surf started to get rough, to the point that we decided we had to abandon the free-diving and get to safety as soon as possible. We were bobbing about in the water under a steep cliff, and it was a good kilometre or so to swim back to the beach where we could climb out of the ocean. We decided it would be easier to clamber from the water straight up the cliff and then walk from there. I guess we were at that age when we thought rock climbing in wetsuits during a storm seemed like a great idea.

Sam went first, clambering up the rocks without incident and I followed behind him. The rain was making everything a bit slippery and muddy, but things were going fine until about halfway up when I reached for a handhold on a very large rock jutting out and felt it move in my hand.

There I was, hanging off the cliff by a handhold that threatened to tumble down at the slightest pressure. I was absolutely frozen, just paralysed with fear. In absolute panic. I was too scared to continue upward or to climb back down.

'I need help!' I called to Sam, and he scrambled down a couple of metres to where I was. Thinking quickly, he took his wetsuit jacket off to use as a makeshift rope and lowered it down to me. I held on to one arm, and he pulled up on the other, and that was just enough to give me the courage to pull myself up and finish the climb to the top. Since then, I've probably been in worse danger, but I've never felt so helpless. That feeling of being paralysed with fear and incapable of helping myself – that really stuck with me. It was a very unpleasant feeling. Maybe that's why *Free Solo* and Alex Honnold's ascent of El Capitan without rope makes for such thrilling, yet uncomfortable, viewing.

*

The first climb of El Capitan was in 1958, when a party of three took forty-seven days in total, over eleven months, climbing in an expedition style with fixed ropes. They used drills for fixing safety cables to the sheer rock face and took necessary breaks when cold weather made climbing too difficult.

Alex, on the other hand, scampers up the vertical face dressed like he'd popped to the shop for a bottle of milk – in t-shirt, slacks and grippy shoes, with no special gear but a bag of chalk and his nerves. If he were to fall, or make the smallest of mistakes on the ascent, he would plummet to his certain death. But he shows no sign of fear.

Even from the safety of my couch, it is almost impossible to watch, so I can't imagine what it was like to see it unfold in real life. Even the people making the documentary are visibly freaked out by Alex's climb. At one point, a camera operator supposed to be filming from the ground can't bear to look and turns away. Veteran climber Tommy Caldwell, famous for his own intrepid climbs and bravery (he was once taken hostage in Kyrgyzstan by rebels and escaped by pushing his captor off a cliff), seems horrified by Alex's ambition. He likens it to attempting a gold medal athletic achievement, in which if you don't get gold, you die. As Tommy points out, 'I think everyone who has made free soloing a big part of their lives is dead now.'

Free Solo is an extraordinary bit of filming. It is a journalistic essay on the sport of ropeless climbing and a document of one man attempting an unprecedented and potentially lethal athletic feat – but also a love story (as Alex is courted by Sanni McCandless, a phenomenally understanding young woman) and a portrait of a fascinating individual.

When we are introduced to Alex in the film, his intensity is immediately evident. Everything about him – from his wiry, ultra-honed climber's physique to his manner, to his seeming inability to stop climbing for more than a few days, even with a severe foot injury – is turned all the way up to eleven. At first, he seems to care about little else except for climbing, although he cares about that to an extraordinary degree.

At times, Alex comes across as unfeeling, but completely driven and entirely devoid of fear. As he inches up the wall like Spiderman, he seems totally unfazed. In a situation where I, and I imagine most human beings on this planet would be 'bricking it', he seems no more rattled than a chess player contemplating a board.

Some offhand statements he makes about the risks involved in the climb seem blasé, almost hinting at a death wish. At one point, he contemplates how his friends would respond if he were to suffer a fatal climbing accident. 'Life goes on, you know, like they'll be fine,' he says. He follows this up by admitting that past girlfriends haven't always been so understanding.

I got the impression that Alex found human interactions slightly baffling. The love story – which comprised much of the film – proceeds in fits and starts. The greater love story seems to be between Alex and the mountain – he seems happiest and most alive when he is talking about the climb. At one point in the film, he tells the camera, 'I will always choose climbing over a lady . . . you know . . . so far.'

Watching it, I was reminded of people I know who consider themselves on a spectrum of neurodivergence and began to wonder if Alex considered himself that way. The fact that this man could do near-impossible and such dangerous feats of athleticism and not seem to be fazed by it made me wonder if his brain was built differently – if he had some sort of neural superpower that made him braver than most. When I actually got to ask him, it was revelatory.

Throughout our conversation, I found myself surprised again and again by Alex. The impression I'd gleaned from the film led me to expect an intense, rather taciturn young man with a superhuman natural gift for climbing. He proved anything but and surprised me with the revelation that he doesn't consider himself a naturally gifted climber.

'I have friends who are gifted climbers who [are] just incredibly talented,' he says. 'I'm definitely not that way. But thankfully, the type of climbing that I've become well-known for . . . you don't have to be super strong to feel comfortable doing it.'

He explains that his own climbing is nowhere close to the limits of human potential. There are rock faces in the world that he cannot physically scale, but which other climbers can manage with appropriate safety gear. It's just not his type of climbing, not what he is conditioned to do. He compares it with asking an ultramarathon runner if they can sprint one hundred metres in under ten seconds – it requires a completely different skill set and training regime. 'Physiologically, it's a completely different thing. I just can't perform in that way,' he says, disqualifying himself from the category of elite, peak-fitness climbers who haul themselves up rock-faces with superior strength and speed. 'If I have any particular gift for climbing, it's just the desire, the moti-vation to go out and [climb] enough to feel comfortable doing it in ways that other people might not.'

Free soloing is a niche speciality within climbing, part of an evolu-tion of climbing in general. The first rock climbers came from alpinism, with early explorers developing rock-climbing techniques out of necessity to scale mountains.

There is an element of adventure baked into climbing because a successful climb means a constant evaluation of safety, concern for one's own life, and the understanding that the outcome could be uncertain. In the days before advanced safety equipment, GPS positioning and helicopter rescue from remote climbing sites, an injury as simple as a broken leg might prove fatal.

The risks attendant with free-solo climbing – the lack of safety ropes, or a partner to catch you in the event of a fall – are elements that Alex loves about his sport. Talking to him, I get a palpable sense of the freedom he must feel on a rock face, finding a path using instinct and experience – unencumbered by the need for a partner, or kilograms of equipment hanging off you. 'If you're climbing a couple of thousand feet, it is tremendously less tiring if you don't have to carry all this stuff up with you. So, you know, those aspects do make it physically more enjoyable like it's just more fun to go free soloing sometimes.'

The freedom that is built into the act of free-solo climbing – in which a climber scrambles over rock to look around the corner and figure out the way forward – is something Alex treasures and feels is lost on a climber who has grown up in the climbing gym.

Since the 1990s, the explosion of popularity in climbing gyms means the element of surprise and danger has largely been stripped from the sport. 'Now you can be an elite climber without ever even having climbed outside. You know, you've never had to make life or death decisions, you've never had to even think about climbing in those terms,' says Alex, who seems to have mixed feelings about rock climbing's move from the wilderness to the safety of indoor gyms, where free soloing is not allowed for insurance reasons.

'I'm not an old curmudgeon about it. I love gym climbing, but there definitely has been a transition from climbing being this big adventure to more of an athletic pursuit, a physical activity for people to do in cities,' he says. 'It does make me a little lonely and the type of climbing that I like to do seems more fringe, for better or worse.'

Sponsors, which are a vital part of a climber's ability to support themselves, have also grown increasingly risk averse. I was amazed to learn that one of Alex's sponsors of six years stopped supporting any free-solo athletes, on the grounds the sport carried too much risk. He has no hard feelings. 'You know, it's their prerogative to do what they think is best and they were actually super cool about it with me – they paid out my contract and kept giving me free products. That is the best kind of sponsorship – you know, where you don't have to do anything, but they still pay you.'

I'm struck that nearly everyone – Alex's sponsors, friends, fellow climbers – consider free soloing and the extreme climbs he attempts to be terribly dangerous. If he is, as he claims, not as good a climber as others, then how does he account for being one of the great free-solo climbers of our era? The only factor I can think of is his mental game, the utter quiet confidence in his talents – for lack of a better word, his 'superpower'. I ask him about his own perception of risk – the way he doesn't seem to recognise danger in the same way others do. I'm not the first to ask the question – Alex has asked himself the same thing. In fact, he's even looked into a medical explanation.

We see in the film how an MRI of Alex's brain found that the amygdala – the part of the brain responsible for the fear response – showed much less activity than a control sample. Essentially – it takes a much greater stimulus to scare Alex. Now I'm not a neuroscientist, however I recall one particularly memorable medical school lecture where we learned that cats whose amygdalae have been removed, became depraved sex fiends. They would hump any animate or indeed inanimate object. So, I can't comment on the veracity of the science in the film, although I missed the opportunity to ask Alex about his libido!

While he appears fearless from the outside, the truth is a little more nuanced. Alex feels fear and knows well the suite of physical sensations that occur in the body. 'But just because you're feeling fear doesn't mean that what you're doing is inherently dangerous. Often at times it is, and you should heed that warning. But many times, it isn't. It's just totally in your head.'

Alex's views on risk-taking and fear and all these things make perfect sense to me. 'If there's any "superpower", it really is just practice,' Alex says. It's the things he does, and the laid-back way he talks about his adventuring that seem extraordinary to me. 'I just go climbing and if I'm going to do something I want to do it well, so I constantly try to do it a little bit better. And then, you know, after twenty-five years, you get pretty good at it. Hopefully.'

Alex draws a distinction between risk and danger. He thinks of risk as having two components – the likelihood of a dangerous event occurring and consequences of that event. For example, it's highly unlikely that your commercial aeroplane will crash, but if it does, the consequences will be devastating. Because the risk to consequence ratio is extremely low, people continue to jet all over the world. 'People conflate those terms, the danger and consequence when they say, "That's really risky."'

According to Alex, a lot of his free-solo climbing isn't particularly risky, because he knows, based on his record of previous successful climbs, that he has an incredibly low likelihood of falling. When he scrambles up a rock face, it will be much like hundreds of other climbs he has mastered without incident. The maths is on his side.

The closest I will come to seeing Alex's sport through his eyes are in the dramatic photos and footage that show him hanging by his fingertips above a drop that would mean certain death – which, given my fear of heights, makes me a poor judge of the true risk. He does concede that while he sees the activity as low risk, 'the consequences

78

are obviously severe. You're almost certainly going to die if you fall off.'

If Alex defines risk and danger as separate ideas, he considers his free-solo climbing as low risk, albeit highly dangerous. I guess I feel the same way about cave diving. The hazards are obvious, but with good training, well-prepared equipment and a sound plan, most cave dives can be performed with a very high degree of safety. The analogy I often use is doing a parachute jump. The hazard is obvious – if your parachute doesn't open, you will die. But if you're trained and you pack your chute carefully, the pastime has an enviable safety record. That doesn't mean I wouldn't be very scared the first time I did it.

Human beings are not particularly good at risk assessment in the modern world. From an evolutionary standpoint, we have evolved to avoid certain kinds of risk, those that are tangible and immediate. We know to be wary of tigers and sharks, as we can recognise an apex predator that, given the chance, will happily make us its dinner. Similarly, many of us are wary of spiders, snakes, the dark, being isolated and alone in the wild – hardships and mortal risks our ancestors faced. From an evolutionary point of view, we are born programmed with certain instinctive risk-mitigation strategies that helped to keep my ancestors alive long enough for me to be born.

On a weekend's dive, I'll think twice before jumping into shark-infested waters even though I know, intellectually, the risks of shark attack are very low. For a man of my age, statistically, chronic illness (coronary heart disease accounts for more deaths in Australian males than any other single cause) presents a far more clear and present danger. Mathematically, the great white shark lurking somewhere out in the deep is far less likely to kill me than the beers waiting in an esky up on the dive boat.

Alex attributes his success less to an innate gift, or even physical conditioning, so much as honing his ability to think clearly and assess risk – a benefit of experience. While some climbers prefer not to think about the inherent risks, he tries to be as aware of them as possible. 'Personally, I think that I'm better at evaluating risk and danger than most other climbers, because I think about it all the freaking time. I'm a little bit clearer-eyed about some of those things.'

Alex knows what he is capable of, and what he is not. That knowledge forms the basis of his practice, and therefore his talent. Through tons of preparation, practice and repetition, he can look at certain types of cracks in the rock, or geological features, and know that he's done what is required of him many, many times before. The tools to keep him safe are locked in his muscle memory – in some ways, not that dissimilar from the way a pianist reaches for the keys and finds the right notes for the song at hand.

In this respect, I know exactly what Alex is talking about – I find strong parallels with what I do in cave diving. I regularly do dives now that I would have found too terrifying to even contemplate when I took up the sport twenty years ago. Some of them I wouldn't have even been able to watch a video of. But now, after countless dives, and through incremental increases in experience and complexity, I find tasks that were once challenging are now straightforward.

Along the way, I've had many incidents that test and stretch my ability to respond to danger and risk. For people who are not the ideal personality type for the sport, then those small scares will be enough to convince them to walk away early on, hopefully before they have a major or dangerous incident. In this way, my sport is self-selective. Nobody goes cave diving unless they really, really love it – but those who do, weather those inevitable small experiences of heightened fear, and become more capable of controlling that fear response. With a couple of decades under my dive belt, I know that if danger arises, I've been there before, and take a few deep breaths until I'm in a mental state where I can assess and overcome the problem. That is not to say that panic is beyond me. Just that I have a better ability to maintain rational thought and continue problem solving compared to when I commenced in the sport.

People who go too hard too soon will quickly find themselves in a very unpleasant situation – however, if they build up to it very carefully and slowly, then it's possible to do things that would have seemed, at the start of the journey, to be 'crazy'.

'When people talk about suppressing their fear – I think of it a different way. I expand my comfort zone until it's just not scary anymore,' explains Alex. 'One's comfort zone broadens, until it includes things that you could never have imagined at first. Part of the appeal is to take something that seems dangerous and make it feel safe.'

The science supports Alex's approach. The 'Comfort-Stretch-Panic model' is a theory concerning learning process developed by psychotherapist Dawna Markova and author M J Ryan. This model identifies three separate zones within learning processes.*

The 'Comfort Zone' is where an individual feels most comfortable and safe. There is no fear or discomfort, no challenges to start a learning process. There is little reflection or learning and the status quo remains unchallenged. Importantly, there is no risk.

On the other end of the spectrum is the 'Panic Zone', which is when we face a challenge so far from our comfort zone that it becomes overwhelming. All our energy is spent on managing and controlling our fear and panic. We experience stress and fear to the extent that the effort to control them becomes all-consuming, and it becomes impossible to learn. The risk is omnipresent and overwhelming.

The 'Stretch Zone' is a mental state between the two. In terms of exposure to risk, it is the Goldilocks mental state, where activities and

---

* Source: MARKOVA, D and RYAN, M J (2006) The Comfort-Stretch-Panic model

THE ART OF RISK

situations feel unfamiliar, and uncomfortable, but to a manageable extent. It's operating in this state – activated by risk, but not overwhelmed by it, that we are able to expand our comfort zones and move incrementally towards new accomplishments. This is the state that Alex has spent countless hours levelling up his ability to free-solo.

The longer we chat, the more I begin to think the motivating force behind Alex isn't so much a superpower, but a pure drive to improve himself. As an athlete, yes, but also across every aspect of his life. Jimmy Chin, who knows Alex better than most – they've been friends for nearly fifteen years – considers this to be one of his mate's best attributes.

'I don't know very many people who are like that – where every day, he's trying to be better,' says Jimmy. 'He has that mentality where he's like, okay, to be a better person, I'm going to do this, this, this, this and this, these incremental steps.'

Jimmy recalls meeting the climber in his early twenties and recalls an awkward, 'not very socially developed' young man with an irrepressible need to push himself. When they first started filming together, Alex would complain that stopping to film and photograph his adventures was slowing him down.

'It was just so funny,' says Jimmy, as he recalls trying to explain that recording and sharing the adventure for the benefit of the public was part of being a professional climber. Across their acquaintance, it appears Alex has slowed down just long enough to let the cameras catch him, and the world of adventure documentaries is better for it.

In the years Jimmy has known him, he's seen Alex grow more comfortable with other people, travel the world, fall in love and get married (to Sanni, his very patient girlfriend featured in *Free Solo*) and become a father. In his spare time, he speaks at schools, and runs the Honnold Foundation, a non-profit dedicated to bringing solar power to communities all over the world. On top of leveraging his fame and connections to make this happen, he donates a whopping one-third of his income to the cause. 'It has been really incredible to see him evolve and become who he's become,' says Jimmy of his old friend.

After speaking with Alex, I can only agree with Jimmy. I expected some kind of emotionless climbing machine, but what I found was a kind, passionate, generous bloke. Just one with an extraordinary talent for focus and self-improvement. Not to mention not falling off rock faces.

He is unquestionably a superb athlete. He's got laser focus and he's driven to the point of obsession. But he's far from an automaton. He feels fear. He can be emotional. And while he realises how gifted he is, he is fundamentally humble.

But does he have a neural superpower? I think his power comes from good old fashioned hard work, practice and experience, with a generous serve of fantastic judgement. In Clint Eastwood's *Dirty Harry*, Inspector Callahan says, 'A man's got to know his limitations'. I reckon Alex knows exactly where his limitations lie. And that's his strength.

My initial hunch, that Alex Honnold must have a death wish to pursue his climbing, was way off. Far from it. He loves his family, his friends, being in nature, being alive. Free soloing is just the most visible exemplar of wanting to live every day to the fullest.

'I feel like anybody could conceivably die, on any given day,' he says, in his typically laid-back manner. 'Soloing makes it more immediate.'

I walked away from my conversation with Alex with my preconceptions much changed. The idea that taking steps to confront your own mortality through defying gravity made sense to me. I could understand the appeal of slow mastery over your fear as a way to ground yourself in life.

But what if you took that idea to the furthest extreme? Would I find a similar quest for Zen mastery from someone who practised the most extreme sport I could imagine? Where the difference between an adrenaline rush and a grisly death is the shortest possible route? I decided to find out.

CHAPTER FIVE

ZEN AND THE ART OF BASE JUMPING

'If a friend jumped off a bridge,' goes the classic saying of parents everywhere, 'would you do it too?'

The phrase goes back generations, a handy intergenerational warning against peer pressure. It's deployed when your child wants to go to an ill-advised party, indulge in drugs or alcohol, get a tattoo – I'd be surprised if it ever worked on an errant teenager. I'd be equally surprised if it's ever actually been invoked when someone really wants to jump off a bridge. For most people, jumping off a bridge seems like a reckless thing to do – which makes BASE jumping – the art of parachuting off bridges and other landmarks – seems to me like the most extreme human activity imaginable. It is also, according to its participants, one of the most intense and amazing experiences a human being can have.

'It's a beautiful sport, something to be celebrated. It's man going beyond his limits,' says Sean Chuma, a professional stuntman and BASE jumper when asked to what drew him to the sport. 'It's man learning to fly, being his own superhero, which is a beautiful thing.'

BASE is an acronym that stands for Buildings, Antennae (such as radio towers), Spans (bridges) and Earth (cliffs). Simply put, the sport of BASE involves a parachutist jumping from fixed objects and free-falling before deploying their chute and (hopefully) landing safely. That's BASE jumping in a nutshell, but, as I would discover talking to Sean, there is much more to the sport than pure adrenaline seeking. 'The public is starting to see that it's a very positive thing rather than just seeing us as a bunch of troublemakers. Because we're not all crazy.'

Crazy is not the word I'd use to describe Sean. Relaxed might be the word, but it doesn't seem strong enough. Honestly, I don't think I've ever met a calmer person. He has the demeanour of someone I'd expect to find doing downward dogs at a yoga retreat rather than throwing himself off bridges. Sean has a particularly laid-back attitude to all things – he knows many people think what he does is crazy, but that doesn't seem to upset him. It's hard to imagine Sean getting upset about anything.

Sean is one of a handful of people who make their living as a professional BASE jumper. Now and again, he works as a stuntman, and the rest of the time he runs Inter-Demented BASE, a BASE-jumping school in Twin Falls, Idaho. Considered one of the world's elite BASE training centres, Sean shares his skills with his students, along with his philosophy – both of the personal growth that comes through risk-taking, and a clear-eyed respect for the dangers of the sport.

Sean has over 7000 jumps under his belt, which is the world record by at least a thousand – as far as he knows. Talking to Sean, I get the impression that he is uninterested in keeping score, or in competition. He's not interested in beating anyone or anything but his own limits.

Before I met Sean, I expected BASE jumping to be the domain of fearless, hard-living, party animals. Adrenaline junkies egging each other on to push the limits of experiences. As such, I expected a conversation with the planet's most accomplished BASE enthusiast to be a wild ride. Instead, I found a deeply cerebral guy, a psychology graduate who has thought long and hard about the contradictions of his passion for jumping, and why he's drawn to it.

Within the broader category of BASE jumping, there are several different activities – some jumpers enjoy an optional freefall, perhaps deploying flips, spins and other gymnastic flourishes before deploying their parachute. Others wear 'wingsuits' – specially built harnesses that inflate into a semi-rigid air foil as air rushes into them – essentially giving a BASE jumper the ability to fly.

This allows them to glide forward away from the point of jumping, dramatically increasing their freefall time and travelling long distances over the landscape.

As suit technology and pilot skill have improved, BASE jumpers have developed a practice known as 'proximity flying'. A flier will soar just metres away from typically rugged terrain, skimming across the faces and ridges of mountains, darting through little holes in cliffs and under rock arches at speeds of up to 160 kilometres per hour.

Sean talks with great eloquence about all the things he loves about the sport: the feeling of weightlessness of freefall; how a twist of a foot in the middle of a spinning backflip will send him spinning on the opposite axis in a way that seems to defy the laws of physics; the sensation of freedom from normal life; an incomparable experience of the natural world. 'For me, it's so many different things. I just love being up in the air and that feeling of flying . . . it's just really cool.'

Another perk of the sport which I didn't consider until Sean pointed it out – he has seen the world from a vantage point only a handful of extremely lucky and brave people will ever have the chance to. Which leads me to another revelation about BASE jumping that the general public wouldn't consider – once you've jumped off a mountain you have to pack up your gear and hike back out. This is on top of the jump, which is emotionally draining even for professional BASE-jumpers – the extra hurdle of having to hump your pack out cross-country with a system that's just tapped out its adrenaline response. It's a sport that requires a great deal of fitness and dedication. As the BASE manual, *The Great Book of BASE*, puts it, 'it's a bit like dedicating your life to risking your life and you should expect it to take up a lot of your time and energy.'

Training a new BASE jumper is a long road that involves intense practice and sustained mentorship. The very first step is to become an accomplished skydiver. Sean directs his students to master their parachute technique through repeated jumps from planes. He makes sure they have at least 200 skydives behind them before he lets them near a BASE jump – this is because launching from the height of an aeroplane is the best place to learn to fly a parachute. When launching from a plane, there is a greater margin for error than the few seconds of airtime and small landing area that a BASE jump affords.

'You don't want to shortcut your way into BASE jumping,' says Sean. 'A lot of things can happen.'

When training an aspiring BASE jumper, Sean has them try to think through every situation that could possibly happen in the air, and how to deal with it. Before they get within cooee of a bridge, he wants them to have the skills encoded in muscle memory – how to instinctively turn around a canopy in an instant or deal with an unexpected hazard. 'You do have to be able to slow down time basically,' he says. 'It's only easy until something happens, some kind of malfunction or something that is not what you want to happen. You have to deal with it quickly, or you're done.'

With almost every jumper toting a GoPro camera these days, there's no shortage of footage available, providing a visceral reference point of the speed and dangers BASE jumpers – and particularly proximity fliers – enjoy.

The footage is both breath-taking and horrifying. I can't think of a sport that would scare me more than BASE jumping. For good reason – it's one of the most dangerous recreational activities in the world. A 2020 study found that BASE jumping carries a 0.2–0.4% injury rate and a fatality rate of 0.004% – per jump. In the years since, wingsuit flying, which appears to have a much greater chance of catastrophe, has only grown more popular.

The fatality and injury rate are 43 times higher than that of parachuting from a plane. Between April 1981 when the first official BASE-jumping fatality was marked, and September 2021, 412 deaths have been recorded.

Given that there are fewer than 3000 BASE jumpers accredited in the United States, those are not odds I would be happy to put money on.

For such a dangerous activity, it's also incredibly well documented. Due to the aforementioned GoPros, the internet is full of gruesome footage from jumps that have gone wrong. Multiple camera angles of accidents and fatalities are easy to find. As someone who has spent their working life tending to people as broken bones and shattered bodies are put back together, I find the footage hard to watch. Once you've spent enough time in an operating theatre the full, visceral damage of a BASE jump gone wrong is far too easy to imagine.

In a sport where there is almost no margin for error, Sean's longevity is extraordinary. There's a certain level of calm authority in the way Sean approaches the dangers of his sport. It is, I think, just good-old-fashioned, hard-won wisdom that comes from watching people rush in too hard, too fast, and suffer the consequences. His survival is borne of practice and of caution.

'I think I'm damn good at making good decisions. I think that's what it really comes down to,' says Sean. 'In BASE, as in life, any one bad decision in any moment can lead to something catastrophic. I know from my experience that you have to be very aware in every moment, and not to be too eager to do something difficult or more dangerous . . . that's when the mistakes happen.'

Sean has found the only real safety in his sport comes from knowing through experience and instinct when to back down. He will pre-visualise every turn a jump might take, and even then, will often decide to err on the side of caution. 'You can't go full speed all the time. You have to really listen to yourself. If I'm going to do a difficult trick, I make sure that everything feels right.'

In the lead up to a trick, Sean will think about it long in advance. When he was younger, he would visualise a particular jump for days, or even years in advance, decide to do it, and then stress himself out on the way to the exit point of the jump, so that when he arrived, he was too wound up to jump effectively, let alone enjoy it. In time, he learned to prepare for every possible outcome, and then learned to trust his gut.

'These days, I visualise things that I want to do for a long time, and I think about them, but I don't decide what I'm going to do until I'm out there. At first, I just feel everything and I just decide right before I jump, because then I'm not stressing myself out. If I get too stressed out and I become fearful, that fear is pretty debilitating.'

The thing that surprises me is that Sean will often make the final decision about a jump in the last few moments before it actually happens. On a jump from a bridge, he will arrive and then take the measure of everything around him – the wind, the temperature, his own levels of fatigue and stress, 'even the vibe around the people on the bridge', then weigh it all up and decide what to do.

'I've been on several jumps where I just feel that something isn't right.' He describes a tangible feeling between fear and a gut reaction – some deeper instinct warning him off. 'It's hard to decipher between the two, but I know if something doesn't feel right, I just don't do it.'

One of the hardest things in any high-risk venture is knowing when to back down. I recall Bill Stone's explanation for his longevity in cave diving and exploration, which he put down to one factor – knowing when to walk away. It's a truism that in cave diving, like in any extreme sport, the people who survive longest are the ones who know when to pack up their bat and ball and go home.

It's the people who, on the verge of a big technical dive – after spending vast amounts of time, energy, effort and money just to get themselves to the water's edge – find one minor equipment fault and say, 'You know what, today is not the day.'

They've got the strength of character to walk away, despite the fact that it's going to disappoint the people who've helped them get to that point. Supplied money and equipment, and even carried their gear. It takes a lot of personal courage to say 'no'. To admit to yourself and others that at that moment in time, it's not a safe thing to do.

Sean knows this well. In his sport, with its public perception of high adventure and adrenaline, there is the added pressure of sponsors and camera crews.

BASE jumping crops up fairly frequently in pop culture – especially in high-octane Hollywood movies. Wing suits have proven to be an easy way for screenwriters to get a movie star from point A (usually a skyscraper) to point B (usually the middle of a fight). *Tomb Raider*'s Lara Croft has BASE jumped. So has Batman. James Bond has done it four times and counting.

Highly skilled proximity fliers are sought after to shoot action scenes for films, and it takes an entirely new level of bravery to tell a film producer 'not today'. 'Let's say, someone's got a job to do a television show or commercial, or something like that. You've got all this pressure, a company that's spent thousands and thousands of dollars to get this certain shot, and to have to say, "Hey, you know, something doesn't feel right" is not easy. But it's a huge thing. It's so important.'

As I speak to Sean, I start to understand that the Zen quality to his outlook is perhaps the result of careful conditioning. He's an athlete who understands that the most important asset in his sport is a sense of calm and self-acceptance. The ones who survive are the ones with a healthy appreciation of their own limits.

When he walks away from a lucrative stunt jump for safety reasons, there's always the possibility that it would have been fine. Many times, he's walked away wondering if he's wasted an opportunity. 'But it's the wondering versus actually having just gone for it and have it all gone wrong. That's what keeps you alive.'

It goes without saying that Sean understands the value of caution. He also knows, all too well, that despite taking every precaution, all the preparations in the world do not prevent unforeseen accidents – freak weather, slips, failures of reflex or nerve, equipment failure, or just plain bad luck – what Sean calls 'lightning strikes'.

'I mean, I've hit cliffs before,' admits Sean, 'but not super hard.' He has had several '180s', incidents where the parachute opens facing backwards, sending the jumper straight back towards their launching place. If that happens when launching off a cliff, the BASE jumper only has a few seconds to turn it around before they smash into the rock face. The best-case scenario in that situation is that the parachute gets snagged on the rocks, and the jumper gets strung up, rather than falling the entire height of the cliff.

'Then you're hanging there with broken bones until you get rescued. Yeah, it can be pretty scary if it's a cliff,' says Sean mildly, before adding, 'You know, it's still really, really fun.'

Sean recalls five serious accidents across his career, including an incident that totally destroyed his left knee. It was during a fairly routine jump – off a popular bridge in Twin Falls, Idaho, perhaps the only one legal all year around for BASE jumpers to use without special permission – when Sean slipped and found himself falling in an awkward position, so that part of his harness became caught beneath his left leg. When the parachute opened, it snapped his leg sideways, tearing all the ligaments in it. That was nine years ago, and, despite surgery and a long recovery, Sean can still feel it in certain weather.

That's not the only injury that Sean, or those close to him, have suffered.

'I've lost a lot of friends – more than I can even name right now,' he tells me. 'It's very sad, and it causes a lot of trauma in our sport.'

This, sadly, is something I can empathise with. I've had friends who died in the pursuit of cave diving and, logically, I know I will probably lose more before my days are done. With this in mind, I wanted to know if that knowledge ever makes him second guess what he does. Does it ever make him want to walk away from it all?

In grief, as in all aspects of life, Sean is philosophical. 'It's pretty mysterious. You have friends you are really close to and then all of a sudden, they're gone, and you're left wondering what to think. And a lot of people look for something to blame.'

He's seen friends blame BASE jumping for the loss of one of their own and consequently leave the sport and the community and disassociate from their friends who continue to pursue it. He understands that drive. But then, he's seen people express regret when they lose another friend to the sport and wish that they'd spent more time with them while they were alive.

'It's still really hard to lose friends. And it's not like that gets easier. It really makes you grow as a person and think about what's beyond life, helps you realise more clearly your purpose, how you live your life. So, I think in the end, it's a good experience, even though that may sound kind of morbid.'

This, too, is something I can understand. As much as my sport has taken from me, it has provided me with an intangible benefit that I've never found in any other field. There is something existentially confronting about going into a cave, spending hour upon hour in an almost trancelike state in the dark and cold, and then emerging. The proximity to death is life-affirming. It is, for lack of a better word, healing. It is an almost esoteric thing, something every serious cave diver I know shares, that we take the stress and woe of everyday life into the cave with us and leave it there when we surface. Cave diving makes me a better doctor, friend, and (I hope) husband and father. Without it, I'd be a very different person.

Sean found BASE jumping at a crucial time in his life. As a younger man, graduating from the University of Nebraska with a bachelor's degree in psychology, he lived an ordinary life – and found it unbearable. The nine-to-five jobs he held caused him stress, anxiety, the feeling that work was a prison. Since he found a way to live as a full-time BASE jumper, the Zen contentment he seems to greet the world with found him. Whatever he finds in those few seconds of freefall makes the rest of his life much richer.

Sean understands the sport in the way only professional sportsmen and women do. He has obviously spent a great deal of time meditating on the risks, the consequences and the benefits. But what about his family? I know I feel a pang of guilt every time I gear up to head off on a cave-diving expedition with my mates, knowing I leave my wife and kids at home to bear the stress and worry while I indulge myself in adventure. Most risk-takers I know experience something similar. I wonder, does he ever feel selfish for the anxiety his sport must cause his loved ones?

'No.' His answer is emphatic. 'I understand that if something did happen, they would be devastated. But they know that I love [BASE jumping]. And they know that I'm very careful. But that doesn't make me immune from danger.'

Rather than guilt, Sean says he feels gratitude. He is grateful for a family who understands that his sport, risky as it is, is a fundamental part of him.

'My girlfriend is so, so supportive of my sport. She could easily tell me that she hates it and that she wishes I didn't do it. But she knows I wouldn't be the same person without it. It's a part of me – it makes me who I am.'

Sure, some people might consider the way he lives to be mad, but while he is too polite to put it in so many words, I get the feeling he thinks the way most others live to be just as crazy.

To Sean, the greater danger in life is to find yourself in a rut. He points to people who get locked into routines, find office jobs, and live the same day over and over again. It works for some people, but a clockwork life is only comfortable until a spanner gets thrown in the works.

'I think it's kind of dangerous to live in the routines that we live in. Once you have these little deviations during the day, you freak out, and that's kind of a scary thing,' says Sean. 'I wish we could have more of a free life. The main part is the drive for, and necessity of, money, so we do these crazy things that don't feel natural or feel like we're living a natural existence.'

Sean worries that people get bored and depressed living routine, predetermined lives, locked into a society that they might not feel like they belong in. 'I know I do,' says Sean. 'If you're not living on the edge a little bit, I think you get kind of lazy and bored.'

And spending your whole life like that? When you look at it from Sean's perspective, that does seem like the crazier option.

For Sean, the antidote to that existential malaise is the feeling of freefall. For me, it's the slow descent into the gloom. For others, it's motorbikes, or horse-riding, or surfing, or dressing up as a Viking to sword fight in a park. The world is a wide and fascinating place. For each one of us, it will be a different thing, but I do think everyone has a part of them that craves a little danger. I don't think anyone grew up dreaming of spending their weekends filling out Excel spreadsheets.

The longer I spend on this planet, the more I feel that our modern lives are too safe for our wellbeing. Obviously, this doesn't apply everywhere in the world, but if you're reading this, the chances are that you're not in a warzone, that you have ample food and water, electricity, a roof over your head. For modern, industrialised human beings, all things being stable, we can expect to live long and uneventful lives. We don't need to walk for kilometres because cars whisk us to work. We don't go out to explore our environment because screens bring the world to us.

Because of all this, the essential, wild part of us is atrophying. Depression and anxiety are endemic in our society including in our children. The jury is out on why this is, and I believe it's actually important for the human condition to still be exposed to some risk. An inoculation against hardship to make us stronger and more resilient.

That, for me, is the big benefit of risk-taking activities – it actually encourages personal growth. When I look back over my life, I see the times that I was confronted with my own fallibility and mortal fragility as formative in making me who I am today. If I'd never faced my fears as a young man, then there would have been no way I could have gone into that cave in Thailand and done my part in getting those boys out.

However, I'm not sure I'm qualified to preach about the benefits of encouraging young people to jump off bridges. So, I sought out someone who is.

CHAPTER SIX

THE PSYCHOLOGY
OF RISK

We, humans, are objectively a very strange species. There are a thousand reasons to think this, but my particular interest lies in the field of risk-taking, where humans are a bit of an anomaly. While other species put themselves at peril for sensible reasons – for food or to ensure mating success – unnecessary risk-taking is nearly unique to humans. These behaviours include activities I might categorise as positive, such as skydiving, BASE jumping, rock climbing and other recreational activities. Then you have negative or antisocial activities such as crime, drug abuse and gambling.

While a few studies have shown examples of other species exhibiting unnecessary risk, the extent is much more limited than that of humans and is usually in a domain of activity the animal already carries out instinctively. A goat, for example, will climb an inhospitable mountain in search of a meal or a mate – but will not risk life and limb just for the thrill of it.

There seems to be a quirk in our biological programming that makes some of us crave risk. But why? Was there an evolutionary advantage to our ancestors going out of their way to put themselves in danger?

What does the need to summit the mountain – not as the goat does, but as an ape with aspirations – tell us about the valleys we evolved in?

Professor Bill von Hippel is Professor of Psychology at the University of Queensland and the author of more than 100 peer-reviewed articles. In his book, *The Social Leap*, he attempts to explain modern human psychology and society from an evolutionary viewpoint. His thesis points to a particular moment in our pre-history, when our ancestors migrated from the dense rainforest to the open savannah in East Africa – roughly six million years ago.

'The data suggests that the forests dried out on the east side of the Rift Valley, due to geological upwelling,' explains von Hippel, 'so the trees really abandoned us – not the other way around.'

Our ancestors, who had evolved in one environment, had to adapt to a new one quickly. Life on the sprawling grasslands precipitated a shift from individualistic ways of living to a more cooperative approach. This was the birth of what you might call 'social intelligence', and it was one of the most significant events in the history of human evolution.

According to von Hippel, the move to the savannah produced a cascade of advances in human intelligence and innovation that led inexorably to the world we live in today. But it also cemented pathologies in the human mind that continue to shape how we live, think and judge.

Von Hippel believes this shift explains many of our psychological quirks – including our nebulous and occasionally harmful appetite for risk. When I spoke to Bill, I wanted to know how our ancestors evolved from great apes that walked out of their natural habitat a scant few million years ago, into organisms both capable and fond of Formula 1 racing.

'The question is, when did we gain the capacity to plan for the future?' says the professor. 'That's a super important human ability, one that's highly involved in risk-taking. Most people who take big risks do so very knowingly, with careful planning. So, when did we gain this capacity?'

The clues lie in the fossil record. Approximately 2.7 million years ago, our *Homo habilis* ancestors used tools of sharpened stone, but no evidence exists that they were carried any great distance from where they were made.

Fast forward a million years and *Homo erectus* were also making stone tools – but using them differently. Archaeologists have found *Homo erectus*-era tools were carried great distances from where they were quarried and made.

This suggests that our *Homo erectus* ancestors could envision a world where they would need a tool beyond the moment and purpose for which they fashioned it. They would make a tool, such as an axe, and would then hang on to it, anticipating having to fell another tree in the future.

This appears to be a cognitive capacity our earlier ancestors lacked – as do our evolutionary cousins, the great apes. 'Chimpanzees will use a tool and when they're done with it, they throw it away. They can't anticipate a future where they'll ever need it again,' explains von Hippel.

That fact suggests that when proto-humans developed the capacity to anticipate future needs, they were able to plan against future risks – they could craft weapons for future conflict, for example, or fashion garments to clothe them in inhospitable climates.

The ability to perceive distant, abstract difficulties and then problem-solve and mitigate risks – whether from predators, from climate, or from rival human groups – is a profoundly human ability. Being able to anticipate threats and work to mitigate them gave our ancestors an evolutionary advantage over rival species. This seems to be a key factor in how we became one of the apex species on the planet.

Proto-humans who could plan for and mitigate risk were more likely to survive and pass on their DNA – and hence the ability to perceive and tolerate abstract risks. As such, modern humanity has evolved to seek out risk under certain circumstances.

Our brains seem, for lack of a better term, to 'like' risk. Stressful or painful experiences – such as those stemming from risk-taking – lead to increased physiological arousal. The adrenal glands release greater amounts of adrenaline, noradrenaline, and other hormones in an 'adrenaline rush'.

The human body's 'fight or flight' response is identical, whether triggered by a violent attack, or when jumping out of an aircraft for the first time. For that matter, the same as when we undertake a task which is not physically risky, but which scares us. If you've ever had sweaty palms and a racing heart before sitting an exam, you can thank your adrenal glands.

The stress reaction also induces the release of endorphins – neurotransmitters which act on the opiate receptors in the brain. These stimulate feelings of pleasure and wellbeing, as well as reduce pain.

Endorphins are released during an adrenaline rush to help maintain homeostasis and linger after the rush has passed. That's why it is so much fun to skydive, for example – once your feet hit the ground, your body knows it is safe, but is still awash with feel-good chemicals.

To put that another way – biologically, we are designed to be able to respond to perceived threats, react in a way that ensures our survival, and our biochemistry rewards us appropriately. Science suggests a gendered difference in the risk/reward dopamine response, skewed towards males.

Testosterone – the male sex hormone – is related to dopamine trans-mission in the brain. Elevated testosterone levels may lead to elevated dopamine; the more testosterone there is in your system, the more pleasurable the thrill during athletic and/or adventurous activities.

There's some evidence that the risk/reward centre of the brain doubles down on this mechanism, with risk taking activities actually increasing testosterone levels in the body.*

This suggests that young men, at the peak of their lifetime testosterone levels, may have a stronger response to risk-related endorphins. In a nutshell, they take more risks because their brains give them greater rewards.

Of course, men are not the only ones drawn to these activities – women get just as much a kick out of going fast, going hard, going as far as the most gung-ho males out there. At the risk of generalising, they do tend to be smarter about it though.

Professor von Hippel points to a study by one of his PhD students, now a professor in Amsterdam.** A group of young, male, heterosexual skateboarders were asked to perform a specific, potentially dangerous skate trick they had been working on but had not yet mastered. The control group were spoken to by a male experimenter, while another group was asked by an attractive female experimenter. The scientific study found that the young men pushed themselves harder to impress the attractive woman – statistically pulling off the trick more often and crashing and burning more often. A study of their saliva found their testosterone spiked when given a chance to impress a woman.

The experiment showed that a statistically significant increase in risk-taking behaviour corresponded with a hormonal response to a perceived mating opportunity. Other experiments have observed similar increases in risk-taking in the presence of someone they find

---

* Source: https://www.researchgate.net/publication/8528581_Testosterone_shifts_the_balance_between_sensitivity_for_punishment_and_reward_in_healthy_young_women
https://www.researchgate.net/publication/5340434_A_Social_Neuroscience_Perspective_on_Adolescent_Risk-Taking

** Source: https://www.psychologytoday.com/us/blog/alternative-truths/201012/pretty-women-make-simple-men

attractive. That said, any woman could probably have told you the same thing without the need for a scientific experiment. The male of the species never fails to disappoint me. We are totally transparent and predictable! As we have been since the dawn of time.

As humanity continued to thrive, 'survival of the fittest' – the golden rule of evolution – put a premium on risk-taking. According to von Hippel, our ancestors who had greater tolerance for risk tended to engage in behaviours such as exploration, conquest and dynasty-building, which made them more likely to pass on their genes. Since historically these activities were done by men who then passed on their genes to us, it means our genetics – especially those of us who carry a Y chromosome – make us predisposed to have a healthy appetite for risk.

'Males of the species were pressed to seek out risk in order to reproduce,' explains von Hippel. 'The best thing that they could possibly do was take big risks to try to take an opportunity to get into the gene pool.'

This is perhaps a rather brutal, testosterone-driven theory, but human history has for the most part been a fairly tough, testosterone-driven journey.

If, right now, you were to examine the genes of any given human on the planet to track the DNA they had inherited from their male relatives versus those inherited from their female relatives, you would find something unusual. We all have many more female relatives than male. At first, this fact might seem odd, as procreation surely takes two to tango.

Professor von Hippel points to this as evidence of Darwinian natural selection at work. 'Some men were very successful at finding mates and conceived offspring with lots of different women. Some men died before procreating, never passing on their genes, and were left out of the gene pool entirely.'

Scientists like von Hippel see this uneven weighting of our genetic history – the fact that we have many more female relatives than male – as evidence that, in Darwinian terms, risk has its reward.

Take the Mongolian emperor Genghis Khan, for example. He died almost eight centuries ago after conquering much of the known world, siring many children and killing many, many potential rival fathers in those lands.

In 2003, an evolutionary geneticist named Chris Tyler-Smith discovered that 8% of men across sixteen different ethnic populations in Asia shared a common Y chromosome pattern. Together with a genetics reference team and cross-referencing historical data, Tyler-Smith was able to ascertain this as Genghis Khan's bloodline – and that 1 in 200 men in the world today are direct descendants of Genghis Khan.

Another way to look at those numbers – up to 0.5% of the world's population, primarily located in Asia, can trace their lineage to Genghis Khan directly along their paternal bloodlines. The data also indicates that 8% of men who live in the areas that were parts of the former Mongol empire carry nearly identical Y chromosomes. From a Darwinian point of view, you could call that a success. Throughout history, individuals like Genghis Khan – who we can surmise had a strong biological tolerance to risk – are now hugely over-represented in the gene pool, as are their genes.

A team of genetic researchers have linked a particular dopamine receptor D4 gene (DRD4) to a propensity for financial risk-taking. Their research seems to suggest that risk-taking investors tend to be people more prone to accept risk for reasons other than monetary incentives. To put it another way, they enjoy the risk itself that's inherent in investing, as well as the financial rewards. This also applies to problem gamblers who insist they enjoy the game, even when they are losing money.

A growing body of research shows that gene variations on dopamine receptors make some people more prone to risk-taking behaviours. If that's true, I wondered if it is possible to predict behaviour from the genetic blueprint – for example, if a child is born with a particular gene, known as a 'candidate gene', will they grow up to enjoy risk? I put the question to von Hippel, who says that the science is not that clear cut.

'It has turned out to be the case that most candidate gene studies end up being very hard to replicate,' says von Hippel.

When a behaviour is linked to a single gene in an individual, there's no guarantee that the next individual with that gene will display that behaviour. Most geneticists have given up on searching for single genes to explain behaviours, in favour of a polygenic approach.

One of the founders of the field, geneticist and psychologist Robert Plomin, encourages a more pluralistic view of understanding genetics. Whereas once science thought we would find 'gold nuggets' in our genetics – X gene makes us smart or agile, Y gene makes us overweight, or prone to depression – the genes which dictate our existence are closer to 'gold dust'. That is, there are literally thousands of genes which together make up for significant variance in our personality. Research is ongoing, but it appears that if you inherit enough risk-taking 'gold dust' from your parents, then you're more likely to be a risk-taker yourself.

Professor von Hippel stresses that these are scientific facts – not a moral judgement. If our potential for risk-taking behaviour is pre-programmed into us, it's still up to us how we follow the program.

'Evolution is not a moral force. It's not an immoral force. It's an amoral force. We should not base our morality on the way we evolved but how we'd like the world to be.'

It's important, von Hippel says, to remember that genetics are only part of the story. We don't have the capacity to measure every gene that makes up the plurality of a person. Even when we work to find the genes responsible for a complex trait, they don't dictate our behaviour entirely. If, for example, I had a genetic tendency towards problem gambling, but never set foot in a casino in my life, I would never know I had an issue. The best science so far seems to indicate that whether a human being will express the behaviour linked to that trait comes down to environment and personality. In terms of nature versus nurture, it's about a half-and-half split.

'Whether you engage in a particular behaviour is only about fifty per cent to do with your genes,' says von Hippel. 'The other fifty per cent is something about your environment and experiences that causes you to enjoy it.'

This leads me to think about my own life and the fact that I discovered cave diving more or less by accident. In another life, I might have never taken up the initial offer to jump into that hole in a paddock and my life would have turned out entirely differently.

To illustrate his point, Professor von Hippel invites me to imagine that I had an identical twin. This twin might be genetically primed to get as much out of cave diving as I have, but decided to prioritise other things, or perhaps had a bad experience in life that stopped him ever embracing physical risk in his life. 'Environment, our upbringing and our agency, all those things matter,' says von Hippel. 'There's a lot of personal agency and choice involved.'

The intersection of risk and choice is something I've long thought about. As an adult, with some degree of agency in my own life, I can choose the level of risk, hardship or discomfort that I'm willing to tolerate (at least for circumstances within my control). It wasn't always that way.

I remember one of the first physical hardships I ever experienced was on a school hiking trip. Nothing catastrophic – just a hike through the Adelaide Hills in winter with a compass and a backpack. But every little thing went wrong. The hills up there are hardly tropical, but for the whole trip it wouldn't stop raining. Our tent leaked so our sleeping bags were soaked. Nobody could start a fire or cook proper food. It was wet and miserable, basically, day after day.

'This is crap,' I complained to Sam, my old mate who always seemed to be there whenever I nearly killed myself. 'I don't want to be here anymore.'

But you can only wallow for so long. At a certain point, we decided it would be more fun to see the humour in the situation, rather than the misery. 'This is character-building,' we told each other, one of those clichéd phrases that grown-ups used, and we rolled our eyes at, and we laughed. From then on, the whole thing was a joke – when we shivered at night, it was character-building. When we ate our cold, soggy dinners, it was character-building. When we finally walked out of the forest after a shit few days, it was, much to our surprise, truly character-building.

As it turned out, learning to laugh at our discomfort was a helpful sort of strategy to endure those few days. In fact, it ended out being a significant moment in my life. It was the first time I had to actively turn my head around in bad times to try and make things more positive, something that has served me well ever since.

'What the literature shows us is a little bit of adversity in life is a good thing,' says von Hippel. The consensus between psychological researchers is that children who encounter no stumbling blocks tend to fall apart later in life when they inevitably encounter one.

It appears that exposure to risk while a young mind is developing works a little like the immune system. In the same way that a child's natural defences against infection will be weakened if they are never exposed to or primed against pathogens, formative events where a child encounters and overcomes pitfalls in life are necessary for developing resilience.

'The more you've led this protected existence, the more you're just at a loss when things actually go wrong,' says von Hippel. 'The cliched expression, "what doesn't kill you makes you stronger" – there's a lot of truth to that.'

Conversely, science tells us that too much exposure to adversity and endless risk is terribly detrimental to a child's development. For children who grow up in a constant state of heightened arousal, constantly having to fend for themselves – like in an abusive household, for example – this can have catastrophic effects on brain development and future wellbeing. In terms of developmental psychology, there appears to be a sort of 'Goldilocks' zone that leads to optimal development – a child who is neither spoiled by lack of challenge, nor crippled by unfair burdens.

'When adversity is overwhelming, it's a huge problem,' says von Hippel. 'But the moderate level that we're blessed to experience in these industrialised democracies in which we live, is a good thing.'

Professor von Hippel points to the wisdom enshrined in the parenting classic *The Blessing of a Skinned Knee*, by the clinical psychologist Wendy Mogel. In the book, she argues that 'real protection means teaching children to manage risks on their own, not shielding them from every hazard'.

That was certainly in vogue when I was a kid. The institution of parenting was less 'helicopter' and more 'free-range'. Children went out to play when the sun was out, came home in time for dinner, and if necessary, you patched them up then. It wasn't a perfect system, but it had its moments. There was very little limitation on what we were allowed to do. Society in general seemed to have more of a slant towards adventurousness – we were encouraged to get out there and go camping or fishing. Naturally, that came with some risk attached, but, on the whole, my generation got through it with fond memories and a minimum of scarring.

I remember when I was a young doctor, working in the United Kingdom in 1991, being struck by the number of signs saying, 'Keep off the grass'. Everywhere you looked, there were some of the most lovingly-tended lawns in the world, beautiful stretches of green grass – but they weren't meant to be enjoyed. I remember taking a stroll between shifts at my hospital, on a rare beautiful English summer day, coming across one of these tame little signs and finding it wildly offensive.

'What an appalling country,' I said to myself. 'You get one day of the year when you could actually sit on the grass and not suffer hypothermia and you weren't allowed to.' It struck me as a microcosm of a society that was so over-regulated that sitting on the grass on a lovely afternoon was dangerous enough to man or grass that it needed prohibition.

Fast forward thirty years and I find myself in a country that's twice as bad in many ways. Not long ago, I was in Sydney with a spare morning and decided to go for a dip. I went down to Coogee – arguably one of the greatest surf beaches in the world, one of the stretches of golden sand that is the embarrassment of riches of Sydney's coastline. The day was perfect – soft sun, the temperature nudging 28°C, the ocean heaving with glistening twelve-foot waves, sunburned back-packers hurling themselves into the white water, and then popping up moments later after a quick spin-cycle in the surf.

I was just putting down my towel, when a klaxon – the sort of thing you might have heard in 1944 Britain moments before a V-2 rocket plummeted from the sky – went off, and an amplified voice started yelling for the swimmers to clear the water. Apparently, it had been deemed unsafe for swimmers, no matter their ability. It was, admittedly, big surf for a suburban beach, but there had been big surf on that beach for as long as humans had been swimming there. Some bathers ignored the klaxon, which seemed to get louder, and before long, an all-terrain vehicle trundled down the beach to enforce the rules.

The psychology of risk

It had been two years since I'd last sat on that beach, but apparently, during that time, the lifesavers had been radicalised into a paramilitary organisation, one intent that nobody should actually go swimming at one of the world's best-loved swimming locations. I should stress that I am a huge fan of surf lifesaving and consider their volunteers to be amongst the most shining exemplars of selfless community service that embody the Australian spirit. But still, that all seemed like a bit much.

Thirty years ago, across the world, I wasn't allowed to sit on the grass. Now I was permitted to sit on the sand and quietly read, provided I didn't even think about going near the water and was happy to listen to a siren blasting every few minutes.

It seemed like madness to me. Either that or I'm just becoming a grumpy old man, which is, perhaps, a somewhat enjoyable destiny to be relished. In any case, I found myself wondering about the fate of the boys and girls being denied the privilege of their own skinned knees that Coogee surf is famous for serving up.

We live in a society that is inexorably safer. Year by year, medical and safety technology advances. Legislation grows ever more all-consuming and the hazards in our society recede. We now live longer, healthier, less hazardous lives than any generation in history. But what has been lost? If, as von Hippel suggests, we have evolved with risk as a fundamental part of our psychological makeup, what happens to us when we live lives largely devoid of it?

My theory is that managed exposure to risk is an essential part of growing up to be the best version of yourself. To test it, I decided to speak to the bravest young people I could find and see what they could teach me about how risk shaped them.

PART THREE

WATER

Perhaps my favourite saying from the eminently quotable martial artist Bruce Lee is this: 'Be shapeless, formless, like water.' Lee was explaining that there was no substance more resilient than water, which took the shape of whatever vessel it was poured into: a cup, a bottle, a pot. The idea stemmed from training with his martial arts master, Yip Man, who had Lee practise punching water. Of course, no matter how hard he struck the water, Lee would never hurt it. Although it seemed weak, it could penetrate the hardest substance in the world. Given enough time, a river can bring down a mountain. Lee took that idea to his physical training and tried to make his mind and style of movement like that of water. As he said, 'Water can drip and it can crash. Become like water, my friend.'

He may have been on to something. We are creatures of water, literally. Up to sixty per cent of our bodies are composed of water – our blood, brains, lungs, even our bones are knit from water.

Out of all the elements, I reckon humans have the most complicated relationship with water. We need it – we don't survive very long without water to drink. Deprive us of it and our bodies start to break down in very short order.

Ironically, perhaps, we're not great at surviving in water. Not for any length of time. Even the most graceful Olympic swimmer is awkward and slow in the water compared to life forms that have evolved to thrive in aquatic environments. Some dangers are evident – we cannot breathe water – but there are many more. Dive without careful depth management and we get the bends. With enough time in salt water, the salinity does terrible things to our skin. The natural defence mechanisms that saw us become one of the predominant species on land – strength, speed, visual acuity, pattern recognition, fight-or-flight reflexive responses – do not serve us at the bottom of the ocean. If an oceanic apex predator decides to see what you taste like, the odds are not in your favour.

But still, every day, we take to the water. Sailors, workers, surfers, explorers, swimmers and divers are all compelled onto and into the water. Your humble author amongst them.

I've interrogated my own (somewhat selfish) reasons for spending every minute I can with my head in the briny. But what about people for whom water is more than a hobby? The people whose vocation is to sail around the globe, breaking records and prejudices? Who race across impossible waves or work far beneath them on the near-frozen ocean floor?

This part of the book takes us to the seas, and we meet exceptional men and women who have challenged the ocean and, in doing so, done things no human being has ever dreamed possible. People who, through sheer grit, determination and chance, have – to borrow a phrase from Mr Lee – become the water.

CHAPTER SEVEN

THE LIFE-CHANGING MAGIC OF STUFFING UP

There have been moments in my life when I have been struck by the sudden realisation that I might be about to die. I mean beyond the everyday baseline level of risk that everybody lives with – those 'oh shit' moments when you realise that the situation you are in presents a potentially fatal problem and you have a limited time to solve it. Those times when I've felt the panic rising and I find myself wondering if, this time, I've finally gone too far. I've stuffed up many times in caves, on dives, on adventures, but there are a handful of moments when I've been hit by the realisation that maybe this mistake would be my last.

The first was when I was fifteen. I'd recently taken an open water diving course and fallen in love with everything about it. I discovered a whole new world under the sea – this dynamic drama of marine life – the colours and action of red snapper chasing their prey, the alien beauty of giant cuttlefish, striped pyjama squid, and octopuses. I loved every minute of it – learning how to equalise and explore. I revelled in the intricacies of every little piece of diving equipment, how it worked in concert to open up the world under the waves.

The sense of wonder and freedom that comes with slipping off the boat into the underwater world – the feeling of weightlessness and fascination never gets old. There are a few things to worry about while you're underwater, but everyday stress isn't one of them. It's hard to stay wound up about falling behind on your mortgage repayments when you're kicking down to explore a wreck with sharks cruising by at the edge of your visibility. That little hint of danger that comes with every dive – the excitement that came bundled with the sense of tranquillity. I was drawn to that as well – perhaps a little too much.

One warm, sunny February afternoon, fifteen-year-old me went out to explore the wreck of the *Norma*, a four-masted iron barque that had been sunk in 1907 in the Gulf St Vincent, five or six kilometres off the coast near my hometown of Adelaide. With me were our diving instructor, Ron Allum, my mate Sam Hall (still ever-present when trouble was close by!), and two young women we hadn't met before. The boat ride out to the site was rough, but it seemed safe enough even in the small 'tinny' we were in.

The wreck sat in fifteen metres of water, and we had a good time exploring the rusting hulk and the magnificent marine life that had grown up around it in the century or so since it had sunk. We had a great dive, but by the time we got around to calling it a day and started to head back to the ramp around 5 pm, the weather had deteriorated. Suddenly, the waves in the gulf really began to kick up, and our small dive boat was doing its best impression of a runaway train, surfing down each massive wave and crashing into the next in the following sea.

'This can't get much worse,' I remember thinking to myself, and of course, it immediately did. Down the next wave we charged, into the back of the subsequent one, buried the nose of the boat and pitchpoled – the boat flipped end over end and dumped us all unceremoniously into the water. One minute we were enjoying the exhilarating ride, the next chaos, then immersion.

We managed to right the boat, so that it floated the right-way up in the water, but it was swamped. While a second ago it had been moonlighting as a fairground ride, now it seemed to want to be a submarine – the deck of the boat partially submerged, and the motor flooded.

The engine wouldn't start, and we were too far out to swim back in. Our basic safety equipment, such as flares and radios, were too wet to be of use. We threw the anchor over to stop us drifting away from the site, but the end was unsecured and so the rope disappeared under the water. Luckily, we were still in our wetsuits, and quickly donned life jackets. We wouldn't drown, but that was the extent of our good luck. All we could do was cling to the boat and wait as darkness fell, the seas got rougher, and the temperature started to drop.

I remember Sam, who was a little less naive than me, looking at the situation – the waves, the gathering gloom, the upturned boat, and then turning to me and stated that nobody was coming to rescue us that night. 'A: it's getting dark, and B: it's bloody rough out here, and it's going to get worse. There are no boats that are going to be able to come out here and find us until morning.'

'No, no, that's impossible,' I kept telling him. I was utterly incredulous that someone hadn't already materialised to whisk me off home. 'Right now, my parents will be ringing the cops and they'll send someone out.'

As it turns out, we were both right – my mum was on the phone to the police, but nobody was coming to save us.

When I'd failed to return home by 7 pm, like I'd promised I would, Mum started to worry. She tried the dive shop, but they were closed already by the time her alarm bells began to ring. Next, she rang Sam's parents trying to track me down, and they were obviously just as worried.

Mum didn't try the police until around 8 pm, but they didn't exactly jump on the case. The cops were understandably cynical. The dispatcher my mum got on the phone wasn't too worried about a couple of teenagers coming home late.

'You know young boys,' they sighed, 'They've probably met up with some girls or gone out for pizza.'

'No. When my son's been diving, he knows I'll be worrying, so he would have rung me if that's the case.' My mum was very insistent. 'He takes diving and boating very seriously. If he's not home when he said he would be home, there's a problem.' She was beside herself with worry – the police, less so. It wasn't until around 11 pm that they actually went down to the boat ramp to ascertain the situation.

'So actually, the trailer and the car are still there at the boat ramp,' the police admitted, 'so you are right. They are still out at sea somewhere.' By this time, the seas were monstrously rough, and even the big police launch couldn't have safely gone out effectively to search, so any efforts would have to wait until the morning.

Meanwhile, we were cold. The worst cold I'd ever known. For a while, Sam and I had tried to put on a brave face for the others, cracking jokes and trying to get some singalongs going. I was quite proud of our efforts to show resilience and good cheer in a bad situation. That lasted until one of the poor girls started praying out loud for deliverance.

By around 2 am, any attempt to maintain a sense of humour had cooled. Literally. The water off Adelaide at that time of year was still pretty fresh, with only fairly thin wetsuits between us and the sea. After nine hours we were chilled to the bone and psychologically exhausted.

In the distance we could see the city lights while we drifted helplessly around several kays offshore. That gave us some hope but was its own kind of mental torture – to know safety and warmth were so close and yet just out of reach. At one point the brilliant lights of a sheep transport ship approached. The first thought was rescue, the next was that we would be run down by the brightly lit behemoth. It passed less than 500 metres away.

Desperate to do something positive, I went up to the front of the boat and sat on the prow to try and paddle us closer to shore, but that was no help. Although it warmed me to some degree, I'll never forget the feeling sitting on that bow watching my legs hanging into the black water off Adelaide, thinking about the white sharks that live under the waves here. I just couldn't do it, I had to get out of the water and go back to sit in the boat and shiver until sunrise. At around 3 am, our vessel started to fall apart as it was buffeted by the elements. The floorboards of the boat began to pop up, and chunks of the buoyancy foam floated away on the waves. The boat settled deeper into the water and intermittently capsized, throwing us repeatedly into the dark ocean. By then, it was dawning on me that *this really might be it*.

But finally, the new day dawned, bringing with it the coldest temperatures of the whole night. That final hour around sunrise was just miserable. At daybreak, I could see an aeroplane circling far to the south, and big motorboats heading out from the shore. I hoped that they were looking for us, but if they were, that was a problem in itself. It became clear that we'd drifted a fair way north with the wind and tide, and while rescue teams were searching, they were concentrating around the dive site we'd since moved quite a few miles from.

So, there was one more of those heart-squeezing 'oh shit' moments, still not sure we were saved, until I heard the most beautiful sound I could imagine – the *putt-putt-putt* of a clapped-out old motor chugging towards us. In the distance, this weathered old timber boat came rolling over the waves, and an equally weathered old fisherman called out, 'Are you the blokes that are lost?'

The old bloke knew those waters probably better than anyone in Adelaide. He took one look at the rescue effort to the south, another at the weather and the currents, and figured out where we would have drifted to. Then quietly slipped off to save our lives.

We climbed into his boat, where he served us coffee and Vegemite sandwiches, then towed our waterlogged dive boat back to the ramp like a just-below-the-surface submarine.

The whole harrowing adventure was an immensely important episode in my life. I'll never forget the fact that out of all the police, pilots, boaters and divers mobilised to rescue us, the one who actually managed it was this kind old man who kept his head, thought clearly, and knew exactly where the prevailing conditions would place us. He was prepared and knew how to handle the situation.

I've always been proud of the fact that I went back to boating and diving after that. I think it put the two women we were with off diving, but I'd survived a night during which all that stood between me and death was a flimsy wetsuit. I knew I would be back in the water, but that I would do everything in my power to manage the risks more effectively.

Sam and I both became safer operators. We never went out on a boat without flares, radios and an anchor rope tied to the boat. In time I did my coxswain's course and marine radio licence, acquiring more survival and on-water skills as I grew. But as my confidence on the water increased, I knew I'd never forget that feeling of helplessness of being stranded on the lonely seas.

At least I got to go through my humbling near-death experience in the relative privacy of a small dive boat. For one of Australia's most celebrated and beloved sailors, her formative 'Oh shit!' moment occurred around the same age as mine, but on the global stage.

*

Imagine spending 210 days at sea sailing 24,285 nautical miles all the way around the planet alone and unassisted in a 10.23 metre boat. Imagine the fortitude, strength of character, and resilience a feat like that requires. Now imagine doing it all at sixteen years of age. That's when Jessica Watson became the youngest person ever to circumnavigate the globe in her small vessel, *Ella's Pink Lady*.

When she cruised into Sydney Harbour on 15 May 2010, three days before her seventeenth birthday, she was greeted by cheers and an adoring public. For her achievement, Jessica was named the 2011 Young Australian of the Year, and the following year was awarded the Medal of the Order of Australia.

The global fanbase who followed her voyage and greeted her on her return weren't always so supportive. Those fans were hard-won. Naysayers from across the world of sailing and beyond criticised her and particularly her parents for even attempting the journey long before she first set sail.

She had to campaign tirelessly against her parents initially to get them on board from the age of twelve or thirteen, when she became enamoured with this idea. Then she faced all the usual challenges of fundraising, gaining sponsors, building a vessel into something that would be seaworthy and safe enough. And then at the outset, had a near critical incident which nearly cost her both her vessel and her life when she was essentially run over by a 63,000-tonne tanker. By tonnage, that's a little under one-and-a-half times the weight of the *Titanic*, ramming a tiny pink sailing boat so small that media pundits speculated it wouldn't be able to store the food Jessica would need for the journey.

When I spoke to Jessica about that moment, it's hard to imagine the sheer stress and terror of waking up to the crushing blow that, had things gone slightly differently, might have taken her life.

'It was absolutely horrendous,' Jessica tells me when we sat down for a chat about her life of adventure. Then with typical understatement, 'Yeah, it was a bit of an interesting night, that one.'

The collision happened after years of build-up, anticipation, and growing media attention while Jessica pursued her dream of solo circumnavigation with single-minded determination. Her passion and drive had won over her sceptical parents, secured the vessel *Ella's Pink Lady*, recruited sponsors, and a crack ground team who would aid her remotely and maintain contact via satellite phone. Three years of obsessive work and preparation were finally paying off as she sailed her vessel down the east coast of Australia on what was their first full night at sea, 9 September 2009.

Jessica was underway at last. That first night, still quite close to shore, she stood on deck to savour the beautiful, calm night, and experienced a tremendous sense of relief and achievement to finally be beginning her journey. It was the culmination of an exhausting effort. She needed rest but didn't want to bed down for the night so close to shore. So, Jess popped below deck for a five-minute catnap. Four minutes later, the *Silver Yang* collided with *Ella's Pink Lady*. She awoke to the sound of the rig being torn off and scraped down the side of this ship. For some time afterwards, she would have nightmares about that moment, but at the same time, found herself completely in control of the situation.

'What my head did was click into sort of a checklist mode. I knew that I was awfully stuffed, there's no doubt about that, so I had to work out a plan to save myself. I found I could deal with it because my training kicked in.' The situation became so catastrophic, so quickly, that Jessica had no choice but to pull herself together, think through what needed to be done, and how she could save her vessel.

Working quickly, exhausted and in the dark, Jessica was able to cut the headsail free, then retrieve the detached mast, the mainsail and the rigging and haul them back on board, then motor the damaged yacht to Southport, Queensland, the next day.

There, a media scrum was waiting. 'Definitely not a positive one. Everyone demanding – quite rightly – what I thought I was doing continuing the voyage when I had so completely stuffed up.'

'It was a terrible setback,' recalls Jessica, 'and pretty embarrassing really, as someone who was trying to say, "Hey, I've got this, I'm competent and ready to do this".' For the young woman, who through sheer drive and force of will had mobilised family, sponsors and a global network of supporters, to meet with disaster the first night out was disastrous to morale.

Jessica's trip already had some controversy surrounding it and, after the collision, the critics swarmed. Internet forums and mass-media publications speculated wildly on what had occurred and who was at fault.

Jessica described the criticisms as ranging from useless and irrelevant to annoying and distracting.

Armchair experts from around the globe weighed in on the discourse about whether it was appropriate for a woman of Jessica's age and experience to even attempt the journey. Naturally, much of the worst criticism was levelled at her family.

'It was incredibly hard on my family. There were these parenting experts coming out with some pretty bizarre criticisms and some blatantly inaccurate stuff that was very unfair.'

Reflecting on the time today, there's a hint of lingering annoyance in Jessica's recollection of the criticisms of her parents. In her estimation, if they made any mistake in raising her, it was going too far in their efforts to make sure she could achieve whatever she set her mind to.

'Those efforts to build up my confidence went a bit further than they imagined. You tell your kids they can do anything: "Believe in yourself, back yourself" and then your daughter throws this idea of sailing around the world back at you. And I think they were very much thinking "maybe not quite that"!'

*

Jessica is the second of four children and grew up sailing. As a family they lived on board a cabin cruiser for five years and were home schooled.

Jessica, who describes herself as 'quite dyslexic', recalls that reading was a struggle in her early years, remedied by her mum who made a huge effort to build up her confidence and literacy, including reading her Jesse Martin's book, *Lionheart*, which chronicled his own circumnavigation of the world in 1999, at 18 years of age. 'That's what did all the damage and inspired me,' laughs Jessica. 'Here's Mum reading it to me as an innocent bedtime story, but that's what sparked the whole thing.'

Jesse Martin's story, of a normal person who'd gone on an extraordinary and awesome adventure, made her realise that she could be one of those people having those adventures, too.

In Jessica's reckoning, the seed had been planted. Her curiosity grew, and after a couple of years of reading, dreaming and putting posters of big waves and boats up in her bedroom, 'Mum must have been thinking something slightly strange was going on.' Her curiosity evolved into inspiration, and then into ambition.

She first told her mum and dad about her dream when she was 12 or 13 years old and recalls crying her eyes out as she was pleading her case – overwhelmed with the enormity of the task – by just how serious she was about it. 'I was sort of telling them what was happening, rather than asking permission.'

A couple of years passed, during which time Jessica says the idea of the voyage became central to everything in her life, an all-consuming obsession. 'Dad realised the dream had become my whole identity, and that to crush it would have actually been worse for me than having to let me go through with it.'

Soon, her parents understood that on balance the risks of staying home outweighed the risks of sailing. She gathered a team of supporters, sponsors, mentors and guides to make the dream come true. She'd set out from Brisbane with the massive amounts of goodwill and support that all adventurers need to fuel them. Then, on the first night out, she'd nearly lost it all.

The life-changing magic of stuffing up

It was one of those fulcrum moments in a lifetime, those times when people who achieve incredible feats really find out what they are made of. The incident gave Jessica a benchmark to fall back on throughout the rest of the journey. Before the trial had even begun, the horrible collision gave her the opportunity to really test herself, and she had now proven that she could keep her head together in the face of disaster.

'Looking back, it's almost a bit of a cliche, but it is true that that setback set me up for success with the rest of the voyage,' says Jessica. 'Not everything after that was easy, but when it got hard, I would tell myself that I'd been there, and held it together, and I wasn't going to go back to being this scared little girl.' The way she tells it, the last lingering doubts she had in her head that she could make her voyage were knocked out shortly after that ship hit her.

'It honestly felt like I stepped away from that with more confidence. And to me, it was quite honestly the last piece of the puzzle to go, I could deal with that. And I think that must have rubbed off on the people around me who quite rightly might have lost confidence in me at that point. It did become a bit of a desire, to make people challenge their own thinking about what we're capable of.'

*

It's a truism that for every adventurer out pushing the limits of human endurance and experience, there's someone who loves freaking out about the danger they are in.

While Jessica had proven herself a cool head in an emergency, taken every precaution, planned for every eventuality, in consultation with her family and support crew back home, there were more than a few close calls. Halfway across the Atlantic Ocean, about as far away from land as a person can get, she found herself in a nightmare storm.

'We knew we were going to run into them, so [my team] had planned for them, and knew they were going to be pretty grim. The first few weren't too bad, but we hit one that was forecast as terrible. It was, and just got worse and worse. Through that night we had four knockdowns.'

A 'knockdown', in sailing terminology, is when a vessel is rolled well past its normal limits by the force of waves. It can result in a complete roll over. Jessica recalls that all four knockdowns that night were terrifying, but it was the third that was the most dangerous. From below deck, where she was braced against the storm, Jessica heard the roar of a massive wave bearing down on her. It hit with such force that the boat was picked up, turned upside down and hurled into the trough of the next wave, which pushed the boat completely underwater.

The wave forced *Ella's Pink Lady* so deep that her emergency beacon, a device designed to automatically broadcast her position if the ship was sinking, activated. 'Those devices only deploy when a ship is under at least three metres of water, so potentially we had three metres of water on top of the boat. I bobbed back up, but obviously it's horrendous for the team back home to get that call from the rescue centre saying that it looked like I'd sunk.'

Luckily, Jessica's satellite phone was still operational, and she was able to get a message to her team that she was fine, even if the situation was dire. Jessica did what she'd done before, which was fall back on her training, to think logically about her situation and course of action.

'When I thought about it, the chances of the boat holding itself together, and my chances of survival in those conditions are pretty, pretty grim.' There were plenty of waves that night that could have taken *Ella's Pink Lady* to the bottom of the Atlantic Ocean. But, of course, Jessica and her boat made it through, which speaks about the quality of her preparation, her team, and her vessel.

126

That was the most dangerous night of her voyage. There were a few more, but that was the scariest one.

'To be able to look over the boat the next day and realise there's a few little things – dents here and there, some torn sails and a few things bent out of shape, but nothing fatal. After a storm like that, you know fundamentally the boat can handle almost anything. It was a huge confidence boost.'

*

Towards the end of our conversation, Jessica and I found some unusual common ground. We'd both been honoured as Australian of the Year and become suddenly and globally famous for one highly unusual adventure.

Whereas my part in the Thai cave rescue came about more-or-less randomly (there are simply not many cave-diving anaesthetists to be found at short notice), Jessica's was the culmination of hard work, relentless self-belief, and the manifestation of a childhood dream – achieved while she was still, in the eyes of most of her critics, a child.

We found ourselves chatting about the strange experience of picking up regular life after the eyes of the world are upon you.

'That's been a journey in itself, you know,' Jessica says. 'It's ten years now since the voyage, and I've worked pretty hard to escape it. Finally, I accepted that to many people I'm never going to be anything other than the young girl who sailed around the world in a pink boat. That's fine, but I do need other things to keep myself challenged.'

That decade since the voyage has been a rich one for Jessica – finishing her education, working in advocacy and on the speaker's circuit, charity work, and more recently, a corporate job as a management consultant with one of the big four accounting firms. And of course, further (if more modest) sailing adventures.

Any way you look at it, Jessica is an impressive human being. On top of being a pioneering solo sailor, she is a high achieving, articulate, intelligent woman who would make any parent proud.

I can imagine few things more frightening (I know I keep saying that as these adventurers tell me of their experiences!) than finding yourself adrift on an endless, unpredictable ocean, unless it's imagining my children in that position. While I haven't asked Jessica's parents if they ever regret giving their blessing for their daughter to sail alone around the world, I suspect I know what the answer would be – not that far from Jessica's own philosophy.

'If there's one thing I know, be audacious and take on these big dreams. You know, do explore and take on adventures and responsible risk-taking. Because it does lead to some pretty extraordinary things. If nothing else, you build some wonderful resilience and it's a lot of fun. So, give these things a go and dream big. It's scary, but I mean, ultimately that's the point of adventure, right? It's because there is that element of unknown. You don't go out there because you know exactly what's going to happen.'

It was a tremendous privilege for me to speak to such an inspiring young woman, brave beyond measure in her teens, and now wise beyond her years in her twenties. She's a great conversationalist, and a living testament to the value of risk-taking and an adventurous mindset. If a brave teenager alone in a yacht can be thrown under the Atlantic Ocean and pop back up, there's hope for us all. At the very least, you'll get a cracking story or two out of it.

She chased her dreams at enormous personal risk, and apart from a couple of terrifying experiences and blows to her pride, came away unscathed. Of course, not everyone is so lucky. What about those young people who take on the odds and find themselves in the deepest of waters? When risk goes wrong and the blows you take on your way can't be shrugged off so easily? What happens then?

CHAPTER EIGHT

SURFING A SKYSCRAPER

If you live in Australia, chances are you, like me, have had a crack at surfing somewhere along the way. Hopefully, with better results than I've had. When done right, it's hard to think of a more glamorous sport. The word itself is evocative of blue skies, white water and tanned skin. Surfing somehow combines peak athleticism with a kind of Zen solitude, purity of purpose and oneness with nature. All while looking pretty bloody cool.

My youthful attempts at surfing gave me, along with minor abrasions and a bruised pride, a taste of what it's like to be dumped by a wave. I remember well the churning, helpless tumble with eyes and sinuses full of sand and salt water, wondering if I'd be able to make it to the surface and snatch a breath before the next wave knocked me down again.

Remembering that sensation is still enough to give my pulse a little kick. And that was the relatively tame local South Australian beaches with waves of maybe a metre or so high. The power of those waves seemed intense and irresistible, so when I imagine what it would be like to ride a wave five, ten or even twenty times larger, I'm glad I'm not the one doing it. But that's exactly what the big-wave gladiators do – riding waves the height of a ten-storey building that move so fast they can only be caught with the aid of a jet ski.

Surfing, in one form or another, has been around for millennia. Wave-riding has been part of most Polynesian cultures since antiquity. In Hawaii, it was literally the sport of kings – and the Hawaiian tradition from which modern surfing evolved, has been practised since around 400 AD.

For most of that time, humans have only been able to surf fairly close to shore, and only on waves of a limited size. Once waves reached a certain threshold, it became impossible to wrangle a surfboard out to them. The force of the water made it simply impossible for even the strongest swimmer to paddle out, or swim at the speeds the wave travelled.

This only changed with the advent of tow-in surfing. As the name suggests, a surfer clings to a rope and is towed through the surf by a jet ski until they reach exactly where they need to be to catch the wave. The technique was pioneered in Hawaii in the mid-1990s, and suddenly waves once thought impossible to ride were on the menu. Waves to the tune of 100 feet (30 metres).

For a few years, tow-in revolutionised surfing: boards became smaller and surfers increasingly bold. A handful of high-profile surfers rose to the challenge – and with them rose the profile of big-wave surfing itself. Through the early 2000s, rising stars chased monster waves around the world, risking white-water annihilation in their quest to smash each other's records.

In the early days when testosterone-fuelled competition wasn't unheard of, big-wave surfing gave the biggest, boldest surfers a new arena to prove themselves. Back then, the world of big-wave surfing was a decidedly macho one, full of big swinging egos. Waves are essentially measured by eyeballing them from land, and the subjective nature of that has led to many arguments over the exact size of waves and how they might differ in size and velocity. As the author William Finnegan put it in his excellent surf memoir, *Barbarian Days*, 'Big waves are not measured in feet, but in increments of bullshit.' All of which is to say, it's testament to her extraordinary ability that one of the best, and most celebrated big-wave riders in the world, is a woman.

On paper, Maya Gabeira is an unlikely champion in the hyper-macho world of big-wave riding. Somewhat petite at 5 feet 6 inches (168 centimetres), from an intellectual family in Brazil, she's soft-spoken, choosing her words in English carefully in a studied manner which hints at the steely resolve she must have needed to forge her path in big-wave surfing.

Growing up in Rio de Janeiro, she came to surfing relatively late in life, when she was introduced to the sport at thirteen while hanging out with friends on Ipanema Beach. 'I was going to the beach with them a lot, but just sitting on the sand was not my thing. Instantly, I was very passionate about the sport. I just dove in headfirst, and I never looked back,' she recalls. 'I wanted to surf all day, every day.'

By her reckoning, Maya was not the most naturally gifted surfer. She entered some amateur competitions in Brazil but found herself facing stiff competition from other female surfers, 'but I found ways to win here and there', she recalls.

At seventeen, Maya decided to become a professional surfer, resulting in a fight with her family. She came from a family of sophisticates – her father is a prominent environmentalist and politician in Brazil and her mother is an ethical fashion designer. Neither of them understood surfing much and didn't see it as a possible career.

'I finished high school,' explains Maya with a laugh, 'and convinced my dad that I needed to move to Hawaii to learn English.'

Once in Hawaii, Maya worked as a waitress to support herself while she pursued her dream, and it was there that she discovered big-wave surfing. She then knew what she wanted to do with her life. She stopped competing in conventional surfing competitions to focus on big waves. There were no women surfing big waves at the time, and where others might have seen an impossible barrier, Maya saw a chance to be a pioneer. 'The big waves had a strong appeal to me, but women weren't doing it. I saw this empty ocean, with nobody swimming there,' says Maya. 'I had absolute certainty that women can succeed in that field, but for some reason they weren't there yet. I got to establish that route.'

The sport was dominated by men – typically, with big muscles, huge personalities and egos to match. 'It is a very male dominated sport, this testosterone and adrenaline-filled environment that is big-wave surfing,' says Maya, recalling that when she first took the sport up, there was no place for women, either culturally or professionally. Paths of professional progression available to men – winning competitions, securing sponsors – simply hadn't factored in a woman wanting to master monster waves. 'In the beginning, there was no women's competition, that was not even a possibility.'

*

Only one avenue of competition was open to her – an award for Women's Overall Performance that was appended to the several categories of big-wave surfing for men. 'That became my focus because that was the only place where I could get recognition. With that recognition, I could begin to move forward.' When she won that award, it came with a stamp of approval from the international surfing industry, and she signed her first professional contract and started carving a place for women in the industry.

She quickly emerged as the world's top female big-wave surfer, winning the Billabong XXL Global Big Wave Awards on four consecutive occasions from 2007 to 2010.

'You have to expose yourself to big risks when surfing big waves, and as a female pioneer in my field, I was often criticised for doing so. In the early days of my career, bravery wasn't celebrated in women, despite the fact that it's an essential component of the sport.'

She gained her reputation, and sponsors, for riding the most challenging waves in the world – surf spots that are affectionately named Mavericks, Ghost Trees and Dungeons. It was at Dungeons – a South African spot that boasts both shark-infested water and several hidden reefs, that she successfully surfed the biggest wave ever by a woman at the time, at 14 metres (46 feet). That was just the beginning. She wanted to pioneer bigger waves, and that search took her to Nazaré.

*

The biggest waves a human being has ever surfed are found in Nazaré, Portugal. Specifically, Praia do Norte, or North Beach, where each winter Mother Nature serves up waves that theoretically crest at 30 metres. This is the height of a ten-storey building. They crash with enough force to break a man's spine. Usually this would be a figure of speech, but in the case of 36-year-old British surfer Andrew Cotton, it is unfortunately, quite literal. Andrew, who held the world record for big-wave surfing, was wiped-out out in November 2017, and was rescued from the waves with a broken back.

Nazaré is a town that travel guides used to describe as 'quaint'. The local tourism website claims it is 'arguably Portugal's most picturesque fishing village'. It would be hard to disagree. About 15,000 people live there in a postcard perfect jumble of traditional Portuguese houses, with cheerful red roofs over sun-bleached white walls. Below the town lies a stretch of pristine sand and the startling blue of the ocean. Above is a cliff where the centuries-old Forte de São Miguel Arcanjo watches over the wild sea and hosts a stubby red lighthouse which guides the fishing boats back to land. It's here, if you visit from October to March, that you'll get the best view of the action.

Nazaré is the Portuguese word for Nazaréth, appropriately enough perhaps, as it serves as a site of pilgrimage for the bravest, strongest and most ambitious big-wave surfers on the planet. A unique under-sea geological feature allows waves to build dramatically then hit the shore more or less at full force.

Typically, giant surf waves occur when water goes from very deep to very shallow over a short distance. Think of big-wave hotspots near islands such as Hawaii and Tahiti, where a lonely volcanic island rises suddenly out of the deep ocean. Nazaré is unique as far as coastal surf because of a mammoth underwater ravine that lies just off the coast.

The Nazaré Canyon is one of the largest submarine trenches in Europe. It is around 230 kilometres long and 5 kilometres deep in parts – three times the depth of the Grand Canyon. The deep sea abruptly meets the shore at Praia do Norte – where the unique V-shape of the canyon, in conjunction with the currents, serve as a natural wonder of fluid dynamics. As a result, the waves are able to arrive at the coast with virtually no dissipation of energy.

To watch video footage of these record-breaking waves is mesmer-ising – the surfers are just specks in the foam. Despite their incredible velocity of up to 70 kilometres per hour, they seem to move in slow motion across the blue. The surfers are dwarfed by a wall of water the size of a skyscraper.

*

Maya first came to Nazaré in 2013 with a team of three other surfers, including her mentor and tow partner, Carlos Burle. The plan had been to check out the legendary waves and begin training on progres-sively larger swells, working towards mastering a 30-metre (100-foot) monster. However, after just a month towards the end of October, forecasts showed a huge swell was on the way. Reasoning that their experience in Hawaii and California would transfer to the bigger waves of Nazaré, Maya and Carlos decided to try and conquer the wave. In the world of big-wave riding, the most effective risk-mitigation strategy is incremental exposure to risk. By slowly mastering larger and larger waves in a methodical manner, big-wave riders keep themselves alive. Other mitigations – breath control, training for wipe-outs, flotation devices, rescue-crews waiting on land – are a measure of last resort. If all goes well, if risk is carefully managed, then with luck you don't need the emergency measures. On this particular day, Maya did.

With Carlos piloting the jet ski, Maya rode out to the line-up, and found herself amongst the biggest waves she'd ever seen in her life. 'It was a whole new experience for me. Everyone was extremely excited and borderline losing the rational aspect of it all. I don't think we were completely ready,' Maya says, then immediately corrects herself. 'I know we weren't completely ready.'

As they navigated the drop zone with Carlos gunning the jet ski through the waves towing Maya on her board by a rope, they lost the radio they relied on for contact with rescue workers on land. Land communication is an important precaution for big-wave surfing, something Maya knew, but she decided to continue – the waves were too enticing. 'The radio is important, but we had never seen things go wrong, so we didn't know how important.'

They forged on, with Carlos driving into a few waves and Maya holding onto the rope and wrestling with emotions. She was terrified, staring down bone-crushing canyons of water and an unknown test of her limits. Eventually, she had to decide if she was going to risk it or head back to land and the judgement of the other big-wave surfers.

Ahead and behind her were waves bigger than any woman had ever surfed. On land, other male big-wave surfers were watching, judging and waiting for their turn in the surf. 'That pressure made me think,

"Okay, I'm just going to go." And that's when I caught the biggest wave of my life up until that point.'

All of a sudden, Maya was riding a 25-metre (82-foot) tall wave. She was doing something unprecedented for a woman in big-wave surfing. Then, just as suddenly, she wasn't.

'I ended up falling. I couldn't handle the speed,' recalls Maya. She hit the bump at the bottom of the wave and was knocked onto her back, seconds before being crushed by a wall of white water.

The force of that wave kept her underwater until her lungs were burning for air, but she made it back to the surface. When she popped up, she looked around for signs of a rescue jet ski but saw no sign of it. Instead, the tallest wave she'd ever seen was heading in her direction. 'That's when I realised things were going to get really ugly.'

That wave hit her with such force that she was underwater long enough for serious oxygen deprivation to kick in. She recalls a feeling of terrible sadness and loss, thoughts of her family filling her mind as she realised, 'This is it. I'm not going to make it. I'm gonna die.'

Just as she was about to break the surface and a chance to catch her breath, a second wave hit her and she went down, with no air in her lungs, and no rescue in sight. 'That impact was tremendous because I was very close to the surface. It was like being hit by a truck.'

She blacked out. When she regained consciousness, she was still underwater, slowly rising from the deep. While she managed to float back to the surface, she was in terrible shape. The waves had broken her leg, ripped off her life jacket, damaged her spine, and she was suffering auditory and visual hallucinations. 'I was losing my vision and I remember Carlos trying to reach me and screaming for me to grab the rope.' Maya recalls bobbing helplessly in the surf and slipping in and out of consciousness, until some instinct drove her to grab the rope as it whipped by her, and she was dragged unconscious towards the shore.

© Jimmy Chin

Free-solo climber Alex Honnold insists that his only 'superpower' is clear thinking and diligent practice.

American filmmaker and adventurer Jimmy Chin is famous for big-wall climbs. He won an Academy Award for his documentary *Free Solo*, which captures Alex Honnold's climb of El Capitan, a 3000-foot (914-metre) sheer rockface, without ropes or climbing gear.

Professional stuntman and BASE jumper Sean Chuma has found the only real safety in his sport comes from knowing through experience and instinct when to back down and walk away.

At sixteen years of age Jessica Watson became the youngest person ever to circumnavigate the globe in her small vessel, *Ella's Pink Lady*.

Saturation diver Chris Lemons' survival is impossible to explain.

Maya Gabeira riding a wave at the Nazaré Tow Surfing Challenge.

World-class big-wave photographer Russell Ord reveals the beauty and power of the ocean to those of us not brave enough to paddle out ourselves.

Fighter pilot and aerobatic competitor Matt Hall says he hates adrenaline as it means he is not in control.

Top Fuel drag racer Ashley Sanford has to anticipate and correct every possible risk factor before a race begins.

Foreign correspondent Hugh Riminton was drawn to a job which meant regular exposure to risk and trauma.

Heath Jamieson on engagement in Afghanistan.

© Ken Smith

Agnes Milowka was an incredible diver, fearless and agile and famous for pushing into passages that seemed impossible to others.

© Jenny Goodall/*Daily Mail*

Ten years after the 7/7 London bombings, Gill Hicks is reunited with PC Andrew Maxwell who pulled her out of the wreckage of the Piccadilly line train. They were taking part in the Walking Together for Peace march along with leaders from the Muslim, Jewish and Christian faiths.

Craig Challen (right) and myself diving in the Pearse Resurgence in New Zealand where we explored to a depth of 245 metres.

Ron Allum (coincidentally the dive instructor who took Sam Hall and I out in the boat which flipped over in 1980), James Cameron and John Garvin in front of the *Deepsea Challenger* submersible.

By the time Carlos managed to get her back to the sand and a waiting lifeguard, she'd been in the water and deprived of oxygen for nine perilous minutes. Maya was given CPR on the beach and resuscitated, then rushed to the nearest hospital.

*

Maya's survival after her non-fatal drowning and subsequent resuscitation is quite extraordinary. As a medical practitioner who has worked on children and adults following submersion injuries, I've seen first-hand that the outcomes are often not good. Her case was exceptionally fortunate, but she was far from unscathed.

The accident left her with a broken leg, as well as serious spinal injuries that would require three operations to recover from. Doctors advised her that due to the extent of the damage, she'd never be able to return to the sport. Her body was shattered. As was her confidence.

Maya's entire ordeal was captured on video and the footage has since been watched more than half a million times on YouTube. The accident was globally reported, and critics of female big-wave surfing seized on Maya as the poster girl for those who believed that 25-metre swells should remain the domain of the men. Surfing legend Laird Hamilton, a high-profile veteran of Nazaré's big waves, was one of those who weighed in publicly. 'She doesn't have the skill to be in those conditions,' the American told CNN. 'She should not be in this kind of surf.'

It's worth noting that male big-wave surfers rarely copped that kind of flak after wiping out. In the same interview, Hamilton criticised Carlos Burle, not for surfing the same waves Maya did, but for failing to 'protect' his partner.

There was no shortage of critics, and Maya found herself questioning her own judgement in a way she never had before. In a perfect world, Maya says, she would have liked to go straight back out and conquer the wave which had nearly killed her – but it would be years until she was in good enough condition to attempt it again. Those years were marked by self-doubt – over whether her body would ever recover, and in her own ability.

'It became this recurring insecurity.' Maya recalled being beset by doubt. 'Am I brave? Am I capable? Was it just an accident? Or is it not for me? And then there was the physical aspect of my recovery. It took a long time for things to fall back into place.'

If she had decided in the wake of her accident to leave big waves behind forever – with serious injuries, major surgery and a near-death experience under her belt – no one would have blamed her.

But for Maya, giving up was not an option. Big-wave surfing was more than a profession, more than just a passion. She had a calling, and she doesn't seem like the type to let waves (or critics) hold her down.

Despite that, neither was she charging headlong straight back into the highest waves or competing at the levels she had been. From the moment she'd been pulled unconscious from the waves, it would take four long years of recovery, several operations, hard work riding progressively larger waves, and a fundamentally new mindset until she was finally ready to return to the wave that had caused her catastrophic wipe-out.

*

In 2017, Maya moved to Portugal, uprooting her life in order to be closer to the action and to start working within the sport as much as her ongoing recovery allowed. Much of that work was on land, providing support for her team and helping them strategise and plan new attempts at breaking records. In her downtime, she would stand on the hilltop fort overlooking Praia do Norte, studying the wave that had crushed her in order to better understand it.

The way she tells it, she began to believe that her injury, and the perspective afforded by her long recovery, was invaluable. Without the option to compete at the highest levels, Maya was free from worrying about performance, results and rankings, and so had an unprecedented opportunity to work on technique and experience facets of her sport that until then she'd never had time to explore.

'That was defining for me . . . to have so much time to soak up experience and knowledge in so many different areas – that as a top-performing athlete I would have never had the time and opportunity. I wasn't winning anything or catching the biggest wave of the day, all of that was out of my reach,' Maya tells me, 'but I was working very, very hard.'

The way she speaks about her experience, with a sort of pragmatic optimism, is striking. During our chat, I was surprised and moved by her resilience and asked her if, in a way, the accident was a good thing to happen to her.

'The accident was a great thing to happen to me,' she says, with total conviction. Even if Maya was never able to return to the sport, she says she would not look upon the experience as a bad one. Hard, certainly, one which involved a great deal of suffering, a lot of pain, and countless difficult moments. But she believes there's no better way to grow, to become a better version of yourself, than to face challenges like that.

'I was twenty-six years old, and I had already experienced what it is like to die,' she says, matter-of-factly. 'That to me was like a gift from God. He showed me how precious life was.'

Maya had experienced the overwhelming emotion of knowing her life was likely over, far below the breaking waves, and with that came the strength to accept it. 'You know, you feel all of that, and then He lets me come back, and allows me to have a second chance? I mean, if that's not a gift, I don't know what is.'

*

When she returned to the sport, she supplemented her surfing with a regime of intense preparation, both physical and mental, in and out of the water. Training at the gym, running, biking and swimming complemented surfing waves, which escalated in size as her recovery progressed. To prepare for the stunning knockdowns and long submersions underwater, Maya does apnoea training, swimming the length of a pool on a single breath. Above all, when she goes out into the waves now, she is psychologically prepared for a wipe-out. She knows, the way only a handful of people on the planet do, how essential keeping calm is in those moments.

On 18 January 2018, five years after the accident, Maya returned to Praia do Norte, ready to face the wave that nearly ended her life. It was the height of Nazaré's wave season, and the surf was bigger than it had been for years. Maya decided her objective that day was to catch the largest wave of her life.

In temperatures of around fifteen degrees Celsius, she waited for three and a half hours for the perfect wave. She describes being perfectly immersed in the moment, totally connected to the water. She channelled her fear, using its energy to control her mind and remain present and calm. She told herself that she was prepared, she'd gathered experience, that she was doing her best to react to what nature was throwing at her. Then she saw it.

Maya knew that it would be a big wave – a special one – when she saw it popping up on the horizon. She set a goal for herself: she would not fall; she would complete the ride untouched. It was a moment of total concentration, speeding down the wall trying to control her speed while following the wave's line so as not to be swallowed by the white water. Then she was at the bottom, banking gracefully out of the terminus. 'Although I knew it had been a very big wave, I had no idea it would be a record breaker.'

That wave, measured at 21 metres (68 feet) made it the biggest wave ever ridden by a woman. When she hit the bottom of it, she surfed right into the record books . . . eventually. Her achievement was initially snubbed by the World Surf League, and she had to petition, publicly, until the world record was recognised.

'I decided to fight for the recognition of women's surfing,' she says, simply. 'I wanted a woman to be able to break a record in any specific category. To make it fair.'

*

Maya has had to break the glass ceiling along with the world records – although that was certainly not a fluke. Two years later, she again set a new world record at the Nazaré Tow Surfing Challenge. At 22.5 metres (73 feet) it was again the largest wave surfed by a woman – and the biggest surfed by anyone that year according to surfing experts.

I suspect there are even bigger waves in Maya's future. She will be spending this big-wave season at Nazaré, and on her favourite wave in the world. There, as they do every year, crowds will gather to watch waves the size of cities crash against the shore and Maya plans to ride them.

I'd put good money on her smashing her own record sometime in the future, although I get the feeling that's not what drives her in her pursuit of sporting excellence. These days, she's a little more circumspect with risk. Her brush with death beneath the waves of Nazaré has given her perspective on why she chases mastery of big-wave riding. She still has an eye to find the next monster wave, to smash the next record, but tempers her hunger for glory with hard-won wisdom. She still has an irrepressible love for surfing, and a drive to succeed, but it's tempered by a healthy appreciation of the consequence of risk when something goes wrong. Like BASE jumper Sean Chuma, she continues to thrive because she knows, when the risk outweighs the potential reward, to walk away.

'I have been so humbled through my experience,' says Maya. 'I think what happened to me that day was because of reckless young Maya who would do anything to achieve, for experience. There was never a next day, you know? It was now or never.'

And if she encounters a compelling wave that her instincts warn her to stay away from? 'No problem. I'll come back tomorrow.'

CHAPTER NINE

AT THE END OF
THE TETHER

Chris Lemons is a saturation diver, perhaps amongst the most unusual and fascinating jobs on the planet. They are the workers who do construction and demolition work on the bottom of the ocean, at depths of up to 300 metres (1000 feet).

He has spent a fair chunk of his professional life on the seabed – although that's not the most interesting thing about him. Chris has experienced what it is like to die – to breathe his last breath in one of the coldest, most remote environments on Earth.

The story Chris has to tell is one of the most extraordinary I've ever heard. I'm not the first to hear it – a 2019 documentary, *Last Breath,* recounts the tale – but being familiar with the facts does nothing to diminish the power of his account. His tale is one that shatters the existential complacency of the day-to-day. Proof that, despite our best efforts, even in the face of the most thorough preparation and risk-mitigation strategies – we are never guaranteed another day. It's a story of risk gone wrong, and certain doom. And remarkably, he lived to tell it to me.

My own understanding of diving medicine and human physiology is challenged by Chris' story of survival. Even for a medical professional, it is, quite simply, inexplicable. I confess that it took *my* breath away when we sat down to chat; more than once as I went to reach for the next question in my notes, I found myself completely speechless.

Edinburgh-born and Cambridge-raised, Chris speaks in a measured, middle-England accent. Bald, six-foot-five with a worker's build, Chris is friendly, self-deprecating and quietly assured. He's the sort of guy you can imagine striking up a conversation with in the aisles of a hardware store. There's a twang in the way he pronounces certain words, but nothing that hints at where he's been or the unprecedented things that have happened to him. Or for that matter, the extraordinary way he makes a living.

*

In the 20th century, human civilisation – specifically, the insatiable oil and gas industries – started tapping into the resources that were hitherto hidden safely at the bottom of the ocean. That required workers who can build, maintain, and disassemble heavy and intricate machinery at the bottom of the ocean. Remote operated vehicles (ROVs) are useful for scouting and observing underwater construction, but don't (quite yet) have the dexterity, manoeuvrability or judgement to do the more delicate parts of the job. The solution is saturation diving – sending humans on weeks-long expeditions onto the sea floor – an environment where humans are just not meant to survive.

'It's a strange world. That's for sure,' says Chris. He first encountered the profession while working on a dive-support vessel (DSV) at twenty-one, watching the divers clamber into science-fiction-ish diving bells and depart for the ocean floor.

He was fascinated by the work, the extreme nature of it, the unique lifestyle – like being an astronaut underwater. It all seemed very glamorous to a young man unsure of what to do with his life. As did the pay they earned. 'They drove up in flasher cars than I did,' he admits with a little laugh. 'That might have been part of the problem.'

The money is good in saturation diving for good reason. It's a tough, physically and mentally challenging job. It is also a job that carries a great deal of risk. The statistics around commercial diving are not encouraging. An American Centers for Disease Control and Prevention report from 1998 estimated that the occupational fatality rate for all commercial divers is forty times the national average for other professions. Most of that danger is associated with the immense pressures found at great depths. Pressure at sea level is 101 kilopascals (kPa). The interior of a well-maintained bicycle tyre is about 505 kPa. At 130 metres, about the depth of the seabed Chris routinely works on, the water pressure is nearly 1420 kPa.

*

As anyone who has ever strapped on a scuba tank knows, breathing pressurised air carries risks. Inert gases, such as nitrogen, increasingly dissolve into your blood and tissues as the surrounding water pressure increases. At the end of the dive and as you return to the surface, all that extra nitrogen you have absorbed needs to leave the body.

Anyone who has been scuba diving knows about the science of decompression. The long decompression that Craig Challen and I undergo in our underwater habitats is an extreme version of hovering in the water on an ascent. What commercial divers like Chris go through is the most extreme decompression process imaginable.

The gas needs time to diffuse out slowly as the pressure decreases. When a diver comes up too fast, the gas may begin to form bubbles within the diver's tissues. In the worst-case scenario, the effect on a rapidly ascending diver can be like shaking a can of soft drink and then opening it.

Inside that diver's body, a million tiny bubbles form. The bubbles can block blood vessels or destroy the tissues in which they form.

They can produce an inflammatory response which further enhances the mechanical destruction produced by the bubbles themselves. Decompression sickness, or 'the bends', can be extremely painful, often debilitating, and potentially fatal. I have treated divers who have presented paralysed, with strokes or heart attacks and even seen fatalities. Within the group of divers I go on expeditions with, I don't think any of us have escaped unscathed, although fortunately mostly only suffering mild cases.

For a half-hour dive to a depth of thirty metres, it might take another thirty minutes to safely ascend and 'decompress' on the way to the surface. But to dive 150 metres to the seabed and work for a six-hour shift with a welder, it would require roughly two and a half days of decompression.

'Obviously, that's not feasible on a daily basis,' explains Chris. Experiments in the 1930s showed that, after a certain time at pressure, divers' bodies become fully saturated with inert gas, and they can remain at that pressure indefinitely without further penalty, provided they get one long decompression at the end. In saturation diving, divers remain in pressurised environments for weeks on end, letting the inert gas lie harmlessly in their tissues.

Chris and his fellow divers climb into a series of deck chambers, which are slowly pressurised to the equivalent depth they will be working at in the ocean. Divers will live around the clock in these chambers on board the DSV. From the deck chambers, the divers transfer into a smaller capsule, in which they are lowered into the depths. The capsule is a base for the length of the shift from where they can then deploy in diving suits to go about their work in the water. At the end of the shift, the capsule is lifted back into the DSV and the high-pressure living chamber inside the mothership.

In other words, once saturated, they can travel from the pressurised chamber on the DSV, to the ocean floor for a shift, then return, all without the dangers of decompression. 'Basically, what you're doing is one very, very long dive.'

Chris and his colleagues call the process of living and working inside the pressurised environment 'doing sat'. It entails living in a highly pressurised environment for weeks at a time, taking turns to work, eat, and sleep – all the while being monitored 24-7 by a crew on a support vessel topside. It's about as close to living on a space-station as you can get without leaving Earth.

Even flushing a toilet at that pressure is a logistical feat and requires the cooperation of both the diver and a technician operating a series of valves in a particular order. A famous, likely apocryphal story floats around saturation dive crews about a diver whose buttocks created a seal with the toilet seat and met a particularly graphic death when they opened the pressure differential valve to flush. Suffice to say, toilet safety when doing sat is taken very, very seriously.

There is no part of sat diving that isn't carefully regimented. Meals are provided on clean trays and taken away to maintain a sanitary environment. Even a mild cold or bacterial infection in the enclosed habitat could derail a very expensive sat dive.

Every meal, every moment, every conversation is monitored and recorded on CCTV. It takes a certain kind of person to thrive in that environment, but from his first dive, Chris loved it. His favourite part of the job was actually suiting up, clambering into a deep-sea diving bell reminiscent of an Apollo project landing craft, which is then carefully lowered through a specialised 'moon pool' in the bottom of the DSV. The bell is lowered to the desired depth, the pressure inside is equalised with the surrounding water and then the divers will drop through an opened hatch into the briny. In a way, it's a dive within a dive, although the actual dive depth may only be ten metres deeper than the 'depth' they have been living at. It's very cool!

While they are still inside the bell, which is tethered to the DSV above, the divers can feel the bell move about with the mothership above. But to work on the actual floor, they climb from the bell, and jump into an alien world.

'As soon as you jump off the bell you lose the sensation of the weather above you,' explains Chris. 'That's one of my favourite parts of diving. I love the feeling of weightlessness. You're effectively flying down to the seabed. If your visibility is bad, you really don't know what you're dropping into, or when you're going to be landing.'

It is eerily tranquil on the seafloor. The darkness is absolute – a sat diver works with only the lights they bring with them. Footage of divers at work – lit by their headlamp, with a small arsenal of equipment hanging off them, looks closer to a gritty sci-fi movie than the popular image of what a diver looks like.

To work on the sea floor, a sat diver is heavily weighted with tools and weights to stay negatively buoyant. Chris likens the conditions to the moon's gravity – you can jump a little, or haul yourself up a rope, but you can't swim.

'There's none of the grace you see with a good scuba diver, beautifully balanced in the water,' says Chris. 'You try your best to be streamlined but you're wearing a pair of old yellow fishing wellies.'

Saturation divers wear bright, loose-fitting dive suits. From each suit, an umbilical cord containing power and life-support systems tethers them to the diving bell and is their ticket back to the world above. Life support in the form of heating is maintained through a network of hot water pipes which wind around their body. The dive bell pumps hot water to the suit, in order to protect the diver from the cold – at ninety metres below the North Sea that night, it was around four degrees Celsius.

Chris describes the hot water life support as, 'quite pleasant really – like being in a jacuzzi at the bottom of the sea'. Until the day of his accident, his main health concern on the job was getting pimples on his back from sweating in his dive suit.

Typically, three divers will deploy on the dive bell for a shift. Two will suit up and jump down to the sea floor, while one – designated 'the bellman' – will remain in the vessel to keep an eye on things. One of the bellman's primary tasks is making sure the divers' umbilicals remain in good working order. The umbilical provides a physical tether to the dive bell and so to the boat above, as well as providing power, lights, hot water, and the very gas the divers breathe. It is, in a very literal sense, the diver's lifeline. The bellman can control the supply of gas, power and water from the bell to the individual diver – however, most of the time, once the divers are in the water, the bellman can kick back, relax with a book, and wait six hours for their divers to return. Unless something goes wrong.

*

It was late, around 10 pm on 18 September 2012, when the dive support vessel *Topaz* took position for a routine operation to repair an oil drill manifold; a collection of pressurised pipes within a superstructure that collect oil as it pumps from beneath the seabed. The manifold stood about five metres high, thirty metres across, and lay about 90 miles (145 kilometres) east of Aberdeen where the oil fields of the North Sea run in a spine down the sea between the United Kingdom and Norway. It was about as far from land as you could get in that stretch of water and, when the bell deployed, the waters of the North Sea were choppy. As Chris put it, 'it was marginal, but diveable'. Chris had been a professional sat diver for about a year and a half, and he'd seen worse.

That night his partner was Dave Yuas, whom he'd dived alongside several times, and got along with well. The two divers had no indication of the weather on the surface as they worked on the manifold.

Ten metres above them, at a safe height to avoid being snagged on the manifold on the seabed, their dive bell floated in the void. Their bellman that night was Duncan Allcock – a veteran diver who'd been something of a mentor and father figure to Chris while he was learning the ropes of sat diving. Ninety metres above them their support vessel, *Topaz*, kept watch over them.

The support vessel is able to maintain position above the dive bell due to a sophisticated dynamic positioning (DP) system. A series of sensors on the seabed work in tandem with positioning thrusters on the boat, all controlled by a centralised computer on the bridge. The DP system locks the vessel over a designated point on the seabed, with almost no drift. The system is so precise it allows the *Topaz* to hold within a metre of a point in winds of up to forty knots.

'It really is incredible. I could have a thirty-ton (twenty-seven-tonne) load hanging on the end of a crane wire in fairly bad weather and I can ask, "Can you move the crane, five metres on thirty-seven degrees?" and it will very smoothly move across,' Chris says.

When Chris had left the bell to start working that night, the weather had been rough, with swells around five metres. It was getting increasingly windy up top, but on the bottom of the ocean, Chris had no indication that anything was different. The seabed might as well have been a different world to the surface one ninety metres above.

The job was straightforward – remove a piece of pipe and replace it with a new one, which would be floated in by crane from the *Topaz*. That's a delicate operation, but one that Chris had done many times before. Chris was pleased that visibility in the water was fairly clear for the North Sea. As he worked away, he could glance up and see the lights of the dive bell floating above. All in all, 'very much a routine day in the office'.

The umbilical cable also held a hardwired radio link to the surface with a direct line of communication to the dive supervisor on duty, who that night was Canadian Craig Frederick. That radio link allows the supervisor to direct their divers in real time. When the divers are off the boat, the supervisor becomes the most important person in the operation – they gain complete control over the rest of the crew and in an emergency, it's up to them to make decisions to keep their divers safe. With the radio link they talk a diver through complex operations, help them orient themselves in low visibility and provide clear instructions when the unexpected happens. Their callsigns that night were Diver One (Dave) and Diver Two (Chris).

For Chris, Craig was a constant, reassuring voice in his ear, keeping them company on that night's dive. On a typical dive, he'd keep up a stream of chatter – directing repairs, coordinating crane-drops of tools and spare parts, and helping individual divers to orient themselves on the seabed. The environment is so alien that it messes with your perception.

'The seabed plays tricks on you,' says Chris. 'It's very easy to get disoriented, turned around. And plenty of times I've put myself in an embarrassing situation where you're lost on a seabed with a boat that costs 200,000 pounds a day above waiting for you to finish the job.'

That boat, the *Topaz*, was equipped with the gold standard in saturation diving technology. Along with the pressurised saturation habitat, it held two dive bells, an ROV, and the state-of-the-art automatic DP system that kept this ship locked in place even as it was rocked by waves and wind. It was a seamless operation until, that night, a freak software glitch in the bridge computer started a cascading systems failure that disabled the ship's functions, one by one.

The radio link let Chris hear everything that was happening on the bridge and gave him his first awareness that something had gone wrong when he heard alarms going off in the background.

Suddenly, Craig's voice crackled in his ear, telling him to down tools. 'Get out of the structure, boys.'

'I think there was something in his tone,' says Chris. 'He wasn't panicked but you could hear in his voice that this wasn't a drill.'

The suddenness of the command alerted Chris and Dave that something potentially serious was imminent, but they had no concept of what was happening. Chris doesn't remember being particularly concerned or equating the alarms to the sudden evacuation order. Small emergencies requiring quick action often happened on sat dives, so the two divers in the water calmly followed his instructions, downed tools, and left the manifold.

'Dave and I exited in a pretty orderly fashion. There was no real running or panic at that point,' Chris recalls.

Within thirty seconds, they'd cleared the structure and had jumped down onto the seabed, where they expected to see the diving bell hanging in the void straight in front of them. But 'it just wasn't where we left it'.

For Chris, this was disorienting and highly worrying. Without the diving bell as a reference point, the seabed was an endless void. 'In any sort of emergency environment, there is only one safe haven and that is the diving bell.' There is literally no other way to retrieve a sat diver from the seafloor. An emergency ascent from that depth would mean explosive decompression and a certain, agonising death.

The mantra in commercial and saturation diving is that the umbilical is your lifeline – and the protocol here was to follow the umbilical back to the diving bell. In this case, Chris and Dave's umbilicals ran back over their heads and over the top of the structure they'd just been inside.

Craig's voice was in Chris's ear pushing him to follow the umbilical with increasing urgency. To do so meant going up over the structure, so the divers began to climb, using their umbilicals as climbing ropes to haul themselves up.

When Chris finally reached the top, he turned to gather up the slack from the line to prevent a snagging hazard and found a loop of his umbilical had caught on a transponder bucket – a jutting piece of the structure.

'Slack to Diver Two,' he said into his radio. 'Umbilical is stuck. Umbilical is stuck. I need to clear it.'

*

Meanwhile, ninety metres above Chris, the *Topaz* had suffered an unprecedented catastrophic system failure and a total loss of control. Every screen on the bridge was blacked out, and all the automatic systems went with them, including the dynamic positioning system. In seconds, the *Topaz* had gone from a cutting-edge diving vessel into a sailboat.

As the increasing wind and waves began to move the ship away at the rate of knots, it pulled the diving bell with it. And attached to the bell, of course, were the two divers.

Chris found himself snagged with the manifold between him and the retreating dive bell with the force on his umbilical dragging him inexorably into the mass of the structure.

Chris's initial worry was that the force of being dragged would break his legs. His legs were splayed wide as he was dragged, and when he hit the structure, it would have effectively made his body into an anchor. 'You've got 5000 tons of ship one end and me at the other and there's only ever going to be one winner in that situation.' The other option would have been to be pulled underneath the transponder bucket, through a gap significantly smaller than his body. As Chris puts it, rather cheerfully, it would have been 'like going through a cheese grater, really'.

That grisly death was avoided when the DSV was thrown in a new direction by the waves, which in turn caused the diving bell to follow. Chris's umbilical went slack, then dragged him to the top of the structure. There he then became trapped against a solid metal bar a metre across. That was all that was standing between him and the open ocean, where the diving bell was being pulled further away. With it went the precious slack on his life-support umbilical, which was being stretched to breaking point.

'Umbilical's jammed. My umbilical's jammed, Craig,' Chris cried out, asking for more slack.

Chris's umbilical grew tighter and tighter, while Craig watched helplessly as the *Topaz* drifted further and further away, dragging the bell with it. 'Chris . . . we cannot give you any slack,' said his voice in Chris's ear. 'You've got to free that umbilical yourself.'

'It's tightening all the time,' Chris replied with rising panic, struggling to free himself. He could hear it creaking in the water as it was being stretched away.

*

Meanwhile, Dave, scrambling to reach the dive bell, realised Chris was in trouble and turned back to help him. As Dave struggled across the top of the structure he, too, was running out of line, but in the opposite direction. He made it to within two metres of Chris when the lurching ship far above dragged him off into the ocean, leaving Chris pinned against the structure on the seabed.

'I remember this strange moment when we were looking into each other's face plates. I could see the whites of his eyes and he could see mine and there was almost a look of resignation in his eyes. Or, of apology, you know: "There's nothing I can do for you, mate." It was almost a moment of goodbye and then he was being pulled backwards away from me and disappearing into the darkness.'

Now Chris was alone on the bottom of the North Sea, with nothing connecting him to the world above but the umbilical cable, which was stretched to breaking point. Soon, not even that. 'It didn't go all at once. The gas hose was the first to break. I lost my breathing gas pretty much instantly.'

154

At that point, he'd reached to the side of his helmet to switch on the 'bailout', a supply of emergency gas carried in two cylinders on his back. It was a manoeuvre he knew from muscle memory, something he'd practised countless times, but he'd never done it in a moment of imminent danger before. Now, his breathing was on the clock, and he had maybe eight minutes of gas, depending on how hard he was breathing.

'Give me slack, please!' he was shouting over the intercom, 'Slack to Diver Two.' Duncan, the operator in the diving bell, had no slack to give out. Chris's umbilical grew so tight that it began to buckle the steel bracket inside the dive bell where Duncan was trying to feed him some slack. 'I was shitting myself,' Duncan reported later. 'If it broke loose and went through the floor . . . I was going with it.'

The audio link topside was the next to go, with a screeching noise of feedback like a stereo jack being ripped out of a sound system. 'Suddenly I can't hear anybody. That again is panic inducing, not having a comforting voice in your ear. Suddenly you feel very alone.'

Seconds after that, the umbilical snapped entirely, with a noise that rang out underwater like a shotgun – so loud that Dave, who was hauling himself up his own umbilical to the diving bell, heard it loud and clear.

With that blast, Chris went tumbling back down in the dark towards the seabed. All his systems went dark, literally – his light went out and he was plunged into total darkness. 'Darkness I've never experienced before; black, black, black, lying on my back like an upturned turtle on the seabed, wondering what was going on.'

With the loss of the hot-water supply, his suit would have flooded with four-degree water within seconds, and the rapid descent into hypothermia began. Chris claims he never even felt the cold.

*

By now he was in full flight or fight mode and was completely focused on finding the bell. It was impossible – the bottom of the ocean is a disorienting place, even with lights and a compass and a reassuring voice directing you.

This situation was magnitudes worse. After several seconds lying on his back, he realised he didn't have a clue which way to go. Out of options, he scrambled to his feet, picked a direction at random, and moved towards it.

He wandered about blind, 'a bit like trying to find a toilet in the middle of the night. Your hands out in front of you in the dark and you're trying to feel your way through literally the most absolute darkness you've ever known.'

After two or three steps, his hands touched the metal of the structure, a miraculous stroke of luck. It was one of many to follow in the next few minutes.

He groped along the structure, shuffling slowly, terrified of losing it, until he discovered a length of two-inch hydraulic hose running up the side of the structure. It proved heavy and stable enough to haul himself up to the top.

'I clambered ten metres up to the top of the structure and pulled myself over the lip and looked up, fully expecting to see the diving bell somewhere.'

Chris had hoped there'd be lights up there, or something he could aim towards, but there was nothing but more darkness. The panic was absolute – all-consuming.

At that point, he recalls a mental transition; from wild panic to realising that if he was going to survive, he needed to think.

He reasoned he had about five minutes of gas left in his bailout, probably less, because he was breathing pretty heavily with panic and exertion. Chris realised that even if the diving bell had been there waiting for him, it would take three or four minutes to find a way up to it.

That was the best-case scenario, and that's not what Chris was facing. It wasn't that Chris was giving up on being rescued, but the maths told him, even with his thinking muddied by fear and trauma, that the chances of him getting out were pretty much non-existent.

Chris, like anyone who does the kind of work he does, is a fairly calm person. For his final minutes of life, he was able to rationalise and fully take stock of the situation, in the absolute certainty that he would soon be dead. His feelings were of terrible guilt knowing the pain his death would cause his family, and a fearful sense of wonder about what the final moments would feel like.

In my own experience in cave diving, I've had two or three moments when I've suddenly feared for my life. Those 'oh shit' moments where I realise I've made a potentially fatal mistake, and I've got a very limited time to solve it.

Like Chris, in those moments, my first thought is always one of guilt and thinking about my family. *This is so stupid. I can't believe I've put myself in this situation. Soon I'll be dead, but I won't have to deal with the consequences. It's my family who are going to suffer because of this.*

When I was a kid, it was my parents and my sisters who would worry. Now that I'm married with children, obviously, it's my wife and my kids. But that's what the thoughts usually revolve around at least initially. That sense of sorrow and guilt, combined with the rising panic and knowing that I'm perhaps seconds away from not only running out of air, but of losing control of myself entirely.

Each time, when I've been on the verge of that existential panic, I've managed to get control of it, quash those thoughts consciously, and bring my thinking back around to solving the problem at hand.

But I've never been in the situation Chris found himself in – one where even with the clearest thinking and superhuman effort, there was simply no way to cheat the maths. He did not have enough air to maintain life until a rescue could reach him. And the cold was too intense for a human being to survive. There was literally no way to escape.

'A resignation came over me at that point that this wasn't going to be survivable. You know that this was going to be . . . I wasn't gonna make it.' Chris recalls this realisation had a strangely calming effect on him, and he felt the panic subside as he made a conscious decision to regulate his breathing. Instead of fear, he remembers 'A sort of sad resignation; what a horrible, lonely place to die. Why am I, a little boy from Cambridge, going to die down here in the black?'

He doesn't remember being particularly frightened, just overwhelmingly sad, and conscious of what he would be leaving behind – he articulates it simply, but eloquently: 'It was grief. Grief for myself, really.'

More than anything, he was acutely conscious of the people he loved. Chris was engaged to be married the next year; now he would never see his fiancée, Morag, again. They were in the middle of building a house and now suddenly he was aware that he wasn't going to see any of that. All those major parts of life he was looking forward to celebrating had been taken away in a few moments, and he had the chance to reflect.

'I'm sorry, Morag!' he remembers calling out into the deep. 'I'm so sorry.'

He recalls, too, calling out for Duncan with a guttural cry. Duncan, who had been so good to Chris and was now somewhere out there in the dive bell, unable to do anything to help.

'Duncan, come and help me, please,' he begged, even though he knew, logically, that if anyone was coming to his rescue it was Dave, who was suited up and still attached to his umbilical somewhere above him. That too was impossible.

So, resigned to die, Chris lay down on the manifold, gripped it as best he could in the current, and curled up into the foetal position. With his neck craned up to watch for the lights of a rescuer that he would never see, he waited for his life to end.

'It happened faster than I thought it would,' says Chris. He felt the breathing getting tight, the way it does when a cylinder is almost out of gas. 'I can remember thinking "I hope this doesn't hurt", then, nothing.'

Chris describes those final moments as like those before you fall asleep at night, the way you can recall what you were thinking about just before sleep takes you, but not the moment it does. 'I don't have any recollection of it being an unpleasant experience.'

*

While Chris slipped quietly out of consciousness on the seabed structure, up on the surface the crew of the *Topaz* were struggling to regain control of the ship, which had been blown 250 metres away from where Chris was stranded on the seafloor. The *Topaz*'s computers were completely disabled – primary, backup and emergency systems had all failed, something that should have been impossible.

The captain made the decision to switch to manual control – which meant steering the guidance thrusters with thruster handles. The problem was that meant four thruster handles, on two separate consoles, and a pilot only has two hands. In an unprecedented situation, the crew were trying to coordinate steering between two people and four joysticks, in a hectic North Sea storm. Each time they regained course, a huge wave would hit the *Topaz* and knock it back.

For Craig, the dive supervisor on duty, the only tool he had functioning was the remote operated vehicle (ROV) – which the *Topaz* dispatched on a tether of 300 metres to search the seabed for Chris. The footage recorded from the ROV's camera is utterly eerie. It captures the imagery as the ROV's lights search into the gloom – the odd ghostly fish flashing by in the silt, the bulk of the manifold emerging from the dark, and then finally, Chris's body is illuminated by the machine's floodlights. As the ROV settles into position with the camera trained on him, he appears to be waving to it.

The pilot of the ROV called out to the bridge crew, announcing that not only had they found Chris, but he was alive, well, and waving at the camera.

Chris has no recollection of this. He was almost certainly unconscious by then. The longer the footage goes on, the more disturbing it becomes as it appears that his arms are waving without control, either flailing helplessly in the current, or suffering from his dying brain and body.

The ordeal was not over. Although the crew of the *Topaz* had found Chris, recovering him would be another matter entirely. It took them more than half an hour from losing control of the ship to rebooting the computers and regaining the DP system. By then, Chris's body was deathly still.

*

The *Topaz* regained its position above the manifold, then lowered the dive bell to within two metres of the structure. From there, Dave was able to jump down and stand over the body of his friend. The way Dave tells the story, he was sure that Chris was gone, and in his mind, he was retrieving a corpse. 'I wasn't surprised by what I saw. A dead guy on the roof of the manifold.'

Nonetheless, Dave took his pneumofathometer tube (used to measure depth but can be used to provide an emergency supply of gas) and jammed the thin hose into Chris's diving helmet to give him something to breathe while he tried to manhandle his friend back into the dive bell. With the extra weight of Chris, Dave had to climb his own umbilical back to the bell one-handed, dragging Chris and all of his gear. Hard enough in still water, but the bell was being jerked up and down in the water metres at a time as the *Topaz* was smashed by waves far above.

More than once, Dave was sure he would drop Chris, and that would have been the end of that. Later, when Dave was showering after the ordeal, he realised he was so physically fatigued his hands had cramped into claws.

With one last mighty heave, Dave managed to get Chris up to the dive bell, where Duncan was waiting. Chris was too heavy to lift into the bell entirely, so Duncan ripped off his helmet, and was shocked by what he saw.

Duncan had been a diver a long time and had seen cyanosis before – the blueish tint that can affect people's lips, gums or fingers when blood oxygen levels are low – but never like this. Chris's head was a bright, vivid blue. The way Duncan tells it, the clean-shaven dome of his head looked more like a large eight-ball than the face of the man he'd taught to dive.

Duncan leaned down to begin resuscitation, breathing into Chris's mouth. One breath. Then another. Suddenly, just like that, with a massive exhalation, Chris started breathing again.

Chris remembers coming to slowly – flashing lights, a groggy feeling like being very drunk at the end of the night. Then he grunted and slowly, with assistance, pulled himself out of the water and into the dive bell.

Craig, watching from the bridge of the *Topaz*, could not believe what he saw. 'Chris,' he asked over the radio, 'are you alright, buddy?' The briefest pause, and after a moment, Chris gave a thumbs up. Five minutes later, he was coming around, and within a few hours he was walking around.

*

Chris's survival is astounding, to put it mildly. It's an astonishing story to listen to as a layperson, but when I consider the facts with my hyperbaric physician and critical care doctor hat on, I find it impossible to explain.

Chris can't have been in cardiac arrest because no kind of airway intervention would help in that situation. Essentially, his heart was still beating although he'd been without air for – at a conservative estimate – fifteen minutes. I assume that the loss of heating and the sudden immersion in the four-degree water of the North Sea made Chris's core temperature plummet, and the low temperature protected his brain once his breathing stopped.

We all know the stories about kids who fall through the ice and are dragged out and successfully resuscitated after thirty, even sixty minutes. Kids have a high surface area to body weight ratio which means their core cools very rapidly. But that is not the case in a man as large as Chris, so I don't believe it is the whole story.

Perhaps the sudden rush of cold water promoted the 'diving reflex'. This reflex promotes a very slow heart rate and may place the circulation in a 'low flow state'. Essential organs such as the heart and brain are preferentially supplied with the limited reserves of life-giving oxygen. There's just enough blood moving around your brain and body to keep things ticking over for a prolonged period of time. But again, this reflex is less potent in adults.

Even with all that in mind, I still don't understand quite how it's possible that he survived.

The final pieces of the puzzle may be that Chris's blood was hyper-oxygenated. The gas in his emergency tank held a high percentage of pure oxygen – so his lungs, blood and body tissues may have been saturated with oxygen when the water temperature put him into a sort of stasis. Fortunately, his helmet was not flooded. It is possible he lost consciousness from high levels of CO_2 within the helmet which can have a gradual anaesthetic effect. When he passed out, rather than being asphyxiated his lungs may still have been full of an oxygen-enriched gas.

I believe Chris found himself at a precise physiological balance point – his heart running at a fraction of capacity, just enough to keep him alive. His body and brain rapidly cooling offering some protection from hypoxic brain injury. The oxygen-enriched gas in his lungs offering a reservoir that just tipped the balance in his favour.

Frankly, it's still a bloody marvel he survived at all, let alone completely intact.

*

Nobody can really explain how Chris walked away unscathed. He travelled to London's Royal Medical Society to speak with the world's leading experts in hyperbaric medicine, seeking answers. 'I assumed that if I'm going to get answers anywhere, it's here, right? And they didn't really have them.'

It's the sort of infinitely small chance that people refer to as a medical miracle, although I prefer to avoid that term, and it's not the one that Chris prefers. He prefers the more accurate term: 'improbable'.

'But improbable doesn't mean impossible and there was obviously some mechanism that allowed me to survive. The human body is such a remarkable thing. Just because we don't necessarily know exactly what those physiological factors were that kept me alive doesn't mean they didn't happen.

'The most amazing thing is not so much that I survived, but that I came away with no brain damage from oxygen deprivation,' says Chris, deadpan. 'Or nobody's been brave enough to tell me otherwise.'

*

After Chris was rescued and stabilised, returning to the surface still meant four days of slow decompression before he could leave the chamber. There was no way around that, which Chris looks back on as fortunate. Those few days were cathartic and gave Chris time to process what he and his colleagues had been through. It was the best debrief with Duncan and Dave he could have hoped for.

By the time they were ready to come out of saturation, Chris was ready to get back into the bell for another dive. When a sign-up sheet was circulated for divers to register their interest in going back down to finish the job, Chris signed his name without thinking twice, to incredulous laughs from the crew of the *Topaz*.

'It's a competitive job, a lot of people want that position,' says Chris. 'I just wanted to get back in the water as soon as possible, get back on the bike, that kind of thing.'

Just three weeks after the incident, the same dive team returned to the bottom of the North Sea to finish the job: Divers One and Two, Duncan the bellman, and Craig as dive supervisor. Chris recalls some nervous banter, a few awkward jokes, but the second he jumped from the diving bell back into the darkness, he forgot all fear, and had nothing in his mind but the job at hand.

'And Chris,' said Craig over the radio as they descended, 'don't fuck it up this time.'

'Roger that,' Chris replied, without missing a beat.

*

It is an honour to be able to retell Chris's story in this book and frankly, I found him inspiring to talk to. Six years have passed since the accident, and on the whole, he looks back on it as a positive experience in his life. From a diving and work perspective he's come away with a lot more confidence, having experienced the most horrific dive accident imaginable and bounced back. He's also had the chance to be involved in making films, travelling to tell his story.

Chris is contacted on an almost daily basis by people who want to talk to him about what happens to you in your moment of death. 'Sometimes, it's hundreds of people a day. Not long after it happened, a little old lady in my local shop stopped me. She'd just lost her husband and really wanted to know what those final moments were like,' Chris says. 'She took some comfort that it wasn't an unpleasant experience. A very sad and lonely one definitely, I'm not trying to brush it under the carpet or imagine those were moments I enjoyed, but they weren't as terrible as you might have imagined.'

Chris is happy some people find comfort in his experience of death's threshold. 'I've come to realise there is a responsibility as a human being to offer comfort to people if they ask.' Then there are the people who approach him, not with questions but with answers, particularly people of faith who have strong opinions on his survival.

'I'm very much an atheist. I'm very much after the concrete facts. I have sympathy for people faced with an unknown death and they want to fill that gap with something a bit larger, but that's certainly not for me,' says Chris. 'You have to find a rational explanation for these things.'

The thing that strikes me about talking to Chris is how, for a lack of a better word, 'normal' he is. An eminently pragmatic bloke before his accident, he remains so now. While he'd like to be able to say he'd had a life-changing epiphany, he knows – better than anyone perhaps – how random his survival was. In a way, Chris being rescued from the bottom of the ocean was no different than surviving the traffic accident you avoid when the car about to hit you slams on the brakes just in time. There is risk inherent in all life.

'The truth of my story is, whilst it is interesting because it happened in this sort of slightly strange and alien environment, people suffer far, far worse than I did. People who face their own imminent mortality on a daily basis. It was my choice to put myself down there, and to do so you have to accept that risk. It was a close-run thing, but at the end of the day, you still have to put the bins out and remember to get milk down at the shops. Life goes on, doesn't it?'

PART FOUR

AIR

'If you have built castles in the air,' wrote Henry David Thoreau, the 19th-century philosopher and pioneering environmentalist, 'your work need not be lost; that is where they should be. Now, put the foundation under them.'

It's a wonderful reminder of the value of both lofty thoughts and the hard work of actualising them. When Thoreau penned it, he wasn't thinking about high octane engines and the whomping shockwave when a fighter jet breaks the sound barrier – but I still find it something to relate to every time I see an air show.

If you listen to the poets, air is where we snatch our dreams from. For much of our history, it is a frontier we dreamed of conquering. From legend to science, humanity has pursued the ageless quest to fly like a bird. Since the first tentative lift off, aircraft have gone faster and higher, and performed more audacious manoeuvres with every passing decade.

As our civilisations advanced, we have steadily conquered the air. In a physical sense, and in a more abstract one. The world seems to have shrunk, as it became possible for a human being to cross the entire planet in a matter of hours. It has shrunk even further, with advancing media and online platforms making us capable of snatching news and images from the air in a way Thoreau could never have imagined.

At times, it seems the human capacity for adventure is limited only by imagination. Thoreau's writing, while living on the shores of Walden Pond in Massachusetts, remains transcendent. Few people have ever been so inspired by a pond. That said, if I were in his position, I would be curious to have a look underneath the surface and see if there were any remarkable caves to be explored. Cave diving wasn't a popular pursuit back in Thoreau's day, but I wonder if he would have taken to it the way I did. You never know. We all take inspiration from where we find it.

So let's look at the way risk interacts with inspiration. The way technology, innovation and individuality combine with risk-taking in order to push the world forward. My own castle in the air is probably a subterranean expedition habitat – but that's just me. I looked to what inspires other risk-takers, and asked them what inspires them to risk life and limb day after day. That meant talking to adrenaline junkies strapped into rocket-powered vehicles, a broadcast journalist with a bird's-eye view of human nature, and a man who disappeared into thin air – and then returned to find his way of being in the world changed forever.

CHAPTER TEN

THE NEED FOR SPEED

When I first set out to talk to risk-takers, my working hypothesis was that most people who do things that might be considered dangerous by many people would actually be like me. That is, not especially brave or courageous, but rather cautious risk-managers rather than risk-takers. And that most of them would not have the persona of the classic adrenaline junky who might whoop and holler before throwing themselves off a cliff or whatever they were into.

I was perfectly ready to be surprised. To have my preconceptions shattered and my prejudices dismissed – but it turned out my hunch seemed to pan out. Nearly everyone was eminently sensible. The BASE jumper Sean Chuma, who I had expected to be the most gung-ho adrenaline junkie, was perhaps the most adrenaline-phobic man I'd ever met.

Nearly everyone I interviewed stressed the importance of preparation, mental fortitude, staying calm and focused while every nerve-ending in their bodies was screaming – but very few were willing to say that was their favourite part of risk-taking. None of them would admit to actually *enjoying* the feeling of wild abandon that came with risking their lives. I was pleased that my hunch about risk-takers turned out to hold water, but I was still surprised at how few people would admit that they enjoyed a good old-fashioned adrenaline rush.

That is, until I met drag racer Ashley Sanford, a woman who seems to need adrenaline the way most of us need air. She spends her days racing cars that are closer to rockets than they are to your standard motor vehicle, and just as prone to bursting into flames.

'I'm a bit of an adrenaline junkie. I love everything fast,' Ashley tells me, before reeling off a list of extremely thrilling and dangerous interests: 'Off roading, anything four-wheel drive, trophy trucks, racers. I am a person that is, in general, in life, just very fearless. There's a lot I have on my bucket list!'

At first blush, Ashley is the epitome of a young daredevil. Young, cheerful, she's got the easy smile and that all-American mix of friendly courtesy and boundless energy that Southern California seems to produce. Raised on a fifty-acre desert property, she grew up racing four-wheeled all-terrain vehicles (ATVs) across the dunes. Her grandfather and father were sand racers, a form of dirt racing she describes as 'a little more dangerous than asphalt racing just because dirt is a little more . . . let's say, unreliable'.

Unreliable, but great fun, according to Ashley. She raced her first quad ATV at eight years old, and raced them until fourteen, just for fun.

'I learned stick shift when I was nine years old. I was always thrown in a vehicle and wanted to figure it out and figure out how to push the limits with it.'

From there she moved to other forms of sand-racing, escalating in speed and octane as she grew. At fourteen, she graduated to her grandfather's Super Comp dragster. Two years after that, shortly after she'd got her road driver's licence, she was behind the wheel of a full-blown dragster, going 250 kilometres per hour.

The need for speed

Throughout her youth, Ashley took any chance she had to go faster. As her teens passed – around the time she started thinking about college and what route to take in life – all her ambitions kept taking her back to drag racing. So, she sat down with her father, who was also a keen racer, and told him she wanted to pursue it as a career.

'I was like, "Okay, you're gonna call me crazy. Just hold on to your seat. But I want to go into drag racing, full time. That's what I want to do." To my surprise he was totally excited about it,' she recalls.

From that point on, her father threw himself into helping her break into the world of Top Fuel drag racing – and a life that would be the envy of petrol heads everywhere. In 2013, at age nineteen, she moved to asphalt in an A/Fuel Dragster. Sponsors, success, and victory followed – and a lot of burnt rubber.

*

The Top Fuel drag racers are some of the fastest cars on Earth – in fact, some of the fastest vehicles ever created. The driver squeezes into a low-slung, long wheelbase chassis, and sits with their back to a 11,000-horsepower nitromethane/petrol engine – one that will shoot the car from zero to 380 kilometres per hour in less than four seconds. No land-based vehicle accelerates faster – or stops as suddenly.

The standard racetrack is 1000 feet (300 metres) long, and in order to stop at the end, the driver deploys both carbon fibre brakes and parachutes. The acceleration is comparable to that of an astronaut blasting into space – but the deceleration is much worse. Ashley experiences deceleration forces of five times Earth's gravity every time she gets behind the wheel.

'It's the wildest ride,' she says. 'When two cars race, it actually sets off the Richter scale, and registers as a baby earthquake. You feel it in your bones. It hits all five senses – overwhelming in the best way.'

The sheer power required to reach those speeds literally tears the engines apart. After nearly every race, they have to be rebuilt; their exploded or melted parts replaced. For most events, that is a highlight for spectators, who get the chance to walk up and watch the cars get stripped down and repaired.

In order to harness that sort of horsepower, a certain amount of attrition is built into the cars themselves. If that's what this kind of racing does to steel and chrome, imagine, if you will, the potential for injury to the drivers.

A Top Fuel driver wears armour: helmet, gloves, and a bulky fire suit as protection against the very real chance the car might be engulfed in flames. Fully equipped, the only part of a racer visible are the eyes. Then they are strapped into the cockpit with restraints fastened by one of their crew, as it's impossible for a racer to fix their own restraints as tight as necessary. The force of acceleration and deceleration alone loosens the safety restraints nearly three centimetres, even when everything goes to plan.

Sometimes, the engine will simply explode, and the nitromethane fuel creates a fireball that accompanies you down the track. It's happened to Ashley: 'I felt and saw the flames – it felt like I was in an oven. Thankfully, it was put out quickly, but in that second, it was intense. It's not a sport for the faint-hearted.'

In the past, when the technology was less streamlined, now and again a driver's retinas would detach from the jolt when they hit the brakes. Even today, with safety much improved, pilots are known to develop tunnel vision and even black out from the g-force as they accelerate.

Ashley has briefly lost consciousness herself – overheated, and with restricted airflow inside the cockpit, she passed out at the head of the throttle. 'The craziest thing is, I immediately woke back up and went back on the throttle to try to win the race,' she laughs. 'Maybe not the smartest move, but you do what you got to do!'

The need for speed

*

The pressure to perform on race day is immense. Drivers like Ashley aren't racing just for their own glory, but that of their team. While other racing codes, such as Formula 1, seem to put a premium on the driver and their personality, drag racing is very much a celebration of the pit crew – the mechanics and engineering minds who build and customise the vehicles. It's their show, too, and they are involved right up to the last minute, mapping the track to account for temperature on the day. I never thought I would find a more painstakingly methodical group of risk-takers than cave divers, but Top Fuel racers give us a run for our money. If something goes wrong on a dive, at worst we have the length of a breath to correct it. Ashley doesn't have such a luxury. Every possible risk factor – mechanical, environmental, meteorological – has to be anticipated and corrected, and this is before the possibility of human error and the exhilaration of the race itself, begins. For the Top Fuel team, their job doesn't end until the ignition starts.

Then, in a 150-decibel roar (enough to cause physical pain and permanent hearing loss), the custom-built car – representing countless hours of blood, sweat and tears on behalf of the pit crew – roars down the raceway in the time of half a dozen heartbeats. 'It's three and a half seconds but so much goes into those seconds,' says Ashley. 'That's what makes it so exciting!'

In total, from starting the car to coming to a stop trailing para-chutes and melted rubber, the whole race can happen in a minute. When she comes to a stop, Ashley says she is usually screaming with the thrill of it all. 'I'm telling you, when I get out of the car, I could have just run a marathon. My heart is thumping out of my chest. My adrenaline is through the roof; pure excitement.'

Exciting, no doubt, but also dangerous. If something goes wrong – be it driver error, or an unexpected mechanical failure – the potential for disaster is huge. At those speeds, the smallest misfortune can have massive repercussions. Ashley once struck a loose object on the track – a pebble, perhaps, or a nail – and lost a rear tyre at over 320 kilometres per hour. She was able to control the car, and a skid plate at the bottom of the vehicle helped her bring it to a stop. 'But usually when that happens, the car gets "tacoed" as we call it.' This charming bit of Californian slang means that the long, thin car has been concertinaed into a giant ball of crushed metal.

Ashley recalls how a friend Steve Torrence, 'a rock star driver', lost control of and crashed his car and the seemingly endless stretch of time between the crash and finding out if he was okay or not inside the mangled vehicle. In the end, Steve survived without serious injury, but crashing remains Ashley's biggest racing-related fear. It's the reality of a bad crash and wondering what it would be like for her parents or boyfriend if they were to watch her in a similar incident, that gives her pause.

'I've seen some gnarly crashes. Some of them felt like they just went on forever. To me, as a spectator, watching someone crash is devastating. I can only imagine what the driver's loved ones are feeling in that moment.'

At the same time, she knows some kind of accident is likely in her sport. And that when it does happen, it will be a terrifying experience. Still, she is pragmatic about it. 'It's what I'm signing myself up for. The highs of getting on a track and it all goes to plan. It's worth risking it all for that.'

According to Ashley, everyone involved in the sport understands that it is one of emotional extremes. When everything goes right, they are on top of the world. When it goes wrong, it's not unusual for everyone on the team to beat themselves up over it. If a run goes wrong on an elimination day, it is devastating. When a driver is injured or their car destroyed, it is much worse. But even relatively minor setbacks can't be easily shrugged off. A motor sport where the cars are designed to blow themselves up is not an inexpensive one.

*

When we spoke, Ashley's career was on a bit of a pause, as the travel and economic restrictions of the COVID-19 pandemic hit. But I got the impression that a little thing like a global pandemic isn't going to keep Ashley down for very long. It takes a certain resilience to lose control of a car at those speeds and come back hungry for more. She seems to live her life a little like she approaches her racing. 'Every trip down the drag strip you're learning constantly. And so, when things go right, you are just absolutely thrilled. But when they go wrong, hey, at least you learned something and hopefully you can take it with you and not let it happen again.'

Ashley, perhaps the only self-confessed adrenaline junky I've found operating at the coalface of risk-taking, still fosters a similar attitude to risk as everyone I've spoken to. She is not gung-ho in her risk-taking. When she climbs into her highly flammable supercar, she does so knowing that an intricate matrix of risk-factors has been assessed and corrected for. Only then does she hit the accelerator.

Her philosophy is simple. 'Life is going to happen the way it happens, and you can't be afraid,' she says. 'You just have to get in the car, and you have to trust what's behind you: your car and your team. You have to trust your procedures and that you know your instincts will do what's right.'

'They say it takes a certain kind of crazy to do what we do,' she says, and I reckon she's right. In fact, we could all use a little more of her brand of crazy. There's something powering her that seems just as energetic and combustible as her cars.

'Even when I'm talking about racing, I just feel so excited! I mean, my adrenaline feels like it's starting to pump just thinking about it!'

I walk away from our chat utterly convinced of the merits of a good old-fashioned adrenaline rush. From a medical viewpoint, high-intensity stressors like BASE jumping or drag-racing cause the adrenal

177

gland to release huge amounts of the stress hormone epinephrine. For some, this fight or flight response stimulates a heightened sense of emotion. The initial sense of fear makes way for euphoria – a sensation that recreational risk-takers go to extreme lengths to experience. Which (provided the risk-taking is accompanied by a healthy expansion of the 'stretch zone' and safe, incremental increases of skill) can be considered a net gain for the individual. Take the sense of wellbeing you experience after a brisk swim in a cold ocean, and multiply it by magnitudes, and you'll land somewhere around the frame of mind Ashley seems to go through life with.

She is a compelling advocate for the cathartic power of hurling herself down a racetrack at absurd speeds. Of course, hers is just one philosophy. There are others.

*

'I hate adrenaline,' says Matt Hall, a former fighter pilot who flies high-speed aircraft through obstacle courses for a living. 'If my body is firing off adrenaline, it means I'm right on the edge, I don't know what's going to happen. I hate that feeling. I absolutely hate it. I'm a control freak.'

Control freak or not, it's hard to imagine living Matt's life without a healthy appreciation for adrenaline. As a pilot in the Red Bull Air Race, he flew a customised, ultra-fast race plane through a slalom course of 'Air Gates' – mammoth pylons rising up to form an obstacle course. Air Race pilots fly just ten metres off the surface of the Earth, navigating hairpin turns at speeds of up to 200 knots (370 kilometres per hour), weaving, banking and rolling like aces in a dogfight, competing to score valuable points to progress to the next round. Often victory is decided by a fraction of a second and there is no room for pilot error. Watching a race from the ground, it seems miraculous that every second pilot doesn't hit an air gate and explode into flames.

Incredibly, since the first official Air Race in 2003, there has been only one serious accident, when in 2010 Brazilian pilot Adilson Kindlemann crashed his plane into the Swan River in Western Australia. He was rushed to Royal Perth Hospital and survived with no serious injuries.

The races were cancelled for the next three years to allow for improved safety measures, and it remains the only crash in the history of the race.

All of which is to say, it takes an extraordinary pilot to compete in the races, let alone take away the championship, as Matt did in the final season in 2019, after which Red Bull announced it would no longer host the race. 'Technically, I am the reigning world champion forever,' says Matt with a laugh. 'Red Bull sold the race to another company. I'm the Red Bull Air Race Perpetual World Champion.'

*

Matt has flying in the blood – he's a third-generation pilot, with a grandfather who served in the Second World War. Matt's first solo flight was in a glider at fifteen, and he gained his pilot's licence at eighteen years of age. He's flown gliders, ultra-lights, stunt planes, combat jets, vintage warplanes – although the way Matt tells it, there's no such thing as a born pilot. It's something you become.

Matt decided at seventeen that he was going to be a pilot. Not just any pilot, but an Air Force fighter pilot. To give some context to this ambition – only a tiny fraction of the top one per cent of pilots will ever sit inside the cockpit of a fighter jet. It's a little like a teenager deciding that they will become a rock star, or a famous actor, or a top ballerina – you can have all the talent and drive in the world, but the odds are stacked against you.

'This was the age of *Top Gun*,' recalls Matt, drily. 'The movie had just come out, and I turn up at school with my Ray-Bans on, telling everyone I'm going to be a fighter pilot.'

Matt got the same advice from everyone – from his career coun-sellor to his dad – that his chances were slim to none. Thinking a career as a commercial pilot would be the next best thing, he got a part-time job and started saving up for his education. At that point, he had a life-changing meeting with a Second World War veteran who'd flown Spitfires – the iconic fighter aircraft that helped win the Battle of Britain and captured the hearts and minds of plane buffs ever since.

'He looked at me and said, "I'd do anything to be in your shoes right now,"' Matt remembers. The veteran, now a successful business-man, would trade it all for a chance to join the Air Force and fly a supersonic jet fighter. He couldn't think of anything more spectacular in the world. Nor, when Matt considered this advice, could he.

'I remember thinking, "What am I scared of?"' Matt soon realised that the key thing holding him back was the fear of failure – of striving for a dream and being told he couldn't hack it. He also realised that he was more scared of the alternative. 'I flipped it in my head. The greater fear should be spending your life wondering what you *might* have done.'

So, he joined the Air Force. After an initial period of adjustment to the strict rules and regulations of the military environment – and nearly failing the officer training course – he took to the air, and never looked back.

Later on, Matt found out his experience of flight training was somewhat unusual, because he enjoyed every minute of it.

'Most Air Force pilots hate their pilot training, because if they don't pass, they don't have a career.' The stress of having to compete at that level, for a handful of places in the elite fighter pilot training program, is often a miserable experience. 'But I enjoyed what I was doing,' says Matt. He couldn't believe that people were actually paying him to fly planes.

'I didn't go to work scared of making a mistake – every morning I took off with a big smile on my face. Boom, let's go! I think that helped me have some pretty great results.'

That's 101 sports psychology. If you're looking forward to competition, you're probably going to do a lot better than someone looking forward to the competition being over. In Matt's case, it seems to have worked – he graduated from his class in 1992 having smashed all performance records.

*

Long story short – Matt became a fighter pilot. A couple more years of specialist training, and he completed specialist fighter training, and was then flying around in a $50 million supersonic jet fighter at twenty-one. 'So that's kind of cool,' Matt observes, drily.

From there, he did a couple of tours flying Hornet supersonic fighters, after which he was selected for the Fighter Combat Instructor course – the Australian version of the Top Gun school. He was then sent to America to work as a Top Gun instructor, flying the F-15 Strike Eagle. From the outset, it was the adventure of a lifetime.

This was in June 2001. On September 11, the Twin Towers terrorist attacks ushered in a new era of global conflict. For the first time since the Cold War ended, flying a fighter jet in a real life war was on the table. Less than two years later, he joined his squadron in the Middle East for Operation Iraqi Freedom, flying F-15 jets as an Australian officer in an American unit.

After honing his skills as a fighter pilot for most of his adult life, he was in a war zone for the first time, taking out enemy targets, getting shot at, and tragically, losing friends: 'We lost a crew, a jet with some mates on board. I heard people screaming on the radios as they were dying. Those experiences are worse than the ones where I nearly died.'

He's had his fair share of those, too. His book, *The Sky Is Not the Limit* is his own account of the extremes of excitement, fear and loss during his time in Iraq. It opens with a hair-raising anecdote about flying in formation, and realising he has been targeted by a tracking surface to air missile, and probably has seconds to live.

When I ask him to expand on that story, he describes seeing the first flash of the missile flare 'like an arc light' and realising the missile was changing direction to follow him, running the maths on a short-range high-speed missile, and then executing a series of evasive rolls he calls his 'last ditch defence' that saw the missile overshoot him.

He tells the story with even humour, finding levity in what must have been a terrifying experience. 'That's the life of a fighter pilot in real quick time. You've got ten seconds of the good life, and then ten seconds in which you might be dead in your next breath. Then it's over, and you tiptoe away, regroup, and go back to bomb the target.'

I'm struck by the analytical way Matt speaks about being in combat, that in the moment of his imminent death, he could look at the problem calmly and mechanically, and choose the right course of action to keep himself and his unit alive. He says that's part of endless conditioning which is what makes him such a confident pilot.

'There's always jokes about how a monkey would make a good pilot, you know, monkey see, monkey do,' says Matt. 'But there's actually some logic to that.'

He subscribes to the idea that it takes 10,000 hours to be an expert in any field – to rehearse an activity until it becomes instinctive. Until you can fly a plane with as little conscious thought as it takes to breathe, then the task will require focus and energy. That's fine, until something goes wrong, and your attention is required to assess and react to an unexpected situation. If even part of your attention is focused on keeping the plane in the air, your capacity to respond overloads, and shuts down. 'That's when things go wrong. So, that's why people that are very, very good at something, who can do it instinctively, have the ability to continue to do something while assessing a problem.' It's an illustration of the concept known as 'mastery'.

It's the extremes of flying – be it in combat or in an air-race – where I imagine adrenaline would be flooding through Matt's system. He says it's just the opposite. When he's doing something that seems high risk, that's when absolute focus and preparation is required. For him, a sixty-second event is just the culmination of preparation and planning – so everything that occurs at the critical moment is deliberate.

The execution is a flow mentality where everything disappears from his thought process except what is necessary in the moment. 'I'm on that perfect line where I'm conscious of what is an immediate threat, and not distracted by what isn't,' he says. 'The feeling of satisfaction coming out the back end of an execution like that is beyond words. I can't describe how good it feels. And that is euphoria, not adrenaline.'

In Matt's reckoning, the times he's nearly lost it all are when an adrenaline spike has pierced his perfect calm. Like a near-miss in 2010, when he stalled his plane while racing over the Detroit-Windsor River on the border of Canada and the United States. The plane rolled over onto its back, and while falling the ten metres to the ground, he was able to right it just as it hit the water. He bounced off the water a few times, but managed to peel back up, and fly it back for a safe landing – with minor damage to the plane, and major damage to his pride.

'I was pretty angry with myself and very embarrassed,' recalls Matt. 'If I was over land (instead of water) I probably wouldn't have bounced so easily. I probably would have rolled into a ball and caught fire.'

He continues, 'That incident was a bit of a wake-up call. I didn't feel I was at risk in the sport, until that point.' The next day, he didn't go out to fly, but sat down to analyse what went wrong. For two weeks, he and his team took apart every single causal factor that might have impacted his performance. Every mechanical variation to his plane, every possible biological explanation: sleep patterns, diet, everything he had eaten in the seventy-two hours up to the incident. Only once every possible cause of error had been accounted for, and plans made to eliminate them, did he take to the air again.

'With this type of sport, you can't just walk in there with your fingers crossed, hoping it works,' he says. 'You've got to get up every morning and go, "Is everything in place? Is the training in effect? Has the risk matrix been ticked? Where's the gap that can actually hurt me?" And on that particular day, we missed it.'

Matt says that the truly dangerous part of a life that involves a lot of high-risk activities is growing complacent about risk when performing at peak capacity. 'You subconsciously carry the acceptance of high-risk levels across into areas that aren't as well planned or controlled, or with as much safety equipment or margin for error,' says Matt.

While I wouldn't compare a cave dive to the interplay between man and machine Matt deals with in a jet fighter, there are sufficiently complex life-support systems involved to allow dangerous errors. Almost all cave-diving fatalities start with human error. The environment is unforgiving enough to allow a small mistake to rapidly send the diver headfirst down a one-way road. Complacency is an especially hazardous trait, something that can transform what should be a simple dive into a close call. This was the root cause of one of my closest calls.

It was on one of my many expeditions to the Pearse Resurgence in New Zealand. The cave is remote, very cold and extremely deep – and necessitates the use of diving habitats – those air-filled 'underwater hotels' explained in an earlier chapter.

The deepest habitat is positioned at a depth of forty metres. And one of the early jobs on the expedition is to fix it in place – actually dive to the requisite depth, construct the habitat, and fill it with breathable air. I was working on this task with my dive buddy, Craig Challen, when I found myself unexpectedly with no air in my lungs.

Not exactly a good problem to have and suffice to say it was entirely of my own making. I broke two of my own rules. Firstly, I used some of my emergency backup breathing gas to fill up the habitat with air. Secondly, I didn't completely check my rebreather before the dive, as I considered this dive to be very straightforward. A minor issue with the rebreather led to a major problem when my backup source of air was not available (I had switched it off after it froze in a 'free-flow' state while filling the habitat). Basically, it was the equivalent of not packing your parachute properly then realising you left your secondary chute in the hangar.

Within thirty seconds I went from having a lovely time to having nothing to breathe. I was at a depth of forty metres vertically and about fifty metres horizontally from the entrance to the flooded cave. With panic just seconds away, I managed to find another solution more by luck than by good planning. By racing upwards towards Craig in the hope I could get air from him (I couldn't have), the air in my rebreather expanded sufficiently to give me enough to breathe for the short time it then took me to resolve the issue with the equipment. I exited the cave much like Matt Hall landed his plane after touching the water – angry with myself and deeply embarrassed.

My analysis of the event brought me to the conclusion that complacency had been the cause of my near-death experience. Because I was building up to an exploration dive of over 200 metres in depth, I had lost perspective on the hazards of a forty-metre working dive in an extremely demanding cave. Had I been younger and less experienced, ironically, I probably would never have made that mistake.

Seen through the lens of a more inexperienced, cautious diver, that forty-metre dive would have commanded enormous respect and comprehensive preparation. It is significant to me that for a deep dive I would use checklists and fuss over my equipment for hours (sometimes days) in preparation, but for a dive where many of the same hazards exist, my attitude was completely different. Nowadays, I try to treat every dive as the one that could cause my undoing. I owe that to myself and to my family.

And, just like Matt – and with apologies to Ashley – it's important to avoid excessive adrenaline coming into play. Swimming through a cave passage is something I generally associate with relaxation, mindfulness and 'being in the moment'. In a sense it is meditative. Not the sleepy kind of meditation, but the kind where your every sense and thought is on the job at hand. With mastery, many of the processes are automated, the scanning of the gauges, the referencing and navigating through the cave, the regular check on your buddy and yourself.

When the dive becomes more challenging or potentially more hazardous, all those senses become heightened. For example, on an ultra-deep dive, I am listening to every sound the rebreather is making, alert for the first sign that something in my gear is not coping with the enormous pressures. My senses are alert to the first symptoms of the various gas toxicities or the neurological effects of the pressure itself. The level of concentration is intense and, in the end, exhausting. I imagine perhaps in the most integral part of a dive, what it feels like to defuse a bomb – the focus and concentration actually works to keep the fear and adrenaline at bay. But if something occurs outside of my control, that flush of adrenaline is the first signal that the spell is broken. It takes positive action to regain control and quell the response before the visceral reaction becomes the single greatest danger in and of itself. It's a fine line. Those times I've lost that are the closest I've come to the end of the line, so to speak.

One incident, unforgettable for all the wrong reasons, happened in 2004, early in my exploration career. I was exploring a remote cave in Vanuatu and had reached the very back of the cave nearly two kilometres from the entrance. At this point the tunnel was getting progressively smaller and smaller. I had a hunch there was just a little bit more explorable cave and had the irrepressible urge to go just a little further, where no one else had been. In doing so, I managed to squeeze through this very tight restriction, and into the last bit of explorable cave. I was pretty chuffed, until I realised I was trapped. When I turned around to try to go back the way I came, the visibility was zero, and suddenly the tunnel was too small. I had my guideline leading me back, but with all my gear, I was too bulky to fit through the narrowing cave.

I tried to post myself through the slot in a few different ways and failed each time. Now I was starting to feel the fear. That sense of panic – literal, rising panic – is a physical sensation, which starts in the stomach and rises to the head to shatter your ability to think and problem-solve. I couldn't think of a single thing, except for the certainty that if I couldn't control my fear I was going to die. At its worst, I reckon I was around ten seconds from total panic, which in a cave-diving scenario means certain death.

Perhaps by luck, I happened to recall a friend's anecdote, from a time he'd been in an even worse situation. He'd been exploring a similar type of cave in the Western Australian Kimberley, and had swum down a steep, sandy slope on the way into the cave. As he passed and unbeknownst to him, he had disturbed the cache of sand that had been pushed up into a crack in the rock by seasonal flooding. It was poised at the angle of repose and as he passed, it slumped down the hill blocking his exit. So, he went on exploring the cave, using up his precious breathing gas, unaware until he turned back that he'd been trapped by the cascading sand. Back he swam, hanging onto his guide-line against the silted water, until the line he was holding suddenly disappeared into solid silt.

He'd felt the panic, the existential terror start to rise in his body. As it got to his lungs, he felt he couldn't breathe anymore. He knew that if it consumed him entirely, he would lose consciousness and die. He didn't know what to do, couldn't even think about how to approach the problem, but felt he had to just do something that was within his control.

So, he counted down from ten. Ten, nine, eight – all the way down to zero – and told himself that when he reached zero he would be calm again. When he got to five, he began to feel in control of his body again, and by zero, the physical symptoms of panic had receded. He felt clear-headed enough to begin to analyse the problem.

In the end, he managed to dig a little hole at the top of the sand slide, enough to slip through if he was wearing nothing but his wetsuit. He took off all his equipment, tied it together into a long daisy chain, reversed through the hole and then pulled his equipment through. It was an extraordinary solution to a terrifying episode, and one that luckily came to mind for me that day in Vanuatu.

I copied the counting technique, down from ten. It was very effective and helped quell the rising panic. Then I realised my friend's 'daisy chain' solution could also work in my situation and basically did the same thing. I took some equipment off and pushed it through the hole – then I was able to fit through and carry on.

Since then, I've used that calming technique a couple of times, in situations when it seemed all was lost. Those moments in an adventure where you brush up against your own mortality – they are the moments you find out what you are really made of. For me, it's the ability to stay calm, to carefully assess the risk and mitigate it, that brings me back to my family in one piece – so that skill is priceless. All of us have a threshold for full-blown panic, of that I am convinced. The secret to survival is being able to hold that panic at bay for as long as possible until every solution has been considered. Adrenaline is not your friend in a cave. Although I have to admit, Ashley does make driving a rocket-powered car sound pretty good.

CHAPTER ELEVEN

LIVE ON THE AIR

'You can never eliminate all risk, or even what elements of risk might confront you in any environment,' says legendary foreign correspondent Hugh Riminton. 'You have to assess it at a certain level and then have a go. Once I've committed to covering a story, once I'm in it, some other element takes me through.'

Hugh is one of Australia's highest profile journalists. For much of my life, he has been a household name – the guy on the telly reporting from war zones and hotspots around the world. His calm, precise voice has provided context and insight into the wider world – from Fiji to Kosovo to Iraq – for generations of Australians.

Journalism is not a profession that we necessarily associate with risk. When we watch the evening news or read the paper, we're in the privileged position of not having to see how 'the sausage is made'. It's always been a high-pressure job, but in our modern age – of 24-hour news cycles, highly polemic discourse, misinformation and social media – it's increasingly risky. There are few journalists doing serious, first-draft-of-history reporting who don't receive regular threats of death or worse.

Of all working journalists, foreign correspondents like Hugh face the most risk. They fly to war zones, natural disasters, sites of massacres in order to bring the story to the world and do so at risk of life and limb. Not to mention long-term psychological ramifications of endless exposure to risk and vicarious trauma.

Hugh has been an observer of the very best and worst that humanity is capable of. As a foreign correspondent, he's subjected himself to grave risks and witnessed countless atrocities. Over the years, he has been shot at, come dangerously close to being blown up by landmines, very nearly burned alive by a mob in apartheid South Africa, just to mention a few examples.

Suffice to say, he knows what he's talking about when it comes to managing danger. But he insists that's not the scary part of the job. 'In times when there have been bullets flying and bombs going off [and] I've felt very, very close to death, that mortality is a very real, proximate thing . . . I've felt quite calm, quite clear-headed.'

Hugh says the times he feels 'dread, real sick dread' are those when he's in a position of complete safety but contemplating whether to commit to a situation he knows will be full of risk. It's that, not the danger he goes through in the course of doing his job, which is the queasiest part of his day.

Once he's made a commitment, past the point of no return, he describes a feeling I believe I know well – not fear exactly, but a kind of sensory purification, a heightened state of arousal.

'When you're in there, you're alive to what's going on. Even when there is real danger around you, and there can be a certain bowel-emptying element to it, somehow it's always felt to be contained,' says Hugh.

For Hugh, the sense of dread is deferred while the danger is acute, and returns when he is back in a place of safety and able to properly process the danger he's been in. He doesn't ascribe the sense of clear-headedness he gets in the field to bravery, but more a sense of professional obligation to be prepared.

'I try to calculate and assess risk and make the risk/reward calculation. For most people who take an element of risk into their working lives, that's a necessary part of your craft. As a mature operator, no matter what you're doing or saying, this is what we're trying to achieve.'

*

As a boy, Hugh lived in Christchurch, New Zealand, 'where we just looked at the Southern Alps at the end of our street'. He grew up idolising Sir Edmund Hillary and the mountaineers who became household names when they first conquered those peaks. His parents had twice been immigrants – to Sri Lanka and then to New Zealand – so he'd always had an understanding of a wider world. As a child, his favourite book was the atlas.

Hugh recalls looking at the atlas when he was around six years old and realising that all the places described in its pages had already been discovered. The dreadful realisation was confirmed by his parents, who had to break the news to him that becoming an explorer wasn't really a valid career path. The news was devastating and left him feeling that his time had come too late.

Time passed, and Hugh grew into what he describes as a 'slightly disorganised kid'.

As a teenager, this tendency only grew. 'I was bright enough, but for some reason, drank rather too heavily,' explains Hugh. 'When I was at high school, my marks were not improved by this experience.'

He wound up working as a cleaner at a teaching hospital, where he washed out the cages that housed laboratory rats. As far as images for a dissolute youth, it's hard to go past that. 'I did my time around those cages as a medical cleaner, and the stink they produced was so rank that I almost smell it even now.'

Hugh was saved from that life through a lucky break. He happened to run into a local radio news director, who was waiting for a job applicant. The news director mistook Hugh for an aspiring journalist and started asking him questions. Miraculously, Hugh's answers impressed him.

'He hired me,' says Hugh. 'It was bizarre. I never thought of being a reporter, and suddenly, I was one at the age of seventeen.'

*

That was forty years ago, and Hugh is still doing the same job. He's won pretty much every award imaginable for an Australian journalist. 'It was the luckiest stroke that could happen to anyone,' he says. 'In fact, it probably saved me from alcoholism. I had a job that required responsibility – and I wasn't bored. I think the thing which made me so glum as a teenager was the prospect of a life that was boring. Suddenly, I had things to do, to be curious about – to travel, to learn about important stories. It's been the greatest teacher.'

In November 1979, when he was just eighteen years old, Hugh was sent to cover the worst aviation disaster in New Zealand's history – a DC-10 aircraft, carrying 237 passengers and 20 crew, had made a critical error and crashed into Mount Erebus on Ross Island, Antarctica. He spent the night in the search and rescue building in Auckland working alongside emergency staff, filing for news organisations around the world as it became clear there would be no survivors. Tragically, all 257 people on board died.

In the morning he went out on the streets and was struck by the emptiness, the silence of a whole town, a whole nation collectively grieving.

'I had a sense then that history is not locked away,' says Hugh. 'I suddenly realised that things are always moving, how nothing is fixed. And life has proven that to me again and again.'

*

In 1987, Hugh was in Fiji and witnessed the first of what would prove to be two coups d'état in the same year. He arrived in Fiji and was there the evening that the Parliament of Fiji was seized by soldiers. All of a sudden, he was surrounded by men in military uniforms and balaclavas, wielding M-16 assault rifles. While reporting those events, he was chased by mobs through the streets and arrested. He learned endurance – what it's like to report on a rapidly evolving situation day after day, fighting twenty-four hours a day to stay on top of the news.

The sheer magnitude of reporting at that level left an impression. It was exhausting but exhilarating. In the aftermath, Hugh signed up for an Outward Bound course, to build up his physical resilience, in the hope that he might get sent to cover similar events. In doing so, he discovered a love for rock climbing. It became something of an obsession – a means of physical training, as well as mental conditioning. 'I realised that I was actually training myself in a way to manage fear,' explains Hugh. 'To manage myself in a stressful situation, to understand what strengths I had.'

He stresses the benefits of training, preparation, and having the skills to survive a catastrophe or help someone else to do so. In a fairly humbling moment, he brings up the Thai cave rescue, and the intricate teamwork that went into its improbable success.

'It's all the training. It's everything that the team was capable of in those days to be the people who could save those kids,' Hugh says. 'Because maybe the rescue would never have happened. Maybe you would never have been called to do it. But that doesn't devalue all the work that you did. The point is to examine yourself, put yourself through these tests of endurance and discomfort and fear, to be the person who was capable of being there when the hour came. And so, for everybody who is asking a lot of themselves and wondering where it all leads – it has value in its own terms.'

Hugh describes managing the demands of being a foreign correspondent as something of a puzzle, one in which you must constantly refine your understanding of the pieces that you can put together in order to get the best out of yourself.

Physical fitness, the capacity to work ceaselessly, and respond to physical risks as they arise are part of it. Just as important is the mental capacity to manage your moods, your exhaustion and stress – and maintain the mental acuity to report on deeply complex events and issues.

Hugh tells me that reporting from a disaster or conflict zone requires intellectual engagement with the underlying issues that have fed into the calamity. What are the forces that brought about the event? The social and economic factors that primed the country for government change? The cultural and historical groundwork behind that? What effects do they have on the people Hugh is talking to in order to piece the story together? He's found this to be the essential responsibility in reporting from hotspots ranging from Somalia to Russia to Northern Ireland. 'You have to learn the context in which people are living through these calamities, and then give all of yourself to the business of telling the story.'

*

Over the years, Hugh has amassed in-depth knowledge of what is necessary for survival in hostile environments. Part of that has been through specialist courses provided by employers. Much of it, however, is from hard-won experience. He's spent a great deal of time in the field with soldiers, and they've passed on bits and pieces. In new locations and cultures, he's learned to rely on local journalists or 'fixers' to help him understand what's going on. And, naturally enough, he's learned from making mistakes. Many of them inconsequential, some of them grievous, happily none of them fatal.

Take the time Hugh was reporting from Somalia. He was in Baidoa, a town known as the 'city of death' for having the highest death toll in a country racked by civil war and famine. On its outskirts, Hugh made a strange discovery – a field of sorghum grain, in a city where the skeletal bodies of the dead who had succumbed to starvation were all around.

Thinking that it would be a good place to record a report, Hugh climbed over a stone wall and got the cameraman to set up a shot. 'Then I saw some Somalis going by, and they were kind of smiling and laughing, and pointing at me. So, I smiled and waved back.' That's when Hugh's cameraman said, 'I think they're trying to tell you something.'

At that moment, Hugh realised why there was an unharvested mature grain crop standing untouched in the middle of a deadly famine. It was a minefield. And he was standing right in the middle of it.

'I just walked into it, and then I had to try and walk back out again,' recalls Hugh. 'I know in the movies, you just put your steps where your steps came from, but it wasn't like that.'

The ground was baked African earth – rock hard, no marks showing where his feet had previously fallen. The best he could do was take a deep breath and stroll on out. He recalls, 'The army who were with us were overwhelmed that I could be so stupid,' but he lived. He walked away with all his limbs still attached, and a title for the memoir he would one day write – *Minefields*. The book is an absolutely cracking read, packed with extraordinary tales of witnessing four decades of the very best and very worst that humanity is capable of. And bringing the reality of it – albeit somewhat sanitised for the evening news – to the world.

That, in its purest form, is what Hugh has tried to do with his life. He was drawn to a vocation which meant regular exposure to risk and trauma. It's not lost on him that this was a choice. More often than not, the people he was reporting on had no say in the matter. The civilian in a war zone who has to deal with crossfire and minefields is not carefully mapping out and completing a risk matrix. The responsibility to those he reports on, whose lives are shaped by risk gone wrong, and the traumatic consequence of that, is clear to him.

'A lot has been written and said about the notion of objectivity,' he says. 'Pure objectivity has a value. It's an important value in reporting what's going on. But I think there is also a value in saying, here's where I am with these people. And this is what it is like for them now.'

He's not necessarily making a moral, legal, or geopolitical argument for their case, but sees the value in putting a human face on a deeply complex disaster situation. 'You're saying, here's how these people are living now. And here's what's happening to them,' he says, although he also concedes, 'I think human sympathy is always with the people who are being hammered at any moment.'

Still, it's one thing to strive for pure objectivity as the noble ideal of journalism, another to stand by as horrors unfold. Take the tragic story of Kevin Carter, the South African photojournalist. As a member of the 'Bang Bang Club' – a group of four conflict photographers who documented the final years of Apartheid – he was no stranger to violence. His photographs brought the execution practice of 'neck-lacing' – forcing a rubber tyre drenched with petrol around a victim's chest and arms and setting it on fire – to global attention.

In 1993, while covering the conflict in South Sudan, Kevin took a photograph that encapsulated everything about the horror of that particular phase of the civil war. It depicts a child, perhaps two years old, buckled over with hunger in the foetal position. Not far away behind the child, a vulture waits patiently. The picture won him the Pulitzer Prize – and endless recrimination. He was hounded by a public who did not understand how he could stand by and take that photo without helping the child. Four months after winning the Pulitzer, Kevin took his own life.

'I always feel some sympathy for him in that,' says Hugh, his voice cracking almost imperceptibly. He thinks the people who questioned Kevin's integrity didn't understand the reality of the situation. 'I've been in environments again and again where I've seen children dying in the dust. But there's not one child who you might be able to save, there are hundreds. Thousands. You don't have the means to save them. There is nothing you can do. There's just nothing you can do.'

The best that journalists like Hugh can do is tell the stories, and hope that they contribute to a kind of pressure on warmongers to stop the actions that are killing civilians – and on the global community to intervene and provide aid and rescue initiatives.

'So, it's not as if nothing good came of what we were doing,' says Hugh. 'But the people who died – could I pick one up, get them on a plane? Those weren't the rules of the game. It's tragic, and it's tough.'

Of course, tragedy is not something that happens in some far-flung country we are only familiar with from the nightly news. Now and again, it finds us where we live. As Hugh reminds me during our conversation – history is always happening to us, right here, right now.

Hugh covered the 1996 trial of Martin Bryant, the Port Arthur killer, in the wake of the massacre that changed Australia forever. He recalls sitting in the courtroom while the man responsible for the worst massacre in modern Australia eyeballed him and being struck by Bryant's malevolence. 'It can only be said that he had an incredibly low level of intelligence and had no great mastery over his own processes.'

In 2019, he flew to his hometown of Christchurch in the immediate aftermath of the white supremacist terrorist attack on the Al Noor Mosque. The terrorist murdered fifty-one people and injured another forty, many of them children. The shooting took place a kilometre and a half from where Hugh went to school. As he was talking to survivors – still in a state of shock and reeling from the horrendous crime that had just occurred – he could look up to the windows of the building where he had worked as a cleaner forty years earlier.

'And there I was, reporting in the town I'd grown up in, on something that I could not remotely have conceived of as happening in a town like Christchurch,' says Hugh. 'These things, they mark you, they become part of your own timber, really.'

*

The sort of risk-taking that I approve of – the slow, incremental expansion of your comfort zone in order to make positive changes to yourself, and through that, the world – is one thing. To expose yourself to so much risk and associated trauma is another. I can't think of any other occupation that involves the accumulation of a lifetime of confronting experience, of intimacy with trauma and tragedy on a global scale. I wondered if he has some way to process what he has experienced, to bear the weight of what he's been witness to and still sleep at night – so I took the opportunity to ask him.

He says it's important to recognise that humanity is not defined by its worst actions. We are capable of great good, as well as the terrible things that Hugh has seen. To dwell only on the darkness, or conclude that we are irredeemable, is a rabbit hole we shouldn't go down. 'And it's not true,' says Hugh. 'Although we have to recognise that we're capable, collectively, of doing horrible things, wasteful things, and we don't seem to learn particularly well.'

For Hugh, the antidote for witnessing such confronting things is to find and nurture whatever it is that brings you peace. 'Where you can, find your own means – whatever it is – to let the accumulation of these horrible things flow out of you. Whether through tears, or surfing, or hikes in the mountains or through cuddles with your spouse. Somehow, you find ways to make your peace with the strangeness of the world.'

I reckon I could do worse than follow Hugh's example. He's seen more blood, despair, and death than I could imagine from my relatively quiet life as a medical doctor, and he remains one of the gentlest, most thoughtful blokes I've ever had the pleasure of talking to. He must be doing something right.

*

Finding a way to deal with the aftermath, the accumulation of difficult experiences, is something that comes up often in conversations with adventurous people. The need to find, as Hugh articulates, a way to make peace with the strangeness of the world.

Strangely enough, my method of dealing with cave-diving-related trauma seems to be cave diving. Amongst my cave-diving mates, a few have adopted methods of visualisation to deal with anxiety and fear. John Volanthen has a technique where in the days leading up to a dive, he will try to visualise every possible thing that could go wrong. Each possible disaster, every outlier that could kill him in a cave – he imagines it in great detail, works out a solution, and when it's done, he imagines putting the fear in a box, locking it, and putting it away on a shelf inside his mind. There it will stay, until he needs it. No longer a fear, anxiety, or trauma, but a method of risk mitigation.

This type of visualisation is something Matt Hall, the top-gun pilot, uses in his own work. As a fighter pilot, and then as an air racer, he reports that he has, unfortunately, lost many friends over the years in aviation. 'I'm pretty tragic,' he admits. 'I'm supposed to be this steely-eyed fighter pilot and I tear up at the drop of a hat. Unfortunately, I've become quite used to mourning good friends.'

In those times, he turns to a piece of advice a friend and mentor once gave him. His method of dealing with losing a friend to aviation was to imagine his grief as an old hotel, with pigeonholes for messages behind the desk. Matt would visualise the incident as a message on the desk, and he would consider it, then roll it up and file it at the back of the counter. 'Then I just leave it there,' Matt says. 'Because if you keep looking at it every single day, you'll start second-guessing yourself. You'll make mistakes, and you will stop enjoying what it is that you once did together.'

In the theatre of combat there was no time for grieving, but he's learned how important it is to process those feelings. 'You have to grieve, even for a couple of days, and you have to look at the lessons that incident holds, then you have to file it away.'

The healthiest thing to do after losing a friend was to learn from their mistakes. That way, the death would not seem like a waste.

This method of processing grief and trauma obtained through exposure to it is tried and true, at least amongst the risk-takers I know. But what about those who never signed up for combat, or adventure, who found themselves in harm's way through little fault of their own? And what if the loss you were mourning was not that of a mate, or a loved one – but yourself?

CHAPTER TWELVE

CHANGE IN THE WIND

Not everyone who finds themselves in danger signs up for it. The number of people who encounter tragedy by accident, by misadventure, or through no fault of their own, far exceeds those who seek out a dangerous activity with full knowledge of, and preparation for, the risks involved. Right now, statistically, someone in the world is walking out in traffic without checking for oncoming cars, swimming into a rip in an otherwise gentle ocean or falling from a roof while doing some DIY home repairs.

If there's one fundamental truth I've learned through my twin lives as an adventurer and a doctor, it's that there's no such thing as a life without risk. Even if you try to live a life insulated from all perceivable dangers, tragedy might still strike. Further, I wouldn't recommend it. It's not much of a life. And luck, like trauma, doesn't discriminate. No matter how far you go out of your way to avoid risk, some measure of it will find you. In life, outcomes are always uncertain, and the flipside of being alive is the constant possibility of disaster. Given that, what can we learn from those who having taken a risk, have been through a disastrous and life-changing outcome?

Those who have suffered? Who have turned out on the wrong side of the risk/reward equation?

Once, at a medical conference, I had the good luck to be seated at dinner next to a bloke named Dr James Scott. He told me one of the most extraordinary survival stories of the modern era – a man who, depending on how you look at it, is the luckiest or the unluckiest man in the world.

*

On 22 December 1991, James went on a hike and seemingly vanished into thin air. He was twenty-two years old, and an aspiring surgeon in his final year of medical school, when he travelled to Nepal for a four-week practical elective at the Bir Hospital in Kathmandu.

Inspired by the landscape, he and his companion – Mark, a fellow traveller he'd met just a day or two earlier – set off on a multi-day trek through the Himalayan foothills, the gateway to the majestic Himalayan mountains. 'Being twenty-two at the time, the frontal lobes of my brain were about as developed as every other twenty-two-year-old male,' James says. 'I thought this is too good an opportunity to pass up.'

The plan was to rest at the tea houses dotted along the trek, which supplied food, water, and accommodation. As such, James had packed light. A warmish jacket, a sleeping bag, some books, a couple of bars of chocolate. On the first night, James and his new mate spent the night in a teahouse at 3600 metres elevation and woke up to a cold morning. The slightest sprinkling of snow covered the countryside.

That day, they intended to trek over a passage that peaked at 4200 metres, cross that, and descend the other side. A few clouds floated above as the men began walking. A couple of hours into the trek, the clouds closed in, and the snow started coming down quite heavily. James, who'd never experienced snow before, found himself in a complete white out unable to discern between the ground and the air in front of him.

James called a stop to discuss how to proceed. His companion, Mark, decided to continue the trek over the pass. James decided to turn back and try to find the teahouse he had stayed in the night before. This seemed like the safest option at the time, and should have been, were it not for the deteriorating weather chasing him down the mountain pass. At one point, he recognised a landmark that was within 200 metres of the teahouse, but, blinded by snow and howling wind, he was unable to find it as he stumbled further into the white out. He was lost. That's when his real ordeal began.

Unable to orient himself, he stumbled through the storm until he came across a treeline that offered a little shelter from the howling wind. There, he hunkered down. James, who'd never anticipated being in a dire wilderness survival scenario, was shocked by the suffering he went through that first night. Nothing in his experience prepared him for the extreme cold; the wind that ripped through his clothes, the chill that crept into his sleeping bag, and then his bones. A cold so profound it stopped registering as a sensation of temperature, but as pure pain. 'I was sure it would be impossible to be as cold as I was and still survive the night,' he recalls.

But dawn broke. James had made it through the night, but the next day would be even worse. An icesheet cracked underfoot, tumbling him into a creek. The fall soaked his gear and may as well have been a death sentence. Soon afterwards, he came across impassable terrain – the path blocked by treacherous cliffs and deep snow. He had to hunker down exposed to the elements. That night he wrote letters to his fiancée and family to say farewell. If he died alone out there, he wanted to leave some explanation of what had happened.

On the third day, after hours of trudging through waist-deep snow, he came across a house-sized rock which provided some shelter from the elements. Beneath it, he found remnants of an old campfire and broken tools – evidence that this area sometimes saw human beings. James decided to wait here, not necessarily in hope of rescue, but to provide closure for his family. 'At this stage I really didn't think I was going to get out alive,' he says. More than anything, he thought that if he died there, his body would have a chance of being found.

He survived that night, and the next, and another. The full moon came and went. He wrote letters until the pen he'd brought with him stopped working. He read the books in his bag, Charles Dickens' *Great Expectations* and Thomas Harris's *The Silence of the Lambs*. When the novels ran out he read his Nepali guidebooks, with some regret that he would now not see the mountain views and glacial lakes it described. In all, he lived for forty-three days lost in the wilderness without proper survival gear. More extraordinarily, he did it without food – except for a couple of bars of chocolate, which he ate in the first days.

They say we can live for three minutes without oxygen, three days without water, and three weeks without food. Like most neat idioms, it's not exactly accurate. In fact, history is full of examples of people who have lived for extraordinary periods of time without food and only water. Shipwrecked sailors, political prisoners on hunger strike, victims of war, famine, or slavery – it is possible for humans to live through the very extremes of starvation.

But that doesn't go all the way to explaining how James Scott survived. I have, after talking to so many exceptional people, learned to stop using the word 'impossible' lightly. Let's just say his survival was highly improbable, from a medical point of view. Like in the case of Chris Lemons, maybe 'inexplicable' is a better word.

It was James' medical training that gave him some of the tools to survive. To keep his core body temperature up, he tried to avoid eating snow without first melting it, as eating ice would burn precious calories. Similarly, he wrapped his head in whatever dry fabric he had, knowing a lot of heat is lost through the head. Above all, he was an extraordinarily fit and robust fellow before he set off on the hike.

He was a black belt in karate, at the height of physical condition, and, when push came to shove, his body was able to cannibalise itself as a way to survive: 'I had a lot of muscle, particularly on my chest, legs and buttocks. These big muscles are a lot (for the body) to feed off when you're starving,' he says.

His karate training also gave him the mental discipline he needed to stay alive. To conserve energy and stave off despair, he spent hours mentally performing kata, the sequence of intricate techniques that karate practitioners use as a form of moving meditation. 'Karate is a craft, and a way of life,' he explains. 'If you're in a good club, with a good instructor, you're pushed to really challenge yourself every training session, and you get stronger mentally and physically. You cultivate the attitude to face challenges and keep working through them. To not give up.'

James found himself finding solace in unexpected places. 'I can remember days when the sun was so glorious, I could make snow-balls which would melt into clear, sweet water, rather than (melting) ice to eat,' he recalls. 'It was just fantastic. It's amazing when you get everything taken away from you how much you appreciate very small things.'

He compared his lot to that of others he'd known who'd faced bad situations and decided his wasn't that dire. He'd done a stint on a burns ward and seen the horrific injuries some people live with. James reasoned that he wasn't physically injured, and while his situation wasn't good, he had a lot to be thankful for. He thought, too, of the diggers, Australian prisoners from the Second World War who endured torture and forced labour, and still found humour in it. 'I thought, if they can enjoy that, I can enjoy this. Others have had it much worse, so just keep going.'

Your author is a man of science, but the closest I can come to a credible thesis on James's survival is that, for lack of a better explanation, he had decided to live, and he did.

Listening to James tell his story, I found myself thinking of books I'd read about survivors of shipwrecks – observers writing that if you put a dozen people in a life raft you could know within twenty-four hours which of them were going to die, and who had a chance at living. There are those who lose their nerve and curl up in a corner and wait for death, and there are those who start making a plan – take an inventory of resources, make rules and schedule rations. Essentially, they make a plan to survive. These stories recur time and again and suggest that there's some interesting inherent psychology to the way people respond to crises. A sort of self-determination for survival.

But no amount of self-determination can last forever. Christmas passed, New Year's Eve came and went. As his sixth week in the frozen foothills approached, James was in a terrible way. His body was skeletal – his reserves of fat and muscle consumed. As dangerous vitamin deficiencies kicked in, he'd gone from craving fatty, calorie-laden food as his muscles wasted, to craving specific fruit and vegetables. He'd wake from dreams of crisp, fresh greens with his mouth watering. Malnutrition was causing severe discomfort and pain in his body, beyond what he had grown used to from the cold. By his final days, he was suicidal, but was stopped by the drive to live, and be reunited with his loved ones.

'The whole time I was thinking about family and friends, and the importance of getting back to them. There were so many reasons to live, and that's what kept me going.'

*

He never stopped thinking of family, and they never stopped thinking of him. Fuelled by hope but working with bad intelligence about the area he'd been lost in, his family had searched the foothills time and again hoping to find him, with no success. As the weeks passed, hope began to fade.

On 2 February 1992, the Scott family hired a helicopter to do one final sweep across the mountains. They knew that logically James must have perished long ago, but they were desperate for at least the closure of recovering his body.

James, lying under his rock, heard the helicopter circling overhead. It was the third that had appeared in the area since he'd first become lost, but this one was behaving differently – turning slow circles overhead.

'I crawled out to wave at them, I couldn't walk by then,' says James, who signalled as best he could using his red thermal underwear. The helicopter circled, again, and again, and finally stopped, hovering overhead, 'They sort of waved to let me know they'd spotted me, then shot off down the valley.'

The light faded not long after that, and during the night, James heard a voice calling out in the dark: 'Namaste! Namaste!'

James called out in response, 'Namaste!' And not long afterward, two Nepalese villagers, who'd broken off from a larger search party to follow a hunch, found him. One stayed with him, and the other went to mobilise the mammoth search party that had scoured thousands of square kilometres searching for James.

The next day, a helicopter came in, James was strapped into a harness, and airlifted off the mountain. As he got lifted higher and higher, he watched the rock, which had been both his shelter and a prison, become smaller and smaller. The impassable rock wall he'd spent weeks on end staring at fell away beneath him, and beyond it. 'The most magnificent view, sunrise over the Himalayas, just the most magical scenery I'd ever seen.'

The helicopter took him to a nearby village, where hundreds of people from neighbouring villages greeted him, clamouring to meet this young man who'd survived an impossible physical trial. James, who the day before had thought he'd never see another human being in his life, found it overwhelming. Seeing his distress, one of his rescuers took him aside and told him, 'Just relax. They just want to touch you and get some of your good luck.'

They weren't the only ones. The media frenzy that erupted around the world when James was finally rescued was one of the most intense in the latter 20th century. The media swarmed Nepal and overran the tiny hospital in Lalitpur where James was being treated. In Australia, a live broadcast of the cricket was interrupted with the news. In England, where I was working at the time, it was all anyone was talking about. I remember hearing this fantastical story of a guy who'd been lost in the mountains for forty-two days with only one Mars Bar and being one of the sceptics.

'Bullshit,' I remember callously saying. 'That's impossible. The guy just wants to write a book and make a buck. Nobody could survive that. He's probably been tucked up in a hotel.'

It defied any understanding of human physiology. I didn't see how anyone with a basic understanding of medicine could believe his story.

Looking back with the benefit of hindsight, I regret my suspicion. More than regret, I feel ashamed of it. I can't imagine what those days were like for James, although I can vouch that a media storm is a confusing and confronting thing to be at the centre of – even when you haven't just been through an unbelievable ordeal.

*

The Scott family found the intense media scrutiny overwhelming. They engaged celebrity agent Mark Miller who flew to Nepal to secure James as a client. The agent moved quickly, and signed a deal with the Nine Network's *60 Minutes* for an exclusive, paid television interview. Deals were also made with the London *Daily Telegraph* and a Fairfax paper in Australia, but it was the *60 Minutes* TV interview that turned out to be a disaster.

James was released from hospital for the day especially to film what should have been a 40-minute interview. Three hours later it was still going. When James asked to stop, the interviewer came in strongly with a series of antagonising, invasive questions. James lost his temper and with it, control of the story.

The narrative – driven by wild media speculation – began to shift. It went from a sympathetic portrayal of a miraculous survival to outright scepticism. Soon, the consensus was that James 'The Ice Man' Scott was a charlatan, who'd faked his ordeal to sell the story to the media.

All this was unfolding while James was profoundly unwell. Malnutrition and vitamin deficiencies had led to peripheral neuropathy – damage to the nerves located outside the brain. His fine motor control would never recover, nor his eyesight. The part of his brain that controls the movement of his eyes had been damaged by vitamin B1 deficiency, and his eyes would oscillate up and down constantly in their sockets. Every waking moment was spent watching the world bounce up and down. For a while, he couldn't even recognise faces. It would be months until he could read again.

In the long-term, it would be impossible for him to become a surgeon. His emotional health was no better – swinging wildly between euphoria to deep despair. There were times he begged his sister to take him back and put him on the mountain to die.

'I struggled for a number of reasons in addition to the overwhelmingly traumatic situation,' says James. 'Particularly the guilt of putting my family through enormous distress. There's no easy way of saying that I was completely stupid, and the consequences were enormous. It took me a long time to come to terms with this.'

These feelings were exacerbated by the intense scrutiny and public scepticism of his story. The aggressive questioning by journalists, in an information vacuum caused by James not being well enough to talk, led to wild speculation. It was another layer of trauma on top of his physical injuries, to know that the world thought that he was a fake.

'That was exactly what I didn't need at that stage,' says James. 'When anyone's been through a traumatic experience, validation is just so important.' Explaining the importance of acknowledging the experience of a survivor, James points to the survivors of institutional sexual abuse. 'These people have been through so much trauma, then have had their claims denied, their integrity attacked, told they were lying, or that they were responsible for their abuse. It's the worst thing you can do to someone. To do that to a young person, it's terribly unkind.'

After his experiences, after trials both by ice and media storm, James is uniquely qualified to talk about trauma and resilience. As life went on, he put that experience to good use.

These days, James is Associate Professor Scott, a renowned psychiatrist specialising in child and adolescent mental health. After recovering from his ordeal, he went back and did his resident years as a junior doctor – although the damage to his vision and fine motor skills disqualified him from his ambition of becoming a surgeon. Considering other possibilities, he enjoyed paediatrics, and saw the appeal of psychiatry.

'I went and spoke to the senior colleagues in both disciplines. Psychiatrists were this cheerful happy group all talking about how interesting their jobs are. Paediatricians are all tired and cranky from waking up every night to deliver babies,' says James, with a laugh.

So, he went into child psychiatry, which, as an anaesthetist, I find curious. In medical parlance, surgeons and psychiatrists are pretty much opposite character types. Psychiatrists are generally empathetic, curious, kind souls, and surgeons are, well, their own thing!

James hasn't regretted his choice for a day. He is fascinated by people, and now spends his days talking to children and teens with remarkable stories and challenges. People growing up in homes where every day is a struggle for survival – who still manage to get through and find success and happiness in life. 'They are inspiring,' he says. 'Every day, I see the resilience of humans is a real testament to the human character.'

What I want to know is, what about James himself? What is it that made him so resilient? Not only in his physical survival, but his mental resilience in the aftermath? When I put the question to him, he has no easy answer.

'Time heals,' says James. He says his recovery was similar to anyone recovering from a blow, working through it gradually, getting back to the purpose of life, doing good, being with loved ones, enjoying it all. 'The experience cost me a lot in terms of my physical health, but it did provide me with enormous opportunities for post-traumatic growth.'

Post-traumatic growth (PTG) is a psychological phenomenon defined by researchers in the field as, 'life-changing psychological shifts in thinking and relating to the world and the self, that contribute to a personal process of change, that is deeply meaningful'. Essentially, you go through a horrible life-shattering experience, and come out happier on the other side.

As a risk-taker highly aware that one day I may suffer my own deeply traumatic event, the concept of PTG – the idea that some people actually flourish after an horrific event – interests me greatly.

Risk and resilience go hand in hand. You need courage to overcome a natural aversion to danger, and resilience to keep going if something goes wrong. Resilience is worthy of study in, and of, itself.

I've been privileged to talk to living examples of extraordinary resilience, like James Scott, Chris Lemons and Heath Jamieson (see next chapter). But it was Gill Hicks who first introduced me to the concept – someone who epitomises the idea to an extraordinary degree.

*

Gill Hicks, like me, was born in Adelaide and travelled to the UK for work – but there the similarities end. Gill was living a life devoted to architecture, arts, and culture when she was caught up in the 2005 London terrorist bombings.

She was so badly injured she was not initially expected to live. As it was, she was left permanently disabled, with both legs amputated below the knee. Gill is someone I'd admired from afar, so I felt lucky to meet her when we were both billed to deliver a keynote address at a function in Adelaide. To hear the power of her message of forgiveness and her story of personal growth following such a cruel attack was truly inspiring.

I've never had to face the kind of adversity she has. I don't think any of us could know how we would respond in the aftermath. It's hard to imagine many people turning their misfortune into a positive, the way Gill has. She must have possessed incredible strength of mind long before the bombing.

*

Trauma was actually the catalyst for Gill's first big life-changing adventure. After a 'safe and very wonderfully predictable' childhood in the Adelaide beachside suburb of Glenelg, Gill lost both her parents within a year of each other – her father first, then her mother, succumbed to cancer. For her mother, it was just three months between diagnosis and death.

She distinctly recalls holding her mother's hand in the hospice as she died, the precise moment it slipped out of hers, and watching that life leave. 'This beautiful woman who had given so much to so many people. And that was that.'

As Gill mourned, she was struck that her parents died quite young, in their fifties, and had never had the chance to live the lives they would have loved to. With that, came the sense that there had to be more to life than what was on offer in Adelaide. She realised that in order to find out what she was made of, she needed to leave behind a comfortable life, and take a risk on a more exciting life. For Gill, a trained singer with a love of the arts, that meant the bright lights, culture, and boundless ambition of London.

In short order, Gill – who had never left Adelaide, even to visit other state capitals such as Melbourne or Sydney – found herself on a Qantas flight to Heathrow. Her preparation was so perfunctory she didn't even know how long the journey to London was and was nonplussed to find it lasted a full twenty-four hours.

'There's this wonderful naiveté of youth, isn't there? When you don't know what you don't know?' says Gill. 'That wonderful bravado of a nineteen-year-old person, off to meet the world, and the world is going to receive me – "How wonderful that you're here!"'

As she tells it, she wasn't worried about the myriad things that could go wrong for a young traveller so much as what clothes she should pack. She landed in Heathrow airport in a carefully selected travel outfit – blue suede high-heeled boots, perfectly blow-dried hair, sunglasses perched on her head. She landed ready for London glamour, even if she didn't really have a sense of what that would look like.

'I had this mental picture of London being exactly like Rundle Mall in Adelaide. I didn't have a sense of size or scale, or grandeur or history,' she says with a wry smile. It's safe to say her research had been minimal. When she asked for directions into town and a local told her to 'Take the tube, love,' her mind began racing with the adventure ahead of her – London was the future, and it was going to reveal incredible new experiences.

'I didn't know what a tube was. What is a tube? That sounds like it might be a giant wind tunnel, doesn't it? That I might be literally sucked into the centre of London where all the incredible shops are. I was quite disappointed to find out the tube is just an underground train.'

There were other small disappointments and culture shocks. Adelaide is a mild city in pretty much every way you can imagine. We're chatty people, by and large, prone to striking up conversations on public transport – a faux pas in a city like London where people will inch away uneasily if you talk to them on the tube.

More than the frosty reception, she was unprepared for the London cold, the wind that cuts through to the bone. She remembers feeling so cold on Holloway Road that she thought she would freeze to death on the spot – just topple over like a frozen chook. She panicked when she realised she didn't have her passport in her bag, sure she would perish on the high street, and no one would be able to identify her frozen body. Nevertheless, she was determined to make a life for herself, even with the freezing cold and stuffy tube stations.

She ended up walking into the office of *Marie Claire* magazine and asked for work. She was knocked back, so she turned up every day for three months and worked for free until they gave her a job. And that was the beginning of her new life.

This was 1991. Over the next decade and a half, Gill rose through the ranks of the culture industries and held positions including Publishing Director of the architecture, design and contemporary culture magazine *Blueprint*, Director of the Dangerous Minds design consultancy and Head Curator at the Design Council.

With her high-flying career came all the vices of a proper Londoner – smoking forty cigarettes a day and drinking copious amounts of gin when a decent meal would have been a more sensible option. She lived the life of frenetic workaholism of ambitious Londoners, so that if she was not at the office, she was in the pub. 'I look at that person now, and even though I had the understanding of mum and dad's early demise, I thought that I was absolutely bulletproof.'

*

On the morning of the bombing, Gill woke late after a late-night celebration the night before. This was unusual for a woman who describes herself as a creature of routine – normally she was at her desk before 8 am. Flustered, she rushed out the door, stopping to grab a scarf on the way, and ran for the train.

Gill squeezed into the tube carriage, where commuters were in raincoats. 'It was British summer, so that meant it had been raining,' she recalls, laughing. They were packed so tight she could feel the breath of the man next to her on her face.

By then, Gill was a local, and her days of talking to strangers on the tube were behind her. She took no special note of the nineteen-year-old man who waited a few feet away with a home-made suicide bomb.

The last thing Gill remembers thinking is silently urging the driver to close the doors and get going, because she had places to be and was already late. Now, later in life, Gill looks back at those increments of time that led her to board the tube in the same carriage at exactly the same time as the terrorist bomber. She counts those moments before and after the bombing in breaths, rather than units of time. There was one breath, impatient for the train to get moving, and the next, Gill and the world around her was plunged into darkness as the bomb detonated.

Gill felt no pain, just an uncanny sensation of flying through the air and being stuck in hot tar. Her first thought was that she must be dead – that the hot, soupy, thick darkness must be what death felt like.

What happens to us after death, if anything at all, remains a mystery. Scientifically minded people tend to look at the experiences and sensations described during near-death experiences as side effects of brain activity as death approaches. Novel sensations – such as being lifted into the air, or of seeing a bright light approaching – might be explained as the hallucinations of a dying brain. What Gill was experiencing, though, was on this side of mortality, and all too real.

Searching for something to anchor her to reality, she reached out a hand in the darkness, and suddenly, felt another hand grip hers. The two hands, belonging to strangers on the Piccadilly Line moments earlier, now clutched each other in a desperate need to connect.

*

It's no surprise that we seek human contact in an emergency situation. Take the common experience of a crowded elevator stopping suddenly between floors. One moment you're intentional strangers, standing stiff and silent – and the next everyone is laughing nervously and making eye contact. The bonds that can form instantly between human beings in that context are remarkable.

I think back to the connection between the rescuers and the boys from the Thai cave rescue. We divers and the boys were complete strangers from vastly different worlds, but there was an immediate connection and bond because we were sharing an intense experience.

For Gill, it was a similar moment of connection. With that contact and the sounds of distress around her, she determined she was, in fact, alive. She began to yell her name into the darkness, and people called back with their own – a roll call as affirmation of life.

To know that she wasn't alone gave Gill a peculiar sense of safety. There was security in waiting for each person to say their name and know that they were still there. 'We kept that going as long as we could,' says Gill.

The rescue effort took some time to reach the site of the attack. Reading back through the transcripts of the emergency services dispatch that day, two things are striking. The first is the utter calm of the British emergency personnel as they began to realise that they were not looking at a transport accident as initially assumed, but that London was under attack on multiple fronts. Second, is that emergency services were ordered not to go straight into the underground tunnels.

The London bombings occurred three months after terrorist bombings in the Madrid transport system. In those attacks, secondary devices had been laid to deliberately target rescuers as they arrived at the scene. In London, a clear command went out that nobody was to go underground until they knew exactly what they were dealing with.

It wasn't until a paramedic named Tracy Russell defied orders and went down the tunnel that others broke ranks and moved to the site en masse. Gill credits Tracy's initiative as the deciding factor in her rescue, buying her precious minutes.

This element of the story – of people in the emergency services who have broken protocol out of a desire to save lives – is familiar to me. The rules are there for a very good reason, and in any rescue attempt, protecting yourself as a rescuer is paramount. The last thing you want is more people injured or needing to be rescued. But the fact remains that sometimes rescuers seem to have an irresistible instinct, a voice which tells them, 'No, I need to go, and I need to go now,' as is the case with the London response. And sometimes, they lead to spectacularly unexpected outcomes.

I recall an orientation lecture I received when I started working with MedSTAR, the aeromedical retrieval arm of the South Australian Ambulance. An image was shown of a fireman carrying a young unconscious girl out of a building, ablaze and collapsing around him.

The question was posed to us, 'Is this fireman a hero?' He certainly appeared to be one. But the subsequent discussion proposed a very different and alternative view of events. What if the fireman was overcome by the smoke or flames? What if other firefighters then had to search for that individual, and also died in the attempt? What if the attempt meant that four other children died in another part of the building, because this individual didn't have the situational overview that the commander held?

In emergencies, it can be critical to follow orders and not put the rescuers at excessive risk. And yet, sometimes experienced operators have a strong sense of when it is time to act, and in this case it was fortunate for Gill.

*

A case I often reflect on is that of Chris Blowes, who was attacked on the West Coast of South Australia by a great white shark, losing his leg during the attack. The incident occurred on a very remote beach, many miles from a regional hospital. By the time the call was received by the ambulance Emergency Operations Centre, Chris was already unconscious.

And by the time the call was transferred to the desk of the doctor in charge of retrieval coordination, he was receiving CPR. In the medical literature, cardiac arrest in the context of traumatic haemorrhage has a survival rate that is best described as 'extraordinarily low'.

When faced with the decision whether to send a medical team to that rural hospital for a patient who was, for all intents and purposes, already dead, many doctors (including myself) would probably have paused and waited until an initial report came in from the hospital to suggest it would be worth sending a very expensive and finite asset. That sounds harsh, but if another call comes in moments later and you have sent your only helicopter and team off on a wild goose chase, someone else may suffer because of your actions. Such decisions are not without some stress.

But on this day, a friend of mine Dr Kylie Stanton was on duty. For reasons even Kylie has difficulty articulating, she didn't hesitate to send the helicopter to the hospital. The time that was saved by her actions was one of many factors that worked in Chris's favour in keeping him alive that day. And whilst Kylie didn't breach any firm rule or protocol, it was certainly a decision that would have been closely scrutinised had the outcome been as expected. Sometimes, you just have to trust your instincts.

In Gill's case, following procedure would almost certainly have killed her. Time was a resource she did not have. As the survivors waited in the dark, some stopped calling their names in the darkness. One by one, they started to succumb to their injuries and perish.

Gill herself was not far away from death. In time, the security lights came on in the tunnel, and the blackness gave way to a grey hue. It was enough light for her to start to ascertain her injuries. She remembers looking at where her legs had been shorn off by the bomb and trying to make sense of what her eyes were telling her. She felt only a strange sense of calm – there was no pain, no signal to confirm how badly injured she was.

'There's no legs,' she remembers telling herself. 'But calm down, calm down. We need some action here.'

The force of the blast had literally blown her clothes off, so she was naked except for the scarf still tangled around her neck. She managed to remove it and moved to tie it as a tourniquet above the wounds. It was when she reached down to grip her thigh and her hand slipped deep into her flesh, that she got some idea of how badly she was hurt.

When Tracy and the lead rescuers did eventually reach her, her remaining life could be counted in breaths, rather than minutes. Gill was in such bad shape that when one London Ambulance officer finally saw her, he ordered her body to be packed in ice, rather than wrapped in a heat-saving silver blanket.

The bomb had exploded seconds out from travelling from Kings Cross – St Pancras, killing twenty-six people and injuring hundreds more. It was the largest of four bombs targeting the transport system and had the largest loss of life. Gill was the very last survivor to be rescued from the tube that day and was not expected to live.

She was taken by ambulance from Russell Square Station to St Thomas Hospital. Not only had her legs been blown off below the knees, but she had suffered collapsed lungs and all manner of other injuries. Her blood loss was so severe that she was losing fluids almost as fast as the paramedics could pump them into her.

For the entire ride of almost thirty minutes, she registered no heart-beat, despite the efforts of a paramedic named Brian who performed CPR on her the entire time. He later reported that despite the lack of technical life signs, Gill was vocal the whole way.

'Apparently, and I know this is going to be no shock to you,' Gill tells me, 'I was talking the whole way. Brian was yelling to the driver from the back of the ambulance, "It's dead but it's talking!"'

Now, few people like being referred to as 'it', but Brian was working with what he had. At this stage, Gill's injuries were so extensive that little about her could be identified. Her ID tag simply read 'one unknown, estimated female'.

The head of the resuscitation team at St Thomas Hospital initially moved to have Gill declared dead on arrival. Policy dictated that the team weren't in the business of bringing back brain-dead people to be on a life support machine for the rest of their lives. That's textbook stuff, and he was of the view that Gill was too far gone.

Fortunately for Gill, Brian insisted that she had been talking during the CPR and was able to convince the resuscitation team to try and bring her back. They agreed to work on her for another three minutes and thirty seconds. Then, right before they were going to call it and announce her dead on arrival, she began to respond. Again, protocol was broken, and again, Gill's outcome was extraordinary.

Gill's survival defied reasonable medical expectation. Her psychological recovery was even more remarkable. From the very first, she deliberately set the course of her rehabilitation. On first regaining consciousness, her water intake was severely rationed – just six drops at a time. She so desperately craved a proper glass of water that she thought of nothing else. Gill focused completely on what it would take for her to sit up and hold a glass of water. Within a week, she could. With that, confidence began to return to her. Early on she was unable to speak, as both her hearing and vocal cords had been damaged in the bombing. Slowly, by mouthing words and writing notes, her voice began to come back, bringing with it a powerful sense of relief.

'I realised very early on that our thoughts are so powerful, that they absolutely determine what we do and what we don't do in life,' says Gill. 'I've got to be very conscious of what I think because I can absolutely shape my life based on how I approach it in my thoughts.'

*

Gill defied the odds – and astonished her medical teams – by not only surviving but thriving during her recovery process. In those early months in hospital, she remembers a sense of absolute euphoria.

'I think for me, it was the sense of understanding that I was alive,' she says. 'That I was still Gill.'

She was relieved, even overjoyed, to wake up in hospital with the understanding that her mind was intact. She realised that no matter what had happened to her body, she remained her own person, and recognised from the beginning that that was a real triumph.

When the forensics team brought her the pulverised contents of her briefcase, she looked at the mess, then asked, 'You didn't happen to find my legs, did you?'

A few days later, she was taken to the morgue to say goodbye to her legs. The morticians brought them out along with some other personal items destroyed in the bombing – her feet presented on a little cushion. For Gill, it was a pivotal moment, a psychological demarcation line. 'This is an end and now I must start thinking in terms of being given a chance to have a second life. What do I want that life to be like?'

*

Gill was so happy in those early months in hospital that four different psych teams assessed her, unable to account for her mood. By the time the third team had assessed her, Gill surmised that they thought she had lost her mind, and started to second-guess her behaviour, wondering what the etiquette was to convince them she was sane. 'What would a proper patient do at this time?' she wondered. 'Should I offer them chocolates?'

The psychiatrists would ask her if she understood what she had been through – that she was in a bomb blast and lost her legs. To which she answered, 'I absolutely understand that. But you need to understand that I survived it, and that I've got my arms, and that I'm still here.'

Each stage of her recovery was greeted with that unstoppable spirit. Learning how to use a wheelchair brought her such joy that before she'd mastered the basics, she was zooming down corridors while physios urged her to slow down and take it easy.

When the time came for her to be fitted with prosthetic legs, the consultant urged her to consider having them made shorter than her missing limbs, to make them more manageable. Gill, in turn, managed to convince her prosthetics doctors that her new legs should make her much taller than she had been. She had been 165 cm before the bombing. She ended up at 172 cm. After all, who wouldn't want to be a little taller given the chance? These behaviours, and many more like them, were not what her medical teams expected from someone living through the aftermath of a horrific event.

222

The psychiatrists were probably expecting a collapse, for Gill to present with the extreme grief, resentment or anger that is common after an intensely traumatic event. If that was the case, they are still waiting. The big breakdown never arrived. Instead, Gill characterises the ongoing legacy of the trauma as a constant battle with many small disappointments.

The first days of being fitted for prosthetic legs were challenging, the literal first steps of a journey towards walking again that she would be on for the rest of her life. It was something she would never master, and the realisation was painful, in more ways than one. Every step hurt terribly, but urged on by her physiotherapists, those steps meant the difference between really living and not.

'My physios worked out how to motivate me,' Gill says. 'They said if I could do a staircase, then they would take me to the pub and get me a gin and tonic.'

True to their word, Gill's first outing on her new legs was to the pub, where her physios bought her a much-needed G&T – on the condition she could walk out of the pub to her waiting wheelchair. Let the record show that Gill passed the test – two stiff drinks later.

Of course, her recovery wasn't all beer and skittles. One of the biggest heartaches for her was on returning to Australia where she visited the beach and realised she'd never again be able to feel the hot sand under her feet. The carefree vision of a day at the beach many Australians share – walking at the water's edge and leaving footprints which fill with brine, shoes in one hand, maybe throwing a ball for a dog with the other – was gone.

'I think that was the moment for me to realise the permanency of my disability. What I'd really lost was a sense of connection,' says Gill. 'I've spent a lot of time working out how to live with that. For me it was starting to look at it through a different lens – what does a foot-print actually mean?'

If Gill couldn't actually leave a footprint in the sand ever again, then life became a quest to leave footprints in other ways.

*

In the years since that fateful day in London, Gill has led a far richer life than most of us could dream of. She's swum with sharks, abseiled down buildings, taken up painting and exhibited professionally. Undaunted by the fact she's deaf in one ear and missing a lung, she has revived a teenage passion for singing and has performed on stage. Most importantly to her, she has become a mother.

There have been awards and accolades including a Member of the Most Excellent Order of the British Empire (MBE) for services to charity in the Queen's New Year's Honours list in 2009, being named South Australian of the Year for 2015, and being made a Member of the Order of Australia (AM) in 2016 'for significant service to the promotion of peace in the community through public engagement, education and network building initiatives'.

Her most globally celebrated achievement stems from her decision to devote her life to advocacy for humanity and building sustainable peace. She is a sought-after public speaker, sits on advisory boards and consults globally on peace-building initiatives. She has also established an organisation called Making a Difference for Peace (M.A.D. for Peace) where she works alongside former extremists to understand and combat indoctrinated hatred.

She could have given up on life, let bitterness overcome her or be consumed with hatred for the man who attacked her. Instead, she devoted her life to deterring anyone from following a path of violent extremism and the destructive ideologies that seek to divide people within our global societies.

As clichéd as it sounds, her genuine passion for world peace has led her to live a massively productive life, devoting her time to really make a difference. They say the best revenge is to live a happy life, and by that metric, Gill is basically vengeance itself. It's impossible to speak to her and not be inspired – or to wonder where that strength of character comes from.

Suffice to say Gill is a fascinating person – determined to live the fullest possible life in a situation where the best of us would have every reason to curl up in a ball and say, 'Woe is me'. Thankfully, I've never had to face that kind of adversity. I don't think any of us could know how we would respond in the aftermath. I'm fairly certain I wouldn't handle it with the grace that Gill did. For whatever reason, she has found the tools: the strength, courage and imagination to not just come back from death's door, but come back stronger. Certainly, she's made a massive, conscious contribution to society.

Out of everyone I spoke to in my mission to explore the world of risk, she is perhaps the most inspiring. Her injuries were brutal, and brutally unfair. When she was caught in a terrorist's bomb blast, she was doing nothing more dangerous than riding the subway – a task millions upon millions of people do every day without incident.

Her misfortune is impossible to fathom (matched only by her dauntlessness) and a stark reminder that living a life without risk is impossible. On any given day, the safest, most cautious person might suffer tragedy out of the blue – look the wrong way while crossing the road, suffer some fatal outcome from an undetected health condition, board the wrong carriage on an ordinary commute to work. None of us know how much time we have, and none of us can live a life entirely without risk. Nor, and I suspect Gill would agree, should we. Given a choice between a life where a young person gets on a plane to embrace the big, wide world, and a life half-lived, I think that we could all learn from Gill's example.

'I don't fear being dead,' says Gill. 'But it's motivated me a lot. For me, the key to living is knowing that we will end.'

In her view, the knowledge that even if we don't know how or when, our lives will end one day, and this is a philosophy to live by. 'That knowledge should make every day something to really savour. It should motivate us to think about what we are doing with the life that we have.'

*

Leading PTG researchers Lawrence Calhoun and Richard Tedeschi have proposed a model to understand the process of post-traumatic growth in which individual characteristics and cognitive processing are threatened or nullified by traumatic events. Or as they put it, 'The question of what determines the tendency of one person to take a perspective that emphasises the loss whereas another perceives gain.'*

It's a fascinating idea, with a huge question at the heart of it. Why do some people go through hardship and emerge stronger and happier, while others fall to pieces? Why is Gill, after all she's been through, such an optimistic, clear-eyed person?

The idea of post-traumatic growth versus post-traumatic stress disorder (PTSD) is a difficult one, and hard to quantify. I am uncomfortable even using the term PTSD, as it is a vexing, somewhat nebulous disorder to understand. Prince Harry, Duke of Sussex, a former soldier and patron of several non-profit organisations dedicated to people wounded in war or by weapons of war – prefers the term 'Post traumatic injury'. Once, he scolded my wife, 'That's post traumatic injury. It's not a disorder, it's an injury. Okay?' It's a good anecdote but its primary value in the context of this book is to boast that Fiona and I once met Harry and Meghan at a tea party during their 2018 Australian visit!

---

* Source: https://ptgi.charlotte.edu/wp-content/uploads/sites/9/2013/01/PTG-New-Considertrns-2004.pdf

Scientific studies on PTSD suggest that PTSD rates – like trauma rates – differ considerably across different demographic groups.** As such, I'm hesitant to make definitive statements on the concept – although what the research suggests is fascinating to me. A combined study by Calhoun, Tedeschi and colleagues found that the chance of developing severe, chronic PTSD in the wake of a traumatic event is very low indeed.

Which seems to run contrary to the popular understanding of PTSD. Perhaps my work in medicine and the emergency services gave me a skewed world view by bringing me into contact with more than the average number of grisly situations – but I suspect people think PTSD is a more common occurrence than evidence suggests.

It appears that PTG is a statistically more likely response. The data suggests an average person faced with a cataclysmic, life-changing traumatic event – the sort of tragedy that makes you rethink everything you once believed – will come out of the event in a better place than they went in. In a nutshell, if you are the survivor of one horrific but isolated event, once the initial trauma subsides, you're more likely to experience post-traumatic growth than develop PTSD.

We are, the data suggests, much more resilient than we might think. A horrific experience isn't necessarily the catalyst for that sort of mental hardship. In fact, it seems like it can be good for us.

Why is this so? There is evidence that active contemplation of our mortality after a traumatic event correlates with growth. Survivors of singular events who have largely lived a life free of violence, fear or sorrow will be more likely to try to make sense of the experience of trauma. Simply, they're more likely to regard a sudden disaster as an anomaly, and actively search for meaning in it. Often, this means seeking emotional support – from other humans. Those with strong

---

** SOURCE: https://www.ncbi.nlm.nih.gov/books/NBK207192/

existing social support networks are those who have a better chance of bouncing back from trauma – stronger than ever.

James Scott was, in many ways, an ideal candidate for PTG. During his time lost in the Himalayas, he never felt he was truly alone. A man of faith, he felt that God was with him and, in an emotional sense, his family. He replayed happy experiences with his family and friends with as much detail as he could. To this day, he cites the connection he has with family and friends as key for his survival, both of his physical ordeal and his trial by media. 'I think that confers so much resilience. If you've got people who you love, and that love you, that gives you real strength.'

Ultimately, I think James Scott is right. The human capacity for survival and recovery seems to correlate with the strength of human connection. As an anaesthetist I work with patients before and after surgery and am often astounded by the outcomes of people who want to get back to their loved ones. In particular, I am struck by the incredible resilience of new mothers.

Pregnancy, and then childbirth, is a taxing physical experience – but the speed with which some mothers recover is astonishing. I've seen patients where a caesarean section is performed – a fairly invasive operation – where women make a rapid recovery with minimal post-operative pain. A similar procedure for a cancer diagnosis leaves the patient with much greater pain and a prolonged recovery. The happy outcome of the first procedure compared to the frightening implications of the second have a significant impact on a patient's response to surgery.

There's a certain fire that drives us to recover from the most extraordinary injuries and setbacks, and it burns all the brighter when we're looking forward to seeing our loved ones again. And that fire does extraordinary things.

PART FIVE

FIRE

'Most of us will never climb Mount Everest, cross Antarctica, or land on the moon, but we know we can,' Peter Hillary once said, speaking about his family's legacy of legendary explorations. 'The truth is we are all liberated by the success of others because they show it can be done.'

The Hillary family are always reliable for a bang-on quote, but this one speaks volumes. Yes, it's true that only a fraction of people on the planet will ever have the privilege of following in the footsteps of giants such as Sir Edmund Hillary, to say nothing of being the first human being to forge a path in the wild. But it does speak to the possibilities that we are all capable of if we are given the right inspiration.

To me, this quote also brings to mind the special echelon of risk-takers – those who risk their lives for the benefit of others. Professional risk-takers who train, travel, and face their own mortality on a daily basis in order to safeguard the freedoms that make the lives of people like me possible. Those who, for a greater cause, volunteer to take lives, and quite possibly, to give their own.

In these pages I want to talk about fire. Not the comforting kind we sit around for warmth and sip tea. The other kind. The kind you come under. The kind that means you are in harm's way and the danger is not from within, but from something in the environment that is trying to kill you. Something, or someone.

What can we learn from the human beings who are forged under fire, whose mettle is tested in the classical sense? We started with the 'Shed Guys', who risk life and limb out of curiosity and a spirit of adventure, now we arrive at men and women who do so out of a sense of duty: the professional soldier, the bodyguard, the policewoman. At some level, all these professionals have enrolled in a calling that means high levels of risk for a greater cause. How does that feel? How can we factor the behaviour of other people into our risk calculations? To kill or be killed is the quandary that most of us will thankfully never face. But we can still learn from those who have to make those choices.

I sought out those who had been through the fire, people who have brushed up against the very extremes of human experience – and been burned by it. The stories I found were some of the most harrowing of the whole project – and the most inspiring. Here were people whose lives were disrupted with the force of a volcanic explosion – and just like the verdant life that grows from the ashes – came back stronger.

CHAPTER THIRTEEN

THE BEST DAY OF YOUR LIFE

Heath Jamieson never saw who fired the bullet that broke his neck. It was an AK-47 round, fired by an enemy insurgent during an engagement in Afghanistan in 2011. He'd been a soldier for five years and spent most of his time as an elite Recon sniper in the Australian Army 2nd Commando Regiment.

Recon snipers have one of the most demanding roles in all of the armed forces. Traditionally, they hike, climb, or otherwise traverse hostile country behind enemy lines in utter secrecy and remain there, gathering information, watching through a long lens, and, in all likelihood, shooting someone from a great distance, after watching them go about their life for a long time. It's a form of military service that takes a special kind of person to acquit themselves in the role. The sort of person who was probably destined to be a soldier.

'I'd always had an interest in the army,' says Heath, who grew up hearing stories about his grandfather who served in the Second World War and Korea. Recently, while organising some possessions held in storage, Heath found a little play, four or five pages long, that he had written and illustrated when he was eleven years old. It was called *Commando* and contained characters and dialogue inspired by the 1985 American action cult classic movie of the same name. It was a little bit of foreshadowing for his eventual career. 'I couldn't stop laughing. Geez.'

Heath became a commando in the Australian armed forces some two decades later, after going to university and spending his twenties working as a geologist. He liked geology, but the desire to serve kept coming back to him. He played rugby recreationally, and he realised that his favourite part of the game was the pre-season training – the constant drive to push oneself. 'I thought, what better way to test yourself mentally? Special Forces was one of the perfect places to be able to do that. There are many attributes that they look for but endurance, that mental capacity to ignore what your body is telling you, is key.'

For that reason, soldiers in his unit tended to be in their thirties. Maturity and mental toughness were key attributes in soldiers deployed in a war where insurgents and civilians lived side-by-side, and the potential for civilian casualties was high.

This was a somewhat surprising revelation for Heath. On his first deployment, he'd expected every person he'd encounter in the theatre of war to be an enemy combatant. What Heath found was a war against deeply entrenched insurgents and a war-weary civilian populace trying to go about their normal lives while rockets flew overhead.

'You might be in combat, but there are still civilians walking around, people farming. They're so used to it; they'd still be just walking around in the middle of a firefight.'

To fight in that theatre of war meant constant mental vigilance. Is an individual on the horizon a potential threat? Are they not? Is the man hiking through the valley an insurgent moving to a new firing position, or an innocent local on his way to work? The responsibility to protect civilian life in a war zone was the priority for Heath and other snipers. Firing on innocents was not an option. However, he found that when engaged by hostile combatants it was 'surprisingly easy to shoot back at people when they're shooting at you'.

Heath was deployed in 2009 and 2010, often working with small teams of other commandos to support army operations in some of the harshest territory on Earth. In 2011, he was tapped for duty in Afghanistan again, for what would prove to be his final outing as a combat soldier.

His platoon deployed into Afghanistan's Helmand province. The mountainous area – which produced nearly half of the world's opium poppies – was a hotbed of insurgent activity. This, and many other factors, had earned it a reputation for being one of the most dangerous provinces in Afghanistan. In the summer, temperatures regularly soared over forty degrees Celsius, and in the winter the mountains fell well below freezing. All in all, it was a difficult place for foreign armed forces to operate in.

It had been perhaps eight years since Australian or allied troops had been seen in this part of the region. Heath's platoon was deployed to hunt down a particular target – an insurgent leader who was known to be operating in the area. It was far enough away from Heath's base of operations that it required a long flight, then a chopper ride, with Heath and his team taking off just before first light.

*

The inserting helicopter could only manage certain altitudes, so the commandos jumped from the helicopter at the base of a strategic mountain before dawn, 'In the middle of nowhere. We had maybe half an hour to get up the mountain as high as we could without being seen.'

Once insurgent forces became aware of Heath's team he expected to be engaged by the enemy. The Aussies knew their target – a high-value individual – and his forces were close.

While Heath's team scrambled up the mountain then set up an overwatch position, the rest of the platoon set up in a bazaar in a town a few kilometres to the south. The hope was that the presence of Australian troops in the remote village would provoke the insurgents into action. 'If we got this guy to pop above the threshold, we could find him.'

Sure enough, shortly after dawn, the commandos spotted some suspicious activity further down the mountain, with a line of armed men trailing down towards the bazaar. The tension started to ramp up, and then broke, as the insurgents spotted Heath's team up the hill and a firefight broke out. Heath tells the story in the clipped, matter-of-fact way he talks about all things military. 'We got engaged,' he says, 'and started engaging back. We got rid of a few guys down there and then they went to ground.'

After taking causalities, the insurgents took a defensive position, seeking cover behind scrubby vegetation which gave them some protection from small arms fire. In that situation, one of Heath's responsibilities was as a Joint Terminal Attack Controller (JTAC) – the sniper responsible for directing air support. Far above them, a Predator drone hovered, and other aircraft were on call to drop Hellfire missiles and heavy ordnance at targets on the ground. They presented an alternative to engaging the insurgents on the ground, 'and luckily we were able to engage them with those missiles'.

Soon, the engagement stopped. The gunfire ceased and all was quiet while Heath kept overwatch. Through his scope, he surveyed the field of combat. He knew that one enemy combatant, 'the guy running the show', was still active, hiding in vegetation. While he watched over the vegetation, two civilian women walked by and dropped a package. While he watched, the women loitered for a while out of sight behind the shrubs blocking Heath's overwatch, until three people dressed in traditional women's clothing made a break for it.

Uncertain which of the figures was the belligerent one who had just been shooting at them, Heath's team could only watch as he walked into the village, surrounding himself with women and children.

Now that the target was surrounded by civilians, Heath's unit could not engage, nor could air support. Above, a precision Predator drone and manned United States Rockwell B-1 Lancer was available for an airstrike, but the supersonic bomber was not suitable in this situation. All they could do was wait.

'We decided to just keep an eye on him, so we knew where he was. While he was around women, children, you're not going to do anything.' If the situation changed and the possibility for a precision air-strike opened up, it would be up to Heath to call it in.

As such, it fell to Heath to keep the allied air assets updated on the target. He was turning around to grab a piece of equipment for this task when he heard the shot ring out. What happened next took only a few seconds, but Heath remembers it all happening very slowly – an impact across the back of his head like someone had smacked him with a baseball bat, then looking down to find his arms and legs limp, flopping about, and blood pooling beneath him.

'Oh shit, they're shooting at us,' Heath remembers saying to himself, then, 'Okay, I've been shot.' He made to move into a more secure position and realised his legs weren't responding.

His first instinct was to work out where the bullet had come from and return fire, but when he tried to reach down for his gun, which lay across his legs, 'I couldn't control my arms to reach down and get my weapon.' At that moment, another shot rang out, and Heath threw himself down to get out of the line of fire.

*

In the moments after he was hit, Heath's situational awareness dropped away to what he describes as a bubble. He remembers lying on his back, aware of nothing but the sky above him. Slowly the bubble expanded, and he became conscious of the world around him, the team scrambling across the rocks to get close to him, yelling for an update, the radio in his ear, where the other JTAC was talking to the strike jet above them.

Heath knew he had to let his team know he was alive, but he was struggling to breathe. He likens the sensation to lying winded on a rugby field, struggling to take enough air in to speak. This time, instead of the sound of a roaring crowd, there was the crackle of gunfire, and a harsh gurgling sound as he tried to force air into his shattered body.

Heath's radio switch was on his left chest, and he remembers looking at his right hand, and willing it to move to call in an airstrike on the position he ascertained the enemy fire had come from, 'because the sooner the air asset starts dropping ordnance or looking for whoever it was that shot me, the sooner our situation is going to get better'.

Meanwhile, Heath's team commander was scrambling across the rocks towards his downed soldier, yelling out for an update. Heath tried to yell back, to let his mates know he was hit but still alive, but when he opened his mouth all that came out was one word: a broken, gurgled – 'Help!'

'As soon as I said that "Help" I remember being filthy angry with myself, for that weak little call,' says Heath. He wanted to yell out with tactical information – he'd been hit, he couldn't move his arms or legs, but when he saved up all his strength again for another try, the only word that would come out was another 'Help'. The commando had seen enough combat to know that if he couldn't talk, or walk, or even move his hand to the wound to staunch the blood, then he was in real trouble.

Years later, telling the story, Heath would try to replicate the gurgling sound he'd made as he lay at death's door after he was hit, until one of the medics who had looked after him asked him not to. 'Mate, I never want to hear that sound again.'

'That's the only time I really considered the possibility of death,' says Heath. His first thought was of his sister. Just before he had been deployed, they'd lost their brother (Heath's twin) and she'd asked him not to go back to Afghanistan, telling him, 'You're all I've got left, don't go over.' Now here he was, bleeding out on a mountainside.

'If I die here, she's going to hate me forever,' he thought, and started to work out how he was going to survive. What action he and his team needed to do to get out of the situation.

One of the other soldiers, trained in patrol first aid, managed to reach Heath and drag him down a rock ledge out of the line of fire, and started cutting off Heath's shirt and battle rig. The trauma shears cut through the mic cord and the radio chatter in Heath's ear fell silent. Now the only voice he could hear was his teammate trying to treat Heath and ascertain how bad the damage was.

*

The bullet likely came from an AK-47 and entered the back of Heath's head at the base of his skull, travelling at more than 2000 feet (610 metres) per second, just under the hairline on the right side and exiting just under the jawline on the left-hand side. Its trajectory had been on an angle to perfectly sever his carotid artery, which would have cut off blood supply to his brain and meant certain death. In what might be the ultimate silver-lining to his wound, the shockwave from the projectile was so intense it pushed the artery and jugular vein out of the way as it passed, effectively saving his life.

That same shockwave caused significant damage to his spinal column and his brain, as the bullet travelled through. The round itself hit and shattered the C2 transverse process, also disrupting the C1 vertebra. The spinal injuries had left Heath unable to feel or control his limbs effectively. Although the internal damage was severe, the entry wound was actually quite small, and the field medic was initially unable to locate it.

The lack of an apparent exit wound meant Heath's injuries were somewhat confounding to the field medic. The Australian soldiers had lost a mate a couple of weeks earlier when he'd been shot in the neck, but the bullet had ricocheted around inside his chest, destroying his internal organs and ending his life. This loss was fresh in the mind of the field medic, and he and Heath had a spirited discussion while they tried to figure out how badly Heath was hurt, and how he might be stabilised.

The bullet had also caused nerve damage, resulting in a type of grievous pain called allodynia all down Heath's left arm and chest. It meant even the lightest touch registered as excruciating pain. 'It was just like being electrocuted. Probably the most pain I've ever felt,' deadpans Heath. 'It was quite interesting.'

Meanwhile, the tactical situation had gone from a hunt for a priority target to a medical evacuation of a wounded soldier. A medivac helicopter could handle their altitude, but there was nowhere to land. Nor could he be winched up, because the moment a helicopter arrived it would come under enemy fire. Evacuation would mean getting Heath down to a landing zone where he could be safely loaded into a helicopter.

That meant closing in as a group, two soldiers picking him up and getting Heath down the mountain, all while enemy fire was raining down on them.

Out of the corner of his eye, Heath could see smoke further up on the mountain where mortars were landing, and suppressing fire from the rest of Heath's platoon, who were embedded in the village a few kilometres to the south.

'One of the guys had a machine gun and was firing to suppress the enemy,' recalls Heath. The shock wave coming off the machine gun, which previously had only registered as noise to the downed soldier, caused havoc with his damaged nerves. With the allodynia, every burst from the weapon felt like a wave of electricity passing through his chest. 'Every now and again I had to ask him to stop shooting just so I could take a couple of breaths, it was that bad.'

The team managed to get Heath to the landing zone, but then they had to run back up to retrieve his gear – pack, weapons, radio – all of which would be a liability in enemy hands. On that particular mission, the full payload of equipment was around 85 kilograms per soldier, so it was no small task for Heath's team to run up and down the mountain with the gear all while dodging enemy fire. Even for the fittest soldiers, adrenaline can only carry you so far. 'They were working pretty hard.'

*

In the meantime, Heath was lying in the sun, trying to stay conscious. He remembers the medic slapping him to stay awake, while he tried to bargain time for a nap. 'Just give me twenty seconds of my eyes closed,' he argued. 'I just want twenty seconds of rest. Just give it to me.'

All in all, from the moment Heath was shot, until the landing area was clear, it took an hour and a half. That's a long time to lie bleeding in the dust. Battlefield medicine has a rule of thumb – what is called the 'golden hour'. Effectively, if your wounds are not immediately fatal and you can get to a hospital within an hour, you have a very good chance of survival: 'Ninety-five to ninety-eight per cent, something along those lines,' says Heath. 'I remember at one stage realising the golden hour was finished, and thinking I was probably screwed.'

Then, all of a sudden, he was being hauled upright by his team. The medivac had arrived – and with it, the rest of his platoon firing mortars up into the hills, and Apache helicopters raining missiles down to provide cover for the evacuation.

'No one likes a fuss being made over them,' Heath says, a little sheepishly, 'And it doesn't get more of a fuss than bombs and ordnance being dropped everywhere, the helicopter kind of hovering there with one wheel on the ground because you need to be in it.'

The soldiers threw Heath into the helicopter, then climbed in, all while the aircraft shuddered as it absorbed enemy rounds. Heath says he'll never forget the feeling of pure relief of being thrown backwards into the helicopter as it took off and the sound of bullets bouncing off the craft stopped. 'Relief. Too much relief. Like, our role is done and we're in a safe place now. It must have been even more so for the other guys because they had been working their backsides off for the last hour and a half or more.'

It took incredible teamwork to get Heath off the mountain involving hard work and sacrifice. Less than twenty minutes after Heath was hit, the platoon suffered its second casualty, when a burst of insurgent machine-gun fire caught a soldier – callsign Tango One – standing on a village rooftop with a direct headshot. 'I remember hearing the casualty report come in over the radio – "Tango One, headshot."'

Shortly after that, the fire started to calm down, and Heath was told that a helicopter was en route for medical evac and arguing that Tango One should be picked up before him, as a headshot took precedence over a spinal injury.

'I'm feeling good now,' Heath told his teammate. 'Let Tango One go first.'

'You're going first,' the medic told Heath, and after some back and forth, Heath realised that he was the priority, because Tango One was already dead, and they didn't want to tell him.

It wasn't until he'd been evacuated – first to the Australian military base at Tarinkot, then to intensive care in Kandahar – that Heath learned who Tango One was.

'He was one of the senior members of the platoon, and a family man with a wife and four kids under the age of ten.' At the time Heath had no children, no girlfriend, and remembers lying in his hospital bed trying to think of some way to swap positions with Tango One. 'Is there some way we can just change this? To take his spot? Is it too late to go back and swap places? He gets to stay, and I'll pass on? But obviously that type of thing is not reality. It's not going to happen.'

Heath couldn't shake the thought that there were only a few centimetres between the bullets that sailed harmlessly by, and the round which had taken the life of Tango One and the devastating effect that bullet would have on five lives in his immediate family. 'And meanwhile, I'm here to go on, and he's not . . . it's just such a fine line between having a good day and a bad day.'

Clearly, Heath has a different threshold for what constitutes a good day to most people. The soldier was alive but had a long road to recovery ahead of him. It would take years of rehabilitation to learn to use his body again. With the extent of his spinal fractures and spinal cord damage, he couldn't move his left arm for six months, and couldn't really walk for a year. A traumatic brain injury resulting from the shooting robbed him of certain skills. For some years after the incident, he couldn't read. Even today, a decade after being wounded, he has still not recovered full function of his body – but not for lack of trying.

Heath's rehabilitation journey started more or less the moment he woke up in hospital. After a day or two in intensive care in Kandahar, he was transferred back to Tarinkot, where his medical team decided to remove his catheter. Heath decided that if he wasn't held in place by a catheter anymore then he was going to get up and relieve himself when he needed to go to the toilet. His doctors argued against this, pleading his broken spine. They brought him a bottle to urinate in, but he was adamant that he wanted to take himself to the toilet.

243

When Heath first sat up after four days lying in bed, he nearly passed out. Slowly, over the space of twenty minutes, he managed to rise, then stand, catch his breath, then with a couple of mates holding his arms, managed to drag himself the ten feet to the toilet.

'I wouldn't call it walking, but I remember standing there, feeling like a normal person and going, "Okay, sweet."' A small victory, maybe, but the first of many. 'That kind of wanting to do normal things and just pushing myself all the time, was the norm through, well, my whole rehab.'

He was still in hospital when his uncle visited with an iPad, on which Heath watched a documentary on Walking with the Wounded, a British charity whose mission is to help those who've served – and their families – get back on their feet. The documentary followed a group of wounded British soldiers undertaking an expedition to the South Pole. Heath was intrigued, remarking to his uncle, 'How cool would it be to do something like that?'

In December 2013, he got the chance. Heath and another veteran wounded in Afghanistan, Corporal Seamus Donaghue, were invited by Walking with the Wounded and its Australian counterpart, Soldier On, to compete in a trek to the South Pole. On their team, representing the Commonwealth, were two wounded Canadian soldiers. They would compete in a 300-kilometre race – in temperatures of minus 45 degrees and winds of 90 kilometres per hour – against teams from the United States and Britain, including Prince Harry.

In the lead up to the trip, people had suggested he would struggle, that the physical and mental injuries that Heath and the other soldiers carried would make the trip unbearable. As it happened, once he was out on the frozen expanse of Antarctica, Heath discovered he was very much in his element. He and the other soldiers found it easier than the civilians accompanying them to adjust to the expedition environment. For military personnel used to routine and the hierarchies of command, it was an easy transition to learning survival skills from their expert guides. The injuries were incidental to the adventure, not a real detriment.

Here, the mental fortitude, the ability to thrive under adverse conditions – the traits that drew him to service in the first place – came back to serve him.

Heath credits that expedition as a pivotal moment – not just in his recovery, but his path through life. It was a revelation to find himself with a challenge again, with like-minded people working towards a goal. 'It woke me up to the fact that I don't need to be in the military to be able to get the satisfaction of purpose. To be exposed to that in a non-military environment put me in a better headspace ahead of being discharged from the army.'

While he knew nothing would be like his time as a soldier, the experience brought him a familiar sense of achievement and success, one that he'd never expected to find in civilian life. "I feel so privileged to have been able to take part in that expedition. I just loved the whole experience; the environment, the people we did it with. Being there in Antarctica . . . it was good luck.'

Luck is a word Heath deploys frequently in conversation. He describes himself as lucky or having good luck more often than pretty much anyone I've known. I sometimes wonder if I'd be as quick to describe myself as lucky if I were to acquire such a world-shattering injury as Heath. Then again, there's a school of thought that we make our own luck. There are people in the world whose luck seems to improve the harder they work.

As part of being discharged from service, the army offered to help Heath upskill into a new career. He was offered university tuition, but he had his mind made up on another career path. 'The only other thing I was interested in, besides being in the military, was flying helicopters. When I told this to one of the doctors who was involved in my treatment, he just laughed and said, "You'll never fly a helicopter,"' Heath, deadpan again, 'so that became my goal. To fly a helicopter.'

Achieving that goal would be another long stretch of Heath's rehab journey. It would require Heath to learn to read again to master the theoretical aspect of a helicopter pilot's licence. It was also a new challenge to master the fine motor control that a pilot requires. It took a special trip to the United States for advanced rehabilitation treatment before Heath had relearned to master his body to the extent that he could take to the air. Heath ended up getting his civilian helicopter licence, and went on to become an instructor, teaching other civilians how to fly choppers.

While he was in the midst of all this, Heath was exploring his newly discovered passion for the frozen wilderness. In 2014, he embarked on a trip to the North Pole with Eric Philips, the Australian guide from his Antarctic expedition, and found his love for polar trekking undiminished. Two weeks into a break from working as a helicopter instructor, he got a call from Eric asking him if he wanted to help guide a trek across Greenland. He hit it off with those clients, and they invited him to come on another trip across Antarctica.

After several trips, Heath decided to formalise his new career, and became endorsed as a professional guide by the International Polar Guides Association. Since then, he has guided treks across the Arctic and Antarctica, leading adventurous people from all walks of life up to their limits, and then some. 'The last few years I have been very lucky to be able to do that as a job. It takes its toll on the body but for me, it's worth it because it's something I enjoy so much.'

Heath loves everything about the job – the mission, the group, and the simplicity of life on the ice, everything stripped away but the raw work of survival on the journey. 'Life is so simple. You wake up, you eat, you pack up your tent, you ski all day, you put up a tent, you eat, and you sleep. There's no phones, no internet, none of that. It's just living.'

An expedition to the poles typically takes around thirty-seven days. That's more than a month of hard slog, with highly regimented routines necessary for survival, much of it spent in the companionable isolation of arctic survival gear. 'You spend a lot of time by yourself, even though you're in a group. It's windy and you've got all the gear on which is not conducive for a lot of communication. And so, you spend a lot of time in your own head. And I just find it meditative, to have eight hours in a day to think without any distractions. That's pretty rare in today's world.'

I know from my own experience that there can be incredible mental reward from pushing your physical limits. The personal growth and peace of mind that can result from being pulled out of your comfort zone is something I've valued for a long time. Heath, after his long road of rehabilitation, knows this better than anyone.

The extremes of stress that his high-risk profession puts him through have given Heath a rare perspective on the business of everyday living. To fight in combat, take lives, lose friends, have your body shattered by enemy fire, all within a few crowded hours, for someone with a life as comparatively tame and comfortable as mine, is unimaginable. Conversely, Heath finds that my sort of contemporary life, in which the pursuit of professional success means multiple stressors keep us in a constant low-intensity state of fight or flight – leaves much to be desired.

'We've been conditioned in certain aspects of our society, to think in certain ways or behave in certain ways in order to be successful in a financial sense or to gain popularity. It's not conducive to happiness,' he explains. 'I'm at a stage now where I'd like to give back. For me, the big thing is changing the way people think about their lives,' says Heath.

Heath's experience gives him a perspective on life I much admire. He sees a society that stresses itself out for reasons it doesn't really need to and, in his work as a polar guide, offers an alternative – to help people experience the remote frontiers of our planet, and of themselves.

On top of his work as a polar guide, Heath volunteers for Operation Flinders – a charity for disengaged youth that teaches self-esteem building and wilderness survival – which is where we met. As part of that role, we guide young people on eight-day walks through the remote South Australian outback. The idea is to build self-esteem and self-reliance in kids who have had a rough go of it, although, if I am honest, I have learnt as much from Heath as the young people do.

A simple conversation early on one trek radically changed my mindset about suffering. Several days into the trek, in which we carry all our equipment in rucksacks, my back was starting to ache. I made some passing comment about my suffering, and Heath stopped in his tracks to look at me.

'How,' he asked, 'did it help you to tell me that, Harry?'

Taken aback, I wasn't sure what to say, so he continued, 'Did it make your back feel any better to tell me that?'

'No, I guess not,' I replied.

'How do you think it made me feel?' he followed up.

'I guess it made you think less of me, and made you think about your own sore back,' I offered, starting to feel a bit sheepish.

'Exactly right. Instead of saying that, I would first remember that everyone in this party is experiencing the same thing, and that verbalising it serves no purpose whatsoever.'

The lightbulb went on for me. He was right of course, and no doubt his sore back was a thousand times worse than mine. In a few words, he made me realise that my moaning wasn't a good strategy – for me, him, or the youth we were supposed to be inspiring. I took the note – and now use the same strategy on my kids!

'I'm trying to impart some of the things I've been lucky enough to learn onto other people,' says Heath, 'whether they take it on board or not, or whether it just makes a little aspect of their life a little bit easier. That's the bit that I enjoy. It makes me want to get out of bed in the morning.'

I've seen Heath working with these at-risk and disengaged kids and seen what he has to say start to sink in – which is maybe the most astonishing part of his whole story. It takes a special talent to get through to teenagers, even on a good day.

I suspect that the way Heath sees it, every day is a good day. It's safe to say that being shot in the spine isn't on anyone's bucket list, but Heath looks back on that time without a hint of bitterness or regret. There is some sadness, certainly, for Tango One, and all the friends lost in battle, but none for his own injuries.

'It was a bad day for me, in that sense, but it was also the best day in my life. The number of experiences jam-packed into that twenty-four-hour period; I'll never have that again. Good experiences, and bad experiences. But it wasn't all doom and gloom,' says Heath.

Out of all the extraordinary things about Heath's story it's this that I find most inspiring – this irrepressible cheerfulness, the drive to keep on walking, and to have a good time while doing it.

Trauma is not parcelled out to individuals with any sense of fairness. The bullet that caught Heath in the neck might have missed him just as easily as it caught him. Looking at it one way, his wounding was the result of bad luck. But by the same token, it might just as easily be seen as a glitch in what had, until then, been quite a fortunate period of military service. Of the hundreds of bullets fired at him during his career, one finally caught him. What is that, if not incredible luck? Heath prefers to look on the sunny side, as is his nature. He signed up for the job, he got shot, he rebuilt his life – proud to have served, and glad for another chance.

I've often wondered what my own reaction to an extreme personal trauma like that Heath experienced would be. Would I fall in a heap?

Or would I shrug it off like Heath and emerge through it all a better, happier, person?

There is a growing body of literature that supports the conclusion that exposure to the stressors associated with extreme environmental conditions can lead to personal growth and greater reported happiness. Heath, who taught himself to walk again, now takes people who want to challenge themselves into the wildest places on Earth, and brings them back calmer, more centred, happier.

I wonder if the sense of growth and optimism experienced by Heath's clients and other adventures into extreme environments is proof in action of post traumatic growth. Did Heath's time as a soldier – and the immense risk involved – set him up for his extraordinary resilience in civilian life? Is his continuing life of adventure integral in his recovery and joy in life?

I know personally, regularly experiencing discomfort in adventure is immensely important for my own equilibrium. If I go too long between cave dives, I start to feel the impact on my own mental state. Without the relatively safe yet exhilarating controlled risks that I expose myself to in caves, the myriad stresses of everyday life start to feel overwhelming – the task of contributing to society, of practising medicine, trying to be a good friend, husband and father – not to mention more recently, and quite unexpectedly, the added pressures of a public profile. Those little stressors add up and can become a lot to deal with – but they never seem to be able to find me as I squeeze through a freezing cave, deep underwater. Strangely, when I come up again at the end of a dive, they don't seem so bad at all.

I can categorically state that I've found risk-taking to be a net-good in my life. Somewhat paradoxically, I know that this one activity that so enriches my life is more likely to actually end it, unlike most other hobbies.

It's intriguing. While, as a recreational risk-taker, I don't crave a traumatic experience, I know that there's a chance there's one on the horizon. So, in order to understand how I might deal with one, I went looking for other people who have seen horrific things and come out the other end smiling. I felt like I understood what drives people to embrace risk – but what about when the abstract risks become real? When everything goes wrong, how do you find the strength to keep going, and even go harder? Where does that sort of fortitude come from?

What makes Heath shoulder his burden without complaint, where other people might fall apart? Where does the resilience afforded by his elite training and experience end and his natural fortitude kick in? Is the extraordinary mental toughness Heath embodies something we all have the potential for? To get the answers I was looking for, I thought I should talk to blokes a little closer to my own temperament. Regular Australians who have made risk-taking – and exposure to traumatic shock – part of their everyday life. That search took me, as it always seems to, back to the water.

CHAPTER FOURTEEN

AT THE POINTY END OF THE DAY

What makes a human being strong? Not just mentally tough, but strong enough to weather almost anything. Why are there people like Heath, who seem in possession of such a strong will that they can be shot in the spine and literally walk it off? Then again, I've met people who are otherwise intelligent, self-possessed and capable who are profoundly discombobulated by tragic events. At first impressions, it's difficult to tell who will flourish in the face of trauma, and who will unexpectedly dig deep. Honestly, it's hard even to tell how an individual will react from trauma from day to day. I know from personal experience.

An event quite early in my life at medical school had a profound effect on me. It was towards the end of my time as a student, so whilst I was in no way hardened to death, I had already seen a little of the suffering and dying that a career in medicine would entail.

In my downtime, I had taken up rowing at the university. One morning my good mate John and I were training on Adelaide's River Torrens in a coxless pair: just two guys in a tiny boat. It was a perfect morning for a row – and we had the river pretty much to ourselves.

At the pointy end of the day

Before we'd set out, I'd spotted something floating in the river some way out and had casually joked to my pal that I hoped it wasn't a body.

I didn't think of it again until about an hour later when we paused on the river for a chat, the boat still gliding along quietly under the momentum of our strokes. As we came to a halt, I glanced down into the water to see the side of a human face staring back at me. The flotsam I'd made a lame joke about earlier – it really had been a floating corpse.

'John, don't turn around and don't look,' I said quietly, 'but that thing I joked about maybe being a body actually is a body.' I spoke as calmly as I could because I was most concerned about the two of us tipping the boat in a panic. Those coxless pair boats are notoriously unstable and easy to tip, especially for a couple of rank amateurs like us. A couple of centimetres dip towards the water is all it takes.

Naturally John's first reaction was to turn around to look for himself. That twisting motion immediately unsettled the boat. Like in a bad dream, the boat started to violently wobble from side to side, threatening to deposit me on top of my water-logged visitor below. Somehow, we managed to settle ourselves and row gently back to the safety of the bank. We alerted the police to our grisly find then foolishly stuck around long enough to watch the cops pull the body – stiff with rigor and wearing only a woollen jumper – up onto the riverbank.

When I got home that afternoon, I actually felt fine. Apart from the initial surprise of finding myself face-to-face with a dead man who'd bobbed up from the river, I was undisturbed.

That changed over the next couple of days, as news reports emerged that the guy had been bashed on the head with a barbell and unceremoniously thrown into the river. The fact that it was a murder started to play on my mind.

I began experiencing flashbacks of the poor guy's face, beaten, water-logged and gruesome. Soon I wasn't sleeping properly. I remember finishing late at the hospital one night and walking back through the pedestrian tunnel leading to the university car park, and suddenly feeling really freaked out. I kept turning to check if anyone was following me, knowing logically that I was safe, but unable to shake this illogical, existential nervousness. The sleepless nights, bad dreams and heightened state of arousal lasted a few weeks. I was at once surprised and also disappointed with my reaction. It's not like I'd never seen a dead body before. So why did this one frighten me so much?

In time, having thought long and hard about the experience, I have come to believe it is the context of such events that are extremely important. During my work I have seen some extraordinarily unpleasant sights. Far worse than the guy in the river. But these have been within the context of the job. When I am en route to an accident scene, a violent assault or a burns victim, I have time to mentally prepare myself for what I am about to see. On the occasions I have performed underwater body recoveries in caves, I have been able to function perfectly well and complete the job as required. Even during the Thai cave rescue, when I knew my actions might lead directly to the deaths of the children and the coach, I felt calm, even robotic until the work was finished. That's not to say I don't get emotional after the event, because I often do.

Decades later, after much experience and exposure to many deaths, I have some perspective on why that one rattled me to the extent it did. I was a medical student in a competitive and highly sought-after field. My life was safe and comfortable but not without its stresses. I had all the usual coping mechanisms that a young man of my generation used – sports, the beach, a beer or two – and I handled it in the typically stoic way that our blokey culture demanded. But something about that unexpected brush with death hit me for six, which suggested that the coping mechanisms I was using weren't actually all that effective.

At the pointy end of the day

That morning, I hadn't been braced to encounter a murder victim, and its emotional impact upon me was outsized. In the seconds before we'd bumped into him, looking across the still water of the River Torrens, the scariest thing on my horizon was the next exam. You don't expect horror in a beautiful location, and when something like that blindsides you, it really can knock you about.

*

The southwest corner of Western Australia is some of the most gorgeous country on Earth, boasting kilometres of wild and stunning coastline. Even for me, a South Australian who is rightfully defensive of our own excellent beaches, I would have to reluctantly admit that Western Australia has us beat. They arguably boast some of the world's best beaches – endless sand, stark cliffs, massive surf, and extraordinarily large sharks.

It's these last two that brought together Russell Ord and Shanan Worrall, two Western Australian blokes who grew up on, in, and under the water. The two men each make their living from the ocean in very different ways, but bonded over their deep love – and occasionally adversarial relationship with – the sea.

These days they are business partners, producing 'Shark Eyes' wetsuits and surfboard decals, gear designed with stylised eyeballs to deter shark attacks while in the water. The idea was the culmination of a lifetime of shared aquatic experience.

Shanan is amongst the most adept surfers to ever climb on a board. He makes his living beneath the waves as a commercial diver, but he made his name in big-wave surfing – an amateur who puts many professional surfers to shame. In 2016, he took out the World Surf League (WSL) Big Wave Award for Tube of the Year for a 6.5 metre barrel ride at the famous break, 'The Right', knocking several pros out of contention. This win was itself the culmination of a string of positions in the finals of other big wave awards, including the Oakley Big Wave Awards in 2010, 2012 and 2014.

Russell Ord is a world class surf photographer, whose big-wave images reveal the beauty and pure dramatic power of the ocean to those of us who are not quite brave enough to paddle out ourselves.

Russell – who has shot magazine covers and portraits of celebrity surfers and chefs – is not the sort of bloke I would call to mind if you asked me to describe a photographer. He came to the vocation via a past as a rugby player and a member of the fire brigade and is appropriately fit and weather-beaten with a broad accent. For lack of a better term, he is *extremely* Aussie.

He's laconic, using fewer words than someone else might – but perhaps he doesn't need to, given his ability to express himself with his camera. His surf photography reveals a rare talent to capture the ocean in all its moods; meditative, menacing, cruel, capricious. The sort of photos that make you stop in your tracks for a bit of a reverie. They are, in other words, deeply moving, and perhaps all the more surprising to be created by such an unassuming bloke.

Although he'd been surfing since he was five, Russell only came to big-wave photography when he was sidelined by a surfing injury. He couldn't surf big waves but could handle a jet ski well enough. 'So yeah, I just picked up a camera, basically, and started shooting my mates.'

That was twenty years ago. He started off photographing from the back of the surfboard. In pursuit of the perfect shot, Russell went in knowing he'd get smashed again and again, the waves plunging him underwater, and holding him under long past the point of safety. One time, after paddling out on a board with a 300 mm lens and camera in an underwater housing (just to see if it could be done), he was dumped and held down for forty-five seconds with a pack full of gear on his back. He remembers making a choice – just before he started breathing salt water – of leaving his bag and a small fortune in gear to the waves, dumping it to make it back up. After this costly experience, he went looking for a jet ski to take him out.

For the next seven years, he would shoot photos from the back of the jet ski – juggling his camera while gunning through the waves, until an accident broke his leg and sparked a rethink of how he could shoot. He decided he would shoot from the water itself to better capture the experience of being a surfer on the wave. 'You just don't really get the feeling of a surfer sitting on the back of the ski.'

The results speak for themselves, but for someone like me, who prefers the tranquil waters of a cave, the practice sounds mind-bogglingly dangerous. With nothing but a wetsuit, helmet and camera, he happily jumps into waves that have a good track record of crippling and killing the surfers that try to ride them.

By throwing himself at the mercy of the surf, Russell is able to capture the shots which have made him a celebrated photographer. His photos, like the waves themselves, are inanimate objects that seem alive – distinct, intricate, intangible. 'When I look at my own work now, it's those I can look back on and see the effort. They're the kind of shots I like taking.'

It didn't put him off. Two decades on he's still on a quest for the perfect shot. It is that mission which takes him to remote and secret breaks, the sort that are closely guarded by territorial surfers. That's how he first met Shanan, when the surfer called him to warn him away from photographing waves he didn't want the world to know about. What started as a mildly threatening phone call somehow turned into a friendship built on mutual love of the ocean.

'He just wanted to protect his waves,' says Russell. 'He must have heard I was sniffing around his neck of the woods. Pretty ironic now that we're such good friends.'

As you might expect, their friendship involved a great deal of surfing, and a fair amount of that makes it into *One Shot*, a documentary film recording his search for the perfect shot of the perfect wave. Shanan, also on the lookout for the perfect wave, was often on the waves and is the subject of some of Russell's best images. That endless search has also put them in some life-threatening situations.

Shanan recalls the day they visited a favourite surf spot on the south coast of Western Australia and found the beach crowded with big-wave surfers keen to tackle unusually large waves. 'Normally you rock up and you know it's big,' he says, in his understated way. 'But this was probably one of the biggest I'd ever seen. Conditions were perfect.'

Waves were cresting at between ten and fifteen metres – wild enough that no one else was on the water. It was early in the day, and the usual big-wave surfers were either waiting on shore or still unpacking. Shanan decided to go for it and jumped on the rope towed by a jet ski to take him out to the back of the waves.

They turned in as a fifteen-metre wave rose, and he jumped off the rope to catch it. 'I thought it was going to be the best wave I've ever had. Then the water rolled over and pushed me down,' says Shanan, who was forced so deep underwater by the wave that his ear drums threatened to burst.

Russell, who'd only just arrived and was watching from the shore with his young son Kalani, saw Shanan go down. He looked up and saw Shanan on the wave, then saw the wave engulf him and send him cartwheeling towards the ocean floor.

It was clear that Shanan needed help, but nobody was rushing to it. Russell looked around, expecting one of the jet skis packing the channel to attempt a rescue. Nobody was, prompting a moral dilemma – let his friend drown or go in and attempt a rescue and maybe drown himself. Russell and his son headed out on the jet ski.

'I went in and straight to where I thought he would pop up in the swell based on past experiences. And in the ten seconds available before the third wave, we managed to get him on the sled behind the ski.' Shanan was lucky. 'If we hadn't, best case scenario would have been a resuscitation. Worst case scenario, well, we wouldn't be here talking today.'

*

Both Russell and Shanan seem to hold fairly healthy attitudes towards risk, although they regularly participate in activities that a layperson might find a little gung-ho. I asked Russell how he coped with the steady diet of danger. 'I've probably had to be really honest with myself,' he said. 'The scenarios we do put ourselves in . . . if you get it wrong, the outcome is potentially death. You can't hide from that.'

Of course all the training, all the risk mitigation in the world, is sometimes not enough. No matter how well trained and psychologically prepared you think you are, you don't know how you'll react until you're already in the moment that might be your last.

The problem with an adventurous life is that sometimes things go awry. Most of the time you can walk – or limp – away with a couple of knocks and a story to tell. Sometimes, you can't. The consequences can be permanent – even if the physical scars gradually heal.

Both Russell and Shanan lived for the waves but made their living with regular jobs. Russell was a fireman. Shanan was a commercial diver, harvesting wild abalone. Both are professions that come with their own occupational hazards.

Abalone divers are a territorial lot. Like surfers, they tend to jealously guard their favourite stretches of reef. They embark on epic journeys in order to find the perfect spot to ply their trade. This takes them to some of the most remote, wild and untouched submerged reefs along our coasts.

Diving in these locations requires complex logistics. Caravans, tractors and boats that are launched directly from the beach all need to be driven in, often on dirt tracks that it would be optimistic to call a 'road'. Once a team is in place, they might camp out for a month to two, diving all the nearby spots before moving the base camp.

Shanan and his colleague Andrew Rowe had been exploring from a camp near Poison Creek, about 120 kilometres east of Esperance. It was an hour's drive on the road, then another hour down a four-wheel drive track. The two divers hadn't seen another human being for some time, when one morning two other divers turned up.

One was Greg Pickering, a tough, fit fifty-five-year-old and one of Western Australia's most respected abalone divers. The other was his younger deckhand, Callan Turner.

'We were stoked, happy to have their company,' recalls Shanan. 'Even if Greg probably hadn't done as much diving around there as we had which meant he was going to follow us around.'

Sure enough, the two dive boats headed out and dropped anchor just 500 metres away from each other, at a spot about 20 kilometres up from the beach launch. Shanan and Greg jumped from their respective boats while their deckhands drove the boats and managed things topside.

'We were in the middle of nowhere,' says Shanan. It was only at the start of the day. I think I was on my first dive sitting on the bottom of the ocean, chipping away at the abalone, when I got the emergency signal.'

Shanan was breathing with a hose of compressed air which ran from a compressor on the boat down to the ocean floor where he was working. When Andrew, up on the boat, gave repeated pulls on the hose, it was a predetermined distress signal. For Shanan, he knew it meant one of two things: 'It's either your air supply is about to run out, or there's a big bitey around.'

He immediately started an emergency ascent, spinning in the water as he came up, to make sure nothing was going to hit him from his blindside. As he got near the surface, he heard the engines of Pickering's boat roar to life and hammer flat out through the water. That wasn't a good sign.

Shanan surfaced, scrambled onto the deck, where he found Andrew, pale with shock.

'Greg.' He said. 'Greg's been hit.'

Greg was over in the other boat, so they had no idea how bad it was, but they followed procedures. Shanan jumped on the satellite phone to call the Abalone Association – who normally have a helicopter available for emergency evacuations. 'We were assuming we were going to have access to that helicopter to get us out of there. But we ended up learning that that wasn't going to be the case.' It was going to be up to the other divers to get Greg out of there.

Andrew pulled the boat up alongside Greg's and they jumped aboard. Greg's deckie Callan met them at the back of the boat. He was distraught. Shanan stopped to check on him before moving to the front of the boat where Greg lay. He remembers looking at Greg for the first time.

Shanan distinctly remembers exchanging a look with Andrew, who simply asked, 'Is it a white?'

'It's a white,' Shanan stammered. 'He's, he's not going to make it.'

In his own words, he praises young Callan's brave efforts to 'do what he could' to put him back together. 'I'd seen Greg . . . yeah, he was in a terrible way. The visuals are absolutely . . . I guess terrifying is the word.'

*

Greg had been working on the sea floor – leaning forward to pry abalone from where they clung to the rocks – when a great white shark had attacked. It had taken him from the front, completely engulfing him headfirst, down to his waist. If it wasn't for his dive gear with a spare air bottle and a weighted vest covering part of his torso, he would have been cut in two immediately.

By some miracle, Greg managed to work his way free of the shark, and somehow make it to the surface, but 'how the heck he managed to do that I don't know. He just got torn apart,' says Shanan.

Greg's injuries were so severe, and so gruesome, that years later Shanan slows down as he tells the story, searching for the right way to describe what he saw. The word 'horrific' is deployed more than once, with good reason.

Greg had been so badly mauled that his scalp had been half-torn from the skull, creating what Shanan describes as a 'flip-top scalp'. His face was just as badly destroyed. One of Greg's eye sockets still had a shark tooth embedded in it, where the eyeball should have been. Shanan recalls grabbing a dive regulator that delivered pure oxygen to deliver first aid, and having to pause, 'I remember trying to place that pure O_2 reg on his face and not really knowing which . . . cavity to put it in.'

Callan had done what he could to piece Greg back together and stop the blood loss, but the situation seemed hopeless. His torso was so badly mangled that the divers decided it was safer not to move him from the boat, 'because it looked like if we were to lift him up, he'd probably fall in two'.

The divers were still several kilometres offshore, with no chance of an air rescue, and even if they could get Greg into a car, they were still at least two hours down the four-wheel drive tracks east of Esperance. With no other options, they made Greg as stable as they could and made a beeline for the shore. They then loaded the boat straight onto the back of the trailer and made a dash towards the town. 'We thought, all right, we've got to at least try. Let's go for a run.'

Incredibly, the divers kept Greg's blood loss down long enough for their vehicle to reach paved road, where they were able to rendez-vous with an ambulance around 110 kilometres from Esperance. The ambulance took Greg to Esperance hospital, then the Royal Flying Doctor Service airlifted him to Perth for ten hours of surgery.

A nineteen-millimetre tooth fragment was removed from his right eye, with was later identified as originating from the rear jaw of a great white shark.

Greg survived – albeit with an incredible story, and a few equally impressive scars to go with it. 'The crazy kid is still diving nowadays,' laughs Shanan, 'so it's kind of a success story, I guess.'

*

Greg wasn't the only one with scars. Resilience is a finite resource. Anyone put through that situation would find their reserves tested. That same year, Shanan lost another friend to a shark attack in the surf off the west coast of Australia.

'Heck of a year that one,' says Shanan. 'I stopped diving, stopped surfing. I can't remember how long after, but I remember when I tried to get back in the water.'

He'd taken his board to a favourite surf spot in Esperance and stood looking out at the ocean. He describes standing with his board under his arm, before the beautiful, clear water, visibility for 'a million miles', nothing out of place, nothing to fear. But being seized with dread.

'I started crying and throwing up and just couldn't get back in. It just didn't happen. So, I've tried to do the Aussie macho thing and push through it and went and forced the issue. I went and sat out the back for forty-five minutes. Same thing, crying and throwing up.'

'I think it was at that point I probably had to recognise that something was actually going on. And it seemed crazy to say those four letters . . . PTSD. But I think I'd just seen a little bit too much, and it was affecting me. And I had to go and get that sorted before I could re-enter the water and actually enjoy myself back in the ocean.'

Shanan says those first six months of learning to talk about his feelings after a lifetime of being 'that Aussie male who never talked about anything, ever, just masking my emotions with alcohol and bravado,' were the hardest of his life.

Russell, too, has banked up his share of trauma. Russell remembers the first real experience with a predator, when a shark charged him out on the water. A lifetime in the water had prepared him and he knew all the conventional wisdom on how to deal with the situation. He knew that if a shark charged, the best chance of survival was to face it head on – stare it down, make it understand you aren't easy prey, and if it persists, fight for all your worth. Every surfer worth their salt knows the rules.

'Well now, none of that actually happened,' laughs Russell, remembering the day. 'I was basically like a little kid, like when I was five years old, and I thought there was a monster coming into my room and I put my head under the sheet. I basically just turned around, thinking it was all over.'

Not quite. The shark veered away at the last second and disappeared into the face of the wave. But Russell, and the other blokes he was surfing with, never forgot the experience. It was a lesson in how Russell acted in that situation, and he resolved to never let that happen again. Since then, he's encountered the odd copper shark, and has resolutely stuck his head underwater to stare the animal down. So far, so good. 'I'm not sure how I'd go with a great white. I might be that little kid under the sheet again.'

'There's been a handful of days in my life, events that probably shaped a lot of what you do and who you are. That's definitely one of them,' says Russell.

*

I think often about the way people absorb trauma. In both my professional life as a medical practitioner and my personal life pursuing the sport of cave diving, I'm surrounded by people who have experienced, or been witness to, deeply traumatising events. Some people seem able to shrug off the most hectic misfortune without trouble. Others fall to pieces. Most of us, myself included, are somewhere in the middle.

It's very strange how some incidents can trigger profound emotional upset where others seem to have very little effect. I rather like the bucket analogy I've heard used in the emergency services. Every unpleasant job you attend adds a drop of water to the bucket, and slowly your personal bucket fills up. And at some point, one too many drops are added, and the bucket will overflow. Just when you thought it was all watertight. I've seen it happen to highly experienced team members. It can just be that one extra case that sometimes pushes seemingly robust and hardened people over the edge, or it can be a case that has some particular significance.

A very good friend of mine, a physician, also no stranger to death, was once witness to something that never left him. He was driving to a seaside town where his grandfather lived, a place full of joy and happy memories, when he came across a horrific car accident. A single car had come off the road and had ploughed into a massive gum tree. As the first person on the scene, he stopped and went to the open window of the car to assist.

The occupants were a young couple, or had been. The young man was dead, essentially cut in half. The other, a young woman, was gasping for breath, but also obviously dying, beyond help.

This sudden and unexpected tragedy – in a place he associated with only good things – had a profound impact on him. I can still see the sadness in his eyes when he talks about it decades later. So, I am not surprised when I hear stories such as Russell's and Shanan's, that there is going to be some 'baggage' to sort through.

Both men speak about the importance of therapy in sorting out their traumas – how it has changed their perspective on both their lives and the times they've risked it.

Shanan reflects on his past and his shifting attitude to risk. When he was younger, he was less conscious of the risks of big-wave photography. 'There was no calculation because, for myself, I didn't really mind what the outcome was, as crazy as that sounds,' Shanan says. 'And when I was younger, there was probably a little bit of ego involved as well.'

Therapy has given Shanan a new perspective – not just on evaluating risk in dangerous situations, but in everyday life. After spending his first three decades 'doing' rather than making deliberate decisions, he began to realise that the biggest risk most of us will ever take is in not appreciating our lives while we live them.

'One of the biggest things I've learned is being conscious around decision-making. For so many years, life was happening to me, and I was just reacting. Whereas I finally got to a place where it's like, okay, I'm going to actually start setting some goals and trying to shoot in a direction that is positive for me, my family and everyone around me, instead of being a burden to them,' Shanan explains. He tells me he has a beautiful wife, two little kids, and that has changed the way he approaches potential risk. He has so much more to lose. 'Yeah, you have to ask yourself, is this worth it? And do you really want to be doing this?'

The answer seems to be yes, but for different motivations perhaps. Shanan explains that the reason he keeps putting himself in high-risk situations, such as his near-fatal wipe-out, and the shark-infested abalone fields, is that that is when he feels truly alive.

'Those traumas in life are monumental things that are shaping you. I think that is actually living,' he says. 'That's where you'll experience the most growth in your life, and when you can reflect on those moments and learn. And then hopefully, you pass on what you've learned through your experiences, then that can be of benefit to others.'

Russell and Shanan have drifted into public speaking, sharing their experiences in the water. They also train others in water safety, especially in the surf. They emphasise the importance of looking after one's mental health in a sometimes toxic and 'blokey' culture.

'It seems like we've actually had some impact on people, and some feedback that they might actually reach out,' says Shanan. 'Because they look at guys like Ross and me and go, okay, these two melon-heads can talk about their feelings, hopefully we can, too, and maybe go seek out some help, and try to steer ourselves in a better direction.'

Neither of the men has a medical background, but Shanan stresses how grateful he is to be able to give back to the community. 'It's quite a selfish life I've lived on some fronts. To actually feel like you could make a difference to someone's life through shared experiences is probably the best thing, the most rewarding thing I've ever done.'

Which, I think, is the heart of what I'm trying to get to in this book. To go to the brink of experience, to learn something about humanity in your own frame, to bring it back to the world – it's a wonderful thing. For me, the risk/reward ratio seems to skew towards showing a clear benefit of leading a life with a healthy amount of risk in it. Of course, I know that the ratio can swing back in the space of a breath, of a heartbeat. I know it all too well.

CHAPTER FIFTEEN

WHATEVER THE RISKS

Sometimes all the risk mitigation in the world won't keep you safe. I'm aware that, for all my talk of the life-enhancing benefits of risk and all I have personally gained from it, there are losses that are hard to justify. I can spend every moment of my life in thorough, exhaustive planning, but no matter how careful I am, there are always going to be what Sean Chuma calls 'lightning strikes' – those unexpected, out-of-nowhere disasters that happen at random. We can't plan for every possible future, because we can't see the future.

Mark Auricht, an old schoolmate of mine, was one of those people who seemed unfairly blessed with both amazing athletic ability and brains. I think it was way back in the late 80s, he started a personal training business at a time when most people had never even heard of that concept. I certainly hadn't.

'How rich would you have to be to hire someone to go jogging with you? No one would ever do that,' I scoffed. I thought it was madness. But of course, it was genius, and Mark was very successful.

Then one day, I received word that he had died, perishing during an attempt to climb Mount Everest. That really hit me for six. Mark was one of the most physically capable, intellectually methodical people I'd ever met. The idea that something happened on a climb that led to his death was fundamentally shocking to me. It was small consolation that he'd died doing something he loved.

For the record, my dear wife Fiona has always said that if I perish in a cave, and someone tries to comfort her with, 'At least he was doing something he loved', she'll likely punch them in the face. Consider yourselves warned!

Like my late friend Mark, the other adventurers I've known who have perished are largely those I've really respected and admired for their skill and courage. The further I delved into the world of risk, the more I found myself fixating on the existential question: why do some die while practising their craft when others – including myself – have not?

For those who die in remote places, on frozen mountains, or in the caves beneath us, many of the contributing factors remain unknown. The reality of death is ever-present in our sports. And yet adventurers and extreme athletes can, and necessarily must, push this knowledge aside to achieve their goals. It is the thorny logic that underpins everything we do. Without confidence, we invite disaster – but over-confidence is just as bad.

It's not that we have a death wish. We are not courting our demise. But nor can we deny that we have a regular relationship with the concept of potentially dying. It really defies comprehension. And I'm not the first to try and comprehend it.

*

Psychologist William Oigarden, himself a long-time cave diver, has studied personality types drawn to the pursuit and found that some really do suffer from a form of addiction to their sport. It can be quite destructive in terms of their social interactions. Their relationships, particularly those with family, can suffer because of it.

I wouldn't say that it's an antisocial sport, but many cave divers will admit to a certain grumpiness that creeps over them as a big expedition approaches. The anxiety ratchets up and excitement for the dive grows, and that's something that people outside the immediate cave-diving community don't always appreciate. For some cave divers that Oigarden studied, this all-consuming passion for diving begins to eat away at other areas of their life.

One of my favourite things about cave diving is that it's such an equipment-intensive sport. I can fill the weeks in-between a weekend away with tinkering in my shed, playing with equipment and building new gadgets. Actually being underwater is only part of the fun.

The more involved you get with cave diving, the more you become part of this incredibly tight, very rewarding community. The downside is that other communities may become less attractive. It's not that I don't enjoy other social activities, such as watching a play for example, but you don't want to ruin an outing for other groups by launching into a discussion of the pros and cons of breathing Heliox at certain depths. I have it on good authority that this kind of behaviour isn't appreciated on date night, either!

Certainly, it's been a source of discussion within my own marriage. My wife, Fiona, whom I love in part for her fortitude and extraordinary tolerance for my behaviour, has no particular interest in extreme sports. Fiona is a very strong woman, iron-willed, and very courageous – but there's just nothing about that life that takes her fancy. She likes a good book and a nice cup of tea and tries not to think too much about what might happen to me if things go wrong on a dive.

I've never hauled my dive gear to a sump without carrying with it the knowledge that I'm courting fate – that my wife might lose her husband and my children their father. That's the worst-case scenario, obviously – but there's a million ways to inconvenience your spouse. Every weekend I've spent poking around in flooded caves is one that

I've not been home to unload the dishwasher and drive the kids to town. The time away, and the worry and distress my sport can cause my family, is not something I take lightly.

When Fiona and I met and married, cave diving was not an obsession for me, and it probably never occurred to her that she would have decades of worry ahead of her when she put the ring on. Okay, there was a dive bag with us on the honeymoon, but there was nothing in the vows about her having to share me with a rebreather for large chunks of the year, let's put it that way. But still, she has given me amazing latitude to do what I love for the last thirty years of marriage.

My own, somewhat guilty, justification is that if I didn't do this stuff and fulfil my own quest in life, then I wouldn't be the person that I am. And I wouldn't be the person that she fell in love with. I am aware that it might be a slightly mischievous excuse for going on dive trips. There is a constant internal struggle around justifying what I do. At times, it feels totally selfish. At times, it's a compulsion. I feel, at times, the way addicts must.

When I asked Professor Bill von Hippel about the compulsive tendency to dive, even in the face of clear and present danger, he compares some risk-taking behaviour as analogous with drug addiction. For a so-called 'adrenaline junkie', the release of dopamine – and the euphoric feelings that come with extreme sports – can be habit forming.

'A lot of times people feel their activity makes them happier,' says Bill. 'But then by comparison the rest of their life isn't as pleasant.' He cites BASE jumpers who report that they come to find the spaces of time between jumps less enjoyable and they feel less alive. Eventually, just like drugs of addiction, the immense pleasurable high first enjoyed when indulging in the sport subsides into a feeling that is barely a high – rather it's just a method to stave off the low.

'I think that risk-taking can have that addictive quality for some people,' says von Hippel. 'Then, by comparison, in ordinary life they feel dull and half alive.'

I'm lucky. My everyday life – a rewarding day job, a comfortable home, my children and my beautiful wife – gives me compelling reasons to be on dry land. I can imagine that without all the good fortune I've had, the joys of regular life might start to seem pale compared to those to be found on expeditions. Von Hippel calls that sense of creeping dysphoria feeling 'half alive'. Personally, my sport helps me feel fully alive in a way I might not without it. Alive, and I intend to stay that way.

Intentions don't always pan out though. The sad fact is some of us do die in the pursuit of our passion. Every time we meet up for a conference or a gathering, there's a tacit understanding that any one of us might be the one to make a fatal mistake on a dive. What's more, because there are so few people with the skills to reach the site of a colleague's death, chances are that one of us will be the one to conduct the post-mortem retrieval.

I'd signed up as the Search and Rescue Officer for the Cave Divers Association of Australia, so I knew, logically, that one day I might be called upon to retrieve the body of a friend. I had decided I was prepared to do it if it ever came to it. When the day came, it was under the most tragic circumstances.

*

Agnes 'Ag' Milowka was a born cave diver. From the first time I saw her dive, her talents were obvious, and matched only by her ambition. She was as brave as she was bright, with an equally brilliant, easy smile. An extroverted, attractive, vivacious woman, she seemed as comfortable in the limelight as she was in the murkiest caves. She gained recognition not only for her research and exploration into previously untouched depths in Australia and the US, but as a public speaker and author with a wonderfully evocative turn of phrase. Articles she wrote managed to capture not only her exuberance but convey the realities of the highs and lows of cave diving for a layman audience.

'There is no greater feeling in the world than finding a passage that no one ever in the history of the world has seen before,' Agnes says in a video uploaded to YouTube. 'It is like any pursuit that is inherently dangerous. If you are pushing the boundaries of that sport, you will find yourself taking on bigger and bigger risks. To me, those risks are worth it, because the rewards are worth it.'

It was clear that she had a thrilling life ahead of her. Explorers and scientists planning extraordinary expeditions wanted her on their team. Filmmakers and TV producers were already paying attention to her, recognising a talent and personality that could cross over from the hermetic world of cave diving to a more mainstream audience.

And all that early success and excitement, I think, made her lose her judgement to some degree. In a pursuit where patience and knowing your limits can be the difference between life and death, she was eager to push every boundary.

During an internship in Florida working on the archaeological excavation of historic shipwreck sites, she became entrenched in the cave-diving community and laid a lot of fresh line into virgin caves. It was there she developed a habit of sneaking into caves by herself after work. More than once, people saw her car parked outside a cave opening and the alarm bells went up from people who thought that someone had not returned from a dive. There are many rules in cave diving, but the number one golden rule is never to dive alone. Agnes, individual as she was, was known to break that rule.

Back in Australia, she was just as brash. All through her meteoric rise, the rest of the community would urge her to slow down, take her time. She was still young, which, I suppose, was the problem. She was young, smart, fearless and ambitious.

It had made me worry for her, especially when Agnes downplayed the risks of diving in the local caves of Mount Gambier. Her success in exploring far more complex caves interstate and overseas had possibly caused her to disregard the dangers of dying in her backyard. In the end, that's exactly what happened.

*

Piccaninnie Ponds lies twenty-seven kilometres southeast of Mount Gambier. It is a stunning coastal spring system that our diving group had gained permission to further explore in 2011. I had just made a breakthrough into a new deep section at over 100 metres in depth, and at the moment I was hanging in the water performing my decompression, a drama was unfolding fifty kilometres away in another site.

Tank Cave, the major cave-diving drawcard of the area, is only fifteen metres deep. But it makes up for its relative shallowness with over nine kilometres of interwoven tunnels that collectively form a deceptively complex maze.

Agnes loved Tank Cave. She once described it as 'a spiderweb gone wild' and wrote eloquently about the joys of exploring it. Towards the end of 2010, Agnes had been asking some in our community about a spot they'd been working away at for years. A tunnel, sealed by rocks, that they'd been slowly opening up, moving a few rocks at a time.

That sort of exploration – slow, steady, but with the tantalising possibility that a long tunnel could be revealed once the obstacle was finally open – is the dream of every cave diver. To a young firebrand like Agnes, it was irresistible.

When I finally surfaced from my dive in Piccaninnie Ponds in February 2011, I was told that a diver had gone into Tank Cave and had not come out. My heart sank. I knew that it had to be Agnes.

By the time I reached the site, an initial search had found Agnes's line leading into the very tight area she had been so curious about. Taking turns with another dive team, we cautiously pushed forward into a very difficult and silty part of the cave. As we progressed, it became so restricted that it was necessary to move rocks and even scrape away at the limestone floor with tools to enlarge the passage sufficiently for the larger divers who were following Ag's trail. There was only room for one diver to push forward, with the second diver hanging well back out of the silted-up water for safety. Eventually I got far enough forward to find one of Ag's air cylinders lying across the passageway. Peering forward I realised I could see a second white cylinder in the distance, and finally my eyes were able to make out her lifeless body just beyond.

*

Agnes was an incredible diver. She was fearless, agile, small enough to squeeze into spaces other divers could never manage, and famous for pushing into passages that seemed impossible to ford, even if it meant taking off equipment, such as her second tank, to get through. Temporarily shedding gear to manage a tight squeeze is something many divers do, but it's not without risk. But leaving your redundant cylinder behind to move forward is extremely dangerous. If anything goes wrong with your primary gas supply, then disaster is inevitable.

As near as we could make out, Agnes had found a hole leading to a new passage around 600 metres from the entrance, one of the ultra-tight tunnels she was famous for braving. She'd dropped her spare air in order to explore further, and when the cave silted up on her entry, she'd lost her bearings and got turned around. In a cave with no visibility and a lost line, panic is often seconds away. Panic, unfortunately, usually means death. Panic has arguably killed more cave divers than any other factor, by far. However, in a testament to Agnes's courage and calm, I believe she staved off panic until she drew her last breath. Her tank was empty, and she appeared to have been working to solve her dilemma until all options were exhausted.

Her body rested at a ninety-degree angle to the line, and it seemed she'd spent her final moments trying to get out of the tunnel through a tiny crack, not the opening she'd entered through. Her gear was all undone, and it looked as though she'd tried to strip off bulky gear to fit through what she thought would be her escape route. She drowned within three metres of her spare tank, but in her disorientation, she'd been heading in the wrong direction to retrieve it.

She was such a determined diver, a gigantic will in a tiny frame, that she'd lodged herself in one of those tunnels that only she could fit into. It would take days to retrieve her body, and we would need help. A couple of the guys we were working with were already exhausted and understandably upset with the task of retrieving their close friend. I needed someone I could trust, who wouldn't get flustered while doing a grim job – Craig Challen, in other words.

Craig flew in from Perth the day after I'd called him for help. In the end, it took another day to even reach Agnes's body – working in buddy pairs to open the passage, planning each part of the excavation, slowly moving specific rocks with the methodical care of a chess game, all supervised by highly anxious police.

Police divers didn't have the specific skills required for this kind of operation, so – much like during the Thai cave rescue – it defaulted to us. That said, if one of us died, then they'd have some explaining to do. And it was quite a dramatic operation in many regards.

The police were rightly very nervous about using civilians in such a high-risk environment and needed us to debrief them thoroughly every time we came up to rest. Video footage from every excursion became a very important part of the debrief and planning for the next dive.

Once we got into a position where we could remove Agnes from the little hole she was stuck in, we had about forty metres of difficult cave to negotiate until we reached an open passage where it would be relatively easy to manoeuvre. Once I brought Agnes out of the terminal chamber to where Craig was positioned, we started our pre-planned extraction.

To get her out, I swam ahead, leading the path through the tunnel, with Agnes's body in tow. Craig swam at the other end, holding Agnes's feet to guide her, all of us single file through this very tight tunnel.

It was a good plan, and theoretically it should have been fine, but at some point during the excavation we'd broken the guideline – the rope meant to lead us back to the surface and to safety. I got to a broken bit of cave line, which meant I would have to figure the way out by feel.

I knew the stretch of tunnel pretty well, so I wasn't too worried – I'd just keep forging ahead, navigating by touch. What I didn't know was that I'd floated up off the floor and into a tiny little ceiling recess extending up into the roof of the cave. And so, when I went to swim forwards, I suddenly hit a solid wall where I expected open water. Smacking your head into a stone wall only has one winner, and it's usually the wall – and the experience is more jarring in those unique circumstances.

Visibility was at zero, so Craig had no idea what had happened, or why I'd stopped. So, he was still pushing Agnes's body from behind, trying to guide her down to the mouth of the tunnel, which meant that she was being squeezed into the alcove, trapping me in there with her.

Finding myself trapped in an unexpected corner of the cave with the body of my friend pushing up against me and preventing my escape, I began to feel that sense of anxiety and panic start to build up.

I knew I had to keep my head, otherwise there was every chance there would be three bodies to retrieve from Tank Cave. If I was trapped, so was Craig. So, I opted for the only way out I could think of.

I basically just had to grasp Agnes by the shoulders and push her body back out of the hole towards Craig – and hope he got the message. Luckily he did and stopped pushing on his end, giving me time to clear my head, get my bearings, and drop back down to the floor of the cave to a position from which he could push forward again.

The whole incident is not something I'll forget in a hurry. It was mildly traumatising, as you can imagine, but I waited until I got to the surface until I let myself really feel it. When I crawled from the cave for the last time and delivered Agnes's body to the police on the surface, that's when it all hit me.

Up until then, the whole ordeal – losing my friend, discovering her body, three days of highly tense digging to retrieve her – had sort of been boxed away in the part of my mind where I needed it to stay in order to work. I had a job to do and, until that was done, the emotional weight of those days stayed suspended, floating somewhere else in the cave with me.

It was on dry land that I remember my knees buckling and just sort of crumpling into the grass and sobbing. Eventually I pulled myself together, but later, when we got back to the place I was staying, a mate walked into where I was sitting and just staring at the wall.

'Hey,' he said, which set me off again, and I just had a huge blub in front of this poor guy. I was processing it all – the grief, the stress, the exhaustion of three days in the cave.

I was pretty sad there for a couple of days. We all were – not just the divers who'd worked to retrieve Agnes, but the whole community. We were all such good mates and Agnes was the best of us. But, in the words of Chris Lemons, life goes on. For the rest of us.

*

We all process grief and trauma differently – and in a community as tight-knit and driven as the cave divers of the world, events like Agnes's death are bound to stir up feelings. One reaction most of us go through is to ask ourselves, 'How could this happen?'

I don't mean that in the existential sense, the way one feels anytime a young person dies far too soon – but in a practical sense. We want to work out what went wrong that led to the outcome.

Particularly in the days of internet forums, after a cave-diving fatality there's often a lot of very robust discussions in which people are quick to try to work out what the cause of a death was. 'They must have done this, which led to that outcome,' and 'I would never have done that, that's a stupid mistake to make,' people would often say.

That sort of locker-room dissection of a death might strike those unfamiliar with the world of adventure sports as clinical or insensitive, but I don't think that's the case. It's a sort of protective mechanism, the instinct to tell yourself, 'Well, that can't happen to me, because I would never have done the things that they did in that situation.'

Often the call for answers can be quite impassioned, verging on being aggressive and insensitive to the family or friends of the dead diver in their search to know exactly what happened.

It's a method of processing loss that all of us in the diving community are guilty of. I know I've done it. When John Bennett, one of the stars of deep-water diving, lost his life back in 2004, I was stunned. He'd been on a forty-five-metre commercial salvage dive and went missing in Korean waters, never to be recovered. I remember obsessively picking over the details we could glean about his death and concluding that if he could die, any one of us could.

John was an extremely careful, incredibly competent diver. He'd done more to push the sport forward than just about anyone. As he once said, 'Diving, by its very nature, will always move forward and there will always be divers – and groups of divers – prepared to gaze into the darkness and want to know and discover what's hidden there.'

In his pursuit of that goal, he dived to depths no human being had experienced, and smashed record after record – he was the first to make a self-contained dive to 300 metres. But he didn't die on one of his intrepid dives into the unexplored – but a very routine dive that any of us could have done without breaking into a sweat.

There's no real lesson to be learned from John's death – whatever went wrong, it's likely it was not something within his control. Even if we don't make mistakes, there's every chance a 'lightning strike' will find us, even underwater.

In the same way, I wish I could look at Agnes's death and find the positives from it. She died doing what she loved, sure, but that's small consolation. I'm sure she would have loved to keep on doing it for another half century.

No one who ever met Agnes will forget her. In the years following her death, several magnificent geological features have been named in her memory by those who miss her and her irrepressible spirit. I think she would have liked that – she lived to push the boundaries of the sport, and the glory of exploration.

As for Tank Cave, I've only been back twice to the actual spot she died. I wanted to reach the end of the tunnel Agnes was exploring, to see what was beyond that crevice she was trying to fit through when she lost her life. I wanted whatever was behind there to be worth it. In the end, it was just a very small amount of cave: silted, sad. I don't see myself going back there again. That section of cave is no longer something wondrous to explore. It's a cenotaph to someone who died far too young, and to the recklessness that youth fuels.

Now and again, I'll swim into the most magnificent cave the size of a cathedral, and just as breath-taking, and think, 'Agnes would have loved this.' It's bittersweet to imagine the things she would have experienced and explored. The sights she would have shown the world if things had gone differently that day in Tank Cave. For now, all I can do is remember and know that, as tragic as her passing was, she died pursuing her dreams – something she would have always done. Whatever the risks.

CONCLUSION

Last summer, I was down at the beach. A perfect day showcasing one of those unmatched strips of South Australian coast. Hot sand to sink your toes into, bracing waves to dive under. The sounds of seabirds on the breeze; children laughing as they braved the surf. Then out of nowhere came a surreal noise that I've recently learned to associate with Australian beaches; sirens and a warning for swimmers to get to dry land as a matter of life and death.

All up and down the beach, families turned in the water and made their way quickly back to the beach as amplified announcements warned of a shark in the water. Above them, the aircraft banked over the surf, as it tracked the great predator it had spotted somewhere out past the breakers.

From my own perch on the beach, I sighed, resigned to the fact that the beach day I'd hoped for would not eventuate. From where I sat, the response from the authorities to clear the water and shut down the beach seemed a little disproportionate. The chances are, that shark had been out there for weeks, minding its own business, ignoring the unappetising humans that swam and surfed near it. But now, a plane had happened to spot it, and panic ensued. I thought it a bit silly, but on balance, I could understand. The human capacity to properly assess risk is nebulous, even for someone like me who has spent his professional life and recreational hours trying to get my head around it.

On a weekend's swim, it's fairly natural to think twice before jumping into shark-inhabited waters even though I know, intellectually, the risks of shark attack are very low. For a man of my age, chronic illness presents a far more clear and present danger (coronary heart disease accounts for more deaths in Australian males than any other single cause). Mathematically, the great white shark lurking somewhere out in the deep is far less likely to kill me than the beers waiting in an esky back on dry land. The risks of perishing while diving in a cave are admittedly greater, but still, I find a way to justify and manage them.

*

If you've read this far, you've probably got a pretty good idea of how I tend to look at the world. I'm a man of science. I believe in chemistry, physics, mathematics – the scientific method. When I started the conversations that led to this book, I had a scientific hypothesis I wanted to test.

For many years I had put up with people suggesting to me that I must be mad to pursue cave diving, or that I must have a death wish. My theory was that, like myself, people who take risks as part of their profession or recreation were probably like me. Not reckless adrenaline junkies, but careful, measured risk managers who avoided excessive danger in order to excel at their chosen pursuit. Okay, maybe those BASE jumpers are a little crazy, and perhaps the big-wave surfers, too! But maybe even *those* extremists might be so good at their craft, that the fear I would experience if I attempted those activities might merely bring a heightened sense of arousal to them? I believe, having surveyed some of the most experienced risk-takers on the planet, that

I am correct. Those individuals who throw themselves off buildings, surf skyscraper-sized waves, and plummet to the primordial darkness at the bottom of the ocean have more in common than I dared hope. I have to say I'm pleased to find out how my theory hit the mark. Without exception, the extraordinary individuals represented within these pages seem highly intelligent and very measured in their quest to discover the limits within themselves and their craft. I am so grateful that they shared their stories with me.

What a treat to have the chance to talk to extraordinary people – and realise that something unified them all. Despite their talents, rare physical aptitudes and advantages they were born with, each of them became extraordinary quite gradually.

Individually, the people surveyed in this book are people who perform near-superhuman physical feats, or tasks that seem so frightening I have difficulty watching footage of it. Let alone entertaining the thought of repeating them myself. On the top of that list would have to be Alex Honnold, the free-solo climber who insists that his only 'superpower' is clear thinking and diligent practice. I think the same is true of everyone featured in these pages. They all became extraordinary through incremental expansion of their comfort zones. By regularly stepping outside of their established comfort zone and into their 'stretch zone', that is where real learning and development begins.

Looking back over my own development, I can see how learning to push my own boundaries, with the incremental exposure to risks along with the occasional mishap – has been an overwhelmingly positive force in my life. The brash kid who got lost in the forest and capsized in the ocean set me up for a life of adventure and exploration. It meant, when fate tapped me on the shoulder and asked if I could duck down a cave in Thailand and play my part in the rescue, that I had the necessary skills to respond. It's my belief that if it weren't for the bumps and scrapes I'd picked up along the way, I wouldn't have been able to rise to that occasion.

Whilst I certainly never faced death during the cave rescue in Thailand, my involvement in such a momentous event has certainly given me an opportunity to reflect on the somewhat selfish existence I had been living up to that point. When your life has been privileged from birth, living in a middle-class family in a country as safe as Australia, you sometimes need a shake up to make you appreciate what you have. I have had the long-held belief that an absence of risk in one's life is actually a moral, if not a physical, hazard. From a teleological standpoint, life for our ancestors was a constant battleground. The fittest specimens attracted the best mate, captured regular food, and fought off both predator and rival to survive. We walked everywhere, didn't smoke and were as skinny as a rake. Life was dangerous and risk was a daily companion. Unfortunately, death from infection, trauma and childbirth meant life expectancy was short.

Of course, life is very different for human beings today. We all carry around technology that only a few decades ago was the stuff of science fiction. Medical care has advanced just as quickly, and in the coming years will become exponentially better. Just look at the extraordinary effort to develop and distribute a vaccine for the COVID-19 pandemic, just a short century after the Spanish flu wiped out more than 50 million people. I'm fully aware of how fortunate I've been in life – to be born in my generation, with good parents, in a safe city, in a (mostly) functional democratic society.

A child born in similar circumstances today is likely to enjoy health, nutrition and a standard of living that for much of human history was only accessible to royalty. Some of them, however, seem to endure similar levels of stultifying safety. A child living today is connected to so much technology and electronic monitoring it is hard for them to move without vigilance. With parents increasingly nervous about germs, predators, bullies and even 'failure' in their offspring, young people are being smothered in a safety blanket that, instead of protecting them, is stifling their normal instincts to compete, adventure, explore and develop.

Helicopter parenting seems like a quaint phrase to explain modern parenting and the omniscient awareness of danger our safe societies have given us, although I don't know what else you would call it. Predator drone parenting, maybe.

If, as Professor von Hippel suggests, we have evolved with risk as a fundamental part of our psychological makeup, what happens to us when we live lives largely devoid of it?

With every silver lining comes a cloud, and the price of our materially comfortable lives is an existence that runs counter to our biological programming. My distant ancestors have, through their genes, passed down the tools I need to survive the hazards they faced. Their hunger has given me taste receptors that crave high-fat, high glucose foods that maximise life-saving calories with every bite. A necessary survival mechanism for a hunter-gather, but less beneficial when reading the menu at a bistro.

I believe we have a similar biological imperative to retain a little danger in our lives. Our neurological makeup seems designed to be able to recognise, respond and adapt to perceived risks. Again, a crucial survival mechanism against the myriad dangers of the savannah, but easily short-circuited in our modern, materially safe, psychologically relentless existence. In a world of the 24-hour news cycle and constant smart-phone notifications, it's no wonder that anxiety and depression are epidemic in our society. We need some kind of circuit breaker. When there is nothing to physically fear, perhaps our minds take over and we become fearful of what is normal.

My conclusion, after making this journey into the world of risk-takers, is that we need more genuine risk in our lives. And I'm not alone in this. The people I've had the privilege of speaking to in writing this book – and many more who aren't quoted but whose insights are peppered through it – generally share similar experiences. We come from wildly different fields and backgrounds – soldiers and scientist explorers, BASE jumpers and mountain climbers, people who fight fires in the bush, or martial artists in the ring. They grew into people with extraordinary skills, and fascinating lives, through well-managed exposure to risk. This seems to be an essential part of reaching our potential in life. I don't mean in measures of career or commercial success (although those things don't hurt) but in terms of a full, rich and happy sense of self.

The things that I truly value in life – my family and friends, my hobbies and my comfortable home – are all made richer by the risks and discomfort that come with my sport. The intersection of risk and choice is something I've long thought about. As an adult with some degree of agency in my own life, I can choose the level of risk, hardship or suffering that I'm willing to tolerate (at least for circumstances within my control).

I worry a lot about my selfish role as a risk-taker, and the impact on my loved ones should I perish in a cave-diving accident. It's not lost on me that nearly everyone I spoke to has lost loved ones to the very activity they speak with such undisguised joy about.

I think of the story of Rob Hall, the mountaineer who spoke to his pregnant wife on a satellite phone shortly before he perished. Obviously, neither of them expected that would be the last time they spoke. But the possibility that it would be must have been in the back of both their minds – as it is every time I call my wife by satellite before I put on my gear and disappear under the Earth. I justify these risks to myself and my family by convincing myself I would not be the person my wife loves if I didn't do what I do. If I intentionally curtail the sometimes-insatiable quest to go deeper or further than I have been before to find unseen cave tunnels, would I be a miserable and sulking partner? The recharging of my life force that comes from a successful expedition lasts for months. And of course, the benefits to the human race are myriad – who hasn't been inspired by the tales of Shackleton's leadership, or benefited from the explorers who have discovered new pharmaceuticals from remote rainforests or the oceans' depths? The world would be very different if mankind had never set sail to find new shores. It is an inescapable part of the human condition and in my view, should not be quelled.

*

It's possible my profession has given me a somewhat unusual view of mortality. When you work in health care or in the emergency services, on any given day you might be meeting somebody on the worst day of their life.

On a typical workday while I'm preparing a patient for the operating theatre, I'll explain what anaesthetic I'll be giving them, outline the risks and make sure they have all the information they need to give informed consent for their medical care. Ninety-nine per cent of the time everything is routine and exceptionally safe. Bedside manner is a part of that. I'll do my best to help a patient relax before inducing their anaesthesia, even if I'm fully aware that their life is in imminent danger. In my career, I have encountered death and disability on a fairly regular basis. To borrow a phrase from Chris Lemons, I still have to remember to get a carton of milk on the way home. Life goes on.

To me, perhaps, this perspective has given me something of a polarised view of mortality. It's a matter of how life is lived, rather than how it ends. Reading the paragraph above, perhaps I come across as a little fatalistic. Not at all. My experience with death has made me very aware of how fleeting life is. We only have so many days to live. It's imperative we make the most of them. I think my father, Jim, taught me this more than anyone. Suck the marrow out of life, treat others as you would like to be treated yourself, tell those close to you that you love them, and be true to yourself by following your dreams. Quality, not quantity counts. We are all going to die, and the best we can hope for is to die a painless and dignified death in the presence of someone who loves us.

I suppose I try to live my life the same way I approach my diving. Sometimes it's difficult, occasionally it's terrifying. But, it's always worth it. You never know what you'll find around the corner if you take a chance and push the boundaries. Isn't that a marvellous thing? I think so. And I reckon that's well worth the risk.

ACKNOWLEDGEMENTS

When a charismatic publisher like Ben Ball from Simon and Schuster emailed me to say how much he enjoyed my *Real Risk* podcast and 'had I thought about writing a book on risk?', the answer was – yes, but I am far too busy! But ideas like these sometimes refuse to go away. And in a light-bulb moment I realised that I already had the meat for the book in the amazing tales I had been hearing. I just needed to add the bread and salad. Hence, this book is as much the property of the extraordinary adventurers, the intentional and accidental risk-takers, and those who study the human need for risk-taking. All of whom were generous in allowing me to use their words and anecdotes to give my perspective on a life lived in an increasingly safe world.

*

My special thanks go to those storytellers, or those with whom I have shared decades of adventures including Craig Challen, Sam Hall, Peter Horne, Ian Lewis, John Dalla-Zuanna, Ken Smith, Paul Hosie, Brian Kakuk, Dr Bill Stone, James Cameron, Andrew Wight, Jimmy Chin, Alex Honnold, Sean Chuma, Professor Bill von Hippel, Jessica Watson,

Maya Gabiera, Chris Lemons, Ashley Sanford, Matt Hall, Hugh Riminton, James Scott, Heath Jamieson, Gill Hicks, Chris Blowes, Dr Kylie Stanton, Russell Ord and Shanan Worrall. Without these extraordinary people this book would not exist. Thanks also to those adventurers and photographers who contributed images to bring the text to life.

*

From Simon and Schuster, publisher Ben Ball and editor Rosemary McDonald for their belief that there was a book in all of this, and Liam Pieper who helped me organise my thoughts into coherent text.

*

A final acknowledgement to those historical figures who paved the way, in times when it was so much harder. With knitted balaclavas, home-made breathing apparatus, ropes made from natural fibres, journeys made on horseback or on planes made of wood and canvas. The tools have changed, but the spirit of adventure lives on.

ABOUT THE AUTHOR

Dr Richard 'Harry' Harris grew up and still resides in Adelaide, South Australia. He has worked in anaesthesia, diving and aeromedical medicine around the world. His passion for cave diving goes back to the 1980s and it has taken him to the corners of the globe in search of new adventures.

Harry and his friends have explored caves to 245 metres in depth, and shipwrecks to more than 150 metres, in dives lasting more than sixteen hours. He is an enthusiastic underwater photographer and videographer and is now also building a career in documentary film making.

Harry has a professional and voluntary interest in search and rescue operations, establishing the first sump rescue training course in Australasia. The 2018 Thailand cave rescue of a Thai youth soccer team was an opportunity to put this training to work.

In 2018, he received the Star of Courage and the medal of the Order of Australia for his role in the Thailand cave rescue. Harry was the joint 2019 Australian of the Year with his dive partner, Craig Challen.

Harry is an advocate for sensible risk-taking in young people, encouraging youth to get off their screens and outside to build independence, resilience and improve their mental health.